Travels With Lottie

by

Juliet Carron

Obviously to
Lottie

With all my love and thanks for the happiest of times.

ITALY – 2003

A T THE beginning of January 2003 Lottie's father left; within days we were legally separated. Lottie was eight years old, with long thick golden hair, green eyes which could turn blue in some lights, and an infectious laugh. It was a horrid time for her.

At some point in February, I made a decision to spend as much of the forthcoming summer holidays away as possible: as a distraction, as an escape, as a palliative. I gave no thought to the problems of what would happen to the animals (two ponies, a dog, and a cat), the house, and the garden all being deserted for so long. In the event, the ponies got farmed out to my sister-in-law who luckily wanted to borrow ponies for August; neighbours looked after the dog and the cat, and the plants died – at least the ones in the conservatory and the pot plants. (It was one of those rainless, boiling summers that cause environmentalists to mutter even more loudly about global warming.) But all that was six months away, and in the grey chill of early February I had images of blue skies and hot sunshine as our goal.

"I want to see volcanoes," said Lottie. (She'd been learning about them in geography at school). "And I want to see the Coliseum." (A child in her class had given a talk about it).

So, Italy it was. It seemed an obvious choice, suddenly. Lottie had been learning about the Ancient Romans in history classes that year. I hardly knew Italy at all (I had spent a fleeting half day in Florence twenty-five years ago, and two and a half days in Rome seventeen years ago) and so it offered novelty of exploration and experience to me. I'm not sure I had even looked at a map of Italy when I went on the internet to find cheap flights. I had some vague idea of starting somewhere in the south and travelling northwards.

In retrospect, how random. At first, however, I thought I would have to bin the whole idea. The flights were so expensive – even bucket-shop flights. I got it fixed in my mind that I wanted to fly back from Pisa so that I could take Lottie up the Leaning Tower before we came home. Some of the airlines didn't even operate from Pisa. I surfed doggedly. Eventually BA came up trumps. Giving them week long windows for dates was the answer, as well as not caring what time of day or night we flew. I booked us out to Naples, and back nearly three weeks later from Pisa, for under £200 for the two of us. Then I forgot about it until July.

As the school holidays loomed, I began to get excited - and nervous. I bought The Rough Guide to Italy (gosh, quite expensive, but in the event worth all of its £15.99!). I read bits of it out to Lottie over breakfasts, and underlined in pencil, and scribbled in margins. We poured over maps and potted descriptions. Well, I poured, Lottie rather quickly got bored. The names meant nothing to her. Other things were of more immediate interest to her, such as Sports Day. I began to ask friends where they had been in Italy; what places they'd recommend; unmissable cities or spots they could think of. I should have written their "Oh-you-must-go-to" places down. I forgot most of them, but was left with an impression that big Italian cities – except for Milan (unless one wanted to shop) were beautiful and/or interesting and that there was a huge North/South divide in terms of character and atmosphere.

I gave up trying to decide on an itinerary. The point of exploring is to see what happens. I discovered that car hire was expensive in Italy, and anyway Lottie said she wanted a proper adventure, so we agreed we would backpack our way up Italy, travelling by bus and by train, staying wherever we wanted and could, for as long as we wanted or could.

How does an eight year old know anything about backpacking? Well, her big sisters had done a bit in gap months before university. Otherwise I think I am to blame for selling the idea to her. I had missed out on this teenage experience, and suddenly felt that this was an ideal opportunity. (Was it not done less commonly in the late sixties by my generation than it is now by this one, or did it just somehow pass me by?) It was just the sort of mental and emotional elastoplast that I needed.

So, the only other thing I did was to book a rail card. That was difficult. The telephone number in The Rough Guide was no longer relevant. In fact the type of rail card I wanted to get no longer existed either, but it took a good deal of calling and recalling the Italian Tourist Board - and on from there - to discover that. In the end I bought a railcard that gave me and Lottie unlimited travel in Italy for any 10 days in 2 months. It was nearly £300 for us both and I hoped that it would be better value than buying tickets for each separate journey when we were there. I thought that it would be good for 10 days worth of long journeys, and I would use cash for short trips. Now I am not so sure. Rail travel was very cheap in Italy and we were never able to use it between Sorrento and Naples anyway. Its great asset was that we never had to queue (and they were some queues!) at the ticket offices before each journey. The other asset was that having it, I never weighed up rail travel cost as a determining factor in whether nor not to make a journey. Any place, any distance, was fine.

Cost for the whole adventure was a real issue, and I had saved up determinedly. There was a certain pleasure in doing it all on the cheap too; a sort of challenge. I only took 1000 euros. I nearly

didn't take my credit card - but panicked at the last moment and
took it in case of emergencies. Just as well. I felt as if I had a lot of
cash for just two of us, and I even imagined that I wouldn't use
it all - but actually it was really not enough.

By the beginning of August we started to think about
packing. Lottie used her school backpack - because I knew she
could carry it reasonably comfortably. I found a huge old thing
in the attic which seemed to have straps that vaguely did up
in the right places. I think it was the one my second daughter
Annabel had taken to Thailand: if she could use it, so could
I. We took the barest minimum: sarongs not towels; no books
except for The Rough Guide and another book I had been given
called "Travelling by Train in Italy"; no jewellery, no make-up,
no hairdryer; two changes of clothing – nothing smart at all;
swimming things and washing things; a change of shoes; exercise
books for writing our diaries; Milli, Lottie's beloved toy rabbit;
and a pot of marmite – because bread and marmite was more or
less all Lottie would eat.

We were ready. Friends said we were brave; I began to
worry.

"Where will you be staying?" they asked.

"Wherever we find," I answered. They looked at me as if I
were at best mad and at worst negligent as a mother.

"Surely you ought to have somewhere at least for the first
night," they urged. I hadn't even decided whether to stay in Naples
for that first night or whether to go as far south as possible straight
away. I didn't even speak the language. I teach Latin, but as I
discovered when I started to teach myself Italian, it isn't at all the
same thing. The similarities are actually rather confusing. I gave
in to everyone's anxieties on our behalf. I made a decision to take
a bus from Naples airport to Sorrento (the guide book said that
there was one), and allowed a kind friend to book us into a small
hotel in advance. The general consensus was that in August, the
Italian holidays, hotels might well be very full and we could end
up by finding ourselves with nowhere to stay.

Other friends were encouraging and soothed my belated fears. Lottie, they said, would be a chaperone, an asset. Italians love children, they said, and because of her will be kind and welcoming. Because of her I would be safe!

On the Tuesday night before we left Lottie and I were both excited. This was quite an adventure, and we were looking forward to the unknown. I hardly slept, frightened of sleeping through the alarm and missing our flight. I lay in half darkness through those quiet long hours wondering how one could tell the difference between thrill and trepidation; the physical symptoms are identical. Either way the adrenalin gives you butterflies in your tummy. The alarm, when it rang, signalled both a beginning and an end.

Wednesday 13th August

Gatwick is apparently deserted at 5.30 am. I wonder why there aren't more night time flights. Still, the emptiness makes things easy: swift check in (backpacks count as hand luggage), and we go and have coffee, hot chocolate and croissants at Costa Rica. We are rather bleary eyed; other people look pretty grotty too. BA 2606 to Naples leaves on time. It is an easy flight spent mugging up the Italian phrase book – but nothing works as well as using a language. My learning works by deciding what words and phrases I have always found I needed most in France, and then trying to learn them in Italian. It turns out later that this is quite an effective thing to do. By the end of today, thanks to as much practice as I can get, I can ask how much something costs, the way to the beach, and quite a few other neat little quick questions – and I can understand the reply. Lottie spends the flight (since, absorbed in my phrase book, I ignore her) chatting to the man next to her. His wife and children are across the aisle and I bet he was looking forward to a brief respite from children's chatter. Bad luck on him!

I try to encourage Lottie to eat as much as possible on the aeroplane as I don't know what we will do about food for lunch - or when. But Lottie has a dislike for most food and so only nibbles on a roll and butter. At home she exists on bread and marmite and pasta, fruit and yoghurt. I worry a bit about what she will eat while we are travelling, which is why I have brought the marmite with us. I am sure local supermarkets will have everything we need, and I don't intend to eat at restaurants very often, if at all.

The warmth of the sun hits us gloriously as we emerge from the plane. Waiting in the passport queue at Naples airport, the first of several extraordinary coincidences occurs: I bump into Charles Metcalfe, an old boyfriend I haven't seen or talked to for over thirty years; it is amazing that we recognise each other. And he has changed: fatter, greyer, wearing hat and shorts (not clothes I remember him ever wearing when I knew him), but his 'manner' is essentially him, and the years concertina. It is odd seeing someone you think you recognise from years ago. Do you dare say, "Hello, aren't you . . .?" It's embarrassing if you are wrong but worse, alone with Lottie, I don't want it to be mistaken for a chat up line. So you stare and half catch their eye and hope that if it's who you think it is, they will recognise you too, or think they do, and then you can edge together towards that moment of mutual recognition, that smile of pleasure in re-meeting that is half relief that you are right. Also, there he is with a pretty, but rather exhausted looking, wife and three children in their early teens. How do they all feel about Daddy being warmly greeted by a strange woman who clearly once knew him well? How well? You can sense his wife wondering. Did he sleep with her? Is this a threat? I can feel wariness vie with instinctive dislike.

"Where are you going? How long for?" I ask – superficial questions which she hedges, in case, I suppose, I come too or become an intrusion on their family holiday, their unit. Charles – of course a man doesn't consider these things – is open, and openly pleased to see me again. I try to make his children laugh by telling them how he used to be passionate about steam engines and how I have a photo of him driving one, in a funny hat and a boiler suit. (It's so old that it has faded to a strange yellowy colour in my album). The children are enchanted (children like windows into their parents' pre-them days) but I shut up when I realise that the revelations endear me even less to his wife. So I talk to her - about the builders in her new kitchen, her job on the wine magazine she runs with Charles, her children, what Lottie and I are doing, and she thaws. I suppose the possessiveness of the female of the species is not surprising. An instinctive chemical reaction to potential threat. And I suppose a man would react as warily had a strange male blast-from-the-past warmly greeted his wife at an airport.

I practise my Italian, asking the way to the bus for Sorrento. It goes rather infrequently so Lottie and I sit on our backpacks and wait for an hour. It is hot and sunny but not at all unbearable. Even some clouds and a breeze. While we wait I chat to a woman with her son and grand daughter. I strike up the conversation hoping to practise my Italian, only to discover that she is French. Well, it is fun practising my French! I am curious to know whether her son is divorced, or whether this is an annual Granny trip minus a busy or disliked daughter-in-law. Lottie is bored by my chatter (which she can't understand, though I wish she would try); bless the ubiquitous gameboy for such waits.

Eventually we depart once the driver has torn himself away from vivacious chat with a mate, and puffed on the last inch of his cigarette. The traffic is bad, but the hour and a half journey wends through cobbled streets and up hills, past just glimpsed marinas, stalls of huge watermelons dappled green like variegated sycamore leaves, terracotta walls and dark green shutters. We can see Mount Vesuvius to the left: a purple grey cone with the top levelled off. Sorrento, when we get there, is much bigger than I expected – much more sprawled out. The bus stops in the main square of the old part of the town, Piazza Tasso, but the map off the internet is accurate and it is only a ten minute walk away from the direction of the sea to Hotel Savoia. It is simple but friendly, clean and pleasant. The reception area, and where I suppose we will eat breakfast, is through a different door from the one that leads to stairs and bedrooms, almost as if they have bought two adjoining houses. Perhaps the owners live above the reception area. Our room is cool beiges and creams. There are single beds side by side. Lottie likes the air conditioning; I like the balcony with wrought iron table and chairs through the shuttered floor length French windows. We quickly discover that cartoons on Italian TV are great. We both learn to understand and say 'il monstre di caverna' in a trice.

We unpack, change and go to explore the way to the beach. I reckon one croissant and a quarter of a bread roll is not much for Lottie to have eaten between 3.30 am and 3.30 pm so I buy her an ice-cream. She ponders lengthily over the choices, deciding by colour rather than name. We meander over a bridge which drops away to a ruined aqueduct and buildings. They are beautiful; grey and wet in the ravine below us, green fronded ferns thrusting through old window openings and between arches. We find endless steps cut into the cliff down to the port, and eventually swim from an incredibly crowded grey, gritty patch of beach (sitting room only). The water seems clear but I thought we'd have to swim separately because of looking after money etc. But I find a kind Italian woman who 'bag sits' while Lottie and I swim out into the bay to some big rocks. It is good to look up at the cliffs from the sea. It is pretty – even striking with high grey cliffs perpendicular from shore to town – but not as picturesque as I'd expected. Down here on the shore it seems crowded with parasols and beach bars – very bustling and busy.

We only have our sarongs as towels, and it is salt-sticky walking back. The sarongs hug our legs damply. We find another, more direct, way back steeply up through some caves where the wall graffiti includes a glorious winged dragon. Lottie says as we climb,

"It feels like a dream being here, but it can't be because it hurts when I pinch myself." I wonder where she has read that rather old fashioned idea of pinching yourself to know you are awake – it's not a phrase I use. I know what she means. It is the strangest feeling – real but not real – being here. It is the first time I have travelled abroad without another adult. It's quite a responsibility – but exciting too.

We are both starting to suffer from fade, and I am beginning to feel tetchy (always a sign that I am tired), so I buy four tiny biscuits for us to eat from an Aladdin's cave of a patisserie near the hotel. We eat them at our balcony table, then shower, change and watch cartoons. Thank goodness for having this hotel already booked – it is a blessed safe haven. Although it is on a main road there are crickets and palm trees outside the window.

The early start has caught up on us now and we are tired, but we decide to eat out since I have no energy to find a supermarket and I think we need more sustenance than a nectarine from the fruit shop two doors down the road! We eat at the Macine Pizzeria. It is a veranda type restaurant. Peach trees and flowering plumbago grow beside our table. It feels very green and lush, and is empty except for us. But then we are early; it is hardly open. We play cards so as not to feel too impatient with hunger; we have pizza margarita (Lottie) and spaghetti vongole (me). The pizza is only 3 euros – not bad value. There is an odd cover charge also of 3 euros for the 'table'. We talk about tomorrow and what we want to do.

"Definitely Vesuvius," says Lottie. Quite right; first things first: our first volcano. The Rough Guide tells us where and how to do it. We discuss and plan. We know we have to go early to avoid the worst of the heat. The news has been talking of temperatures reaching 40 C in parts of Italy at the moment. Lottie is hoping for fire and brimstone in the crater when we get there and views me scathingly when I disabuse her. I hope she won't be disappointed.

We are back by 8 pm and asleep 15 minutes later. I don't even stay awake long enough to make sure she is asleep first, or to muse philosophically on our first night in Italy. Lottie is right to like the air conditioning; it is wonderful.

Thursday 14th August

We wake up at 7 am – a swift up and breakfast in order to walk to the station to catch the 08.26 train to Herculaneum. The hotel has all the timetables, which is useful for planning. Sadly, the Trenitalia pass doesn't work – the Circumvesuviana line is privately owned (Mafia, so I am told), and so doesn't count with the pass; but it is only 3.60 Euros each. 25 stops! Through blocks of flats interspersed with tiny plots of vine or vegetable, and even a sandy rectangle of ground with a stable, horse, chickens and goats. An amazing aqueduct, now a road, is visible from the train when it stops at Scabia. Travel by train gives time and access to views you never see from a car. 45 minutes later we arrive at Herculaneum and wait for a bus up to Vesuvius. We stop at a ticket shop where a 75 year old rogue called Andreo gives us spiel about Vesuvius – he lives in Tora al Greco, he tells us, which has been destroyed seven times (and he manages to make it sound as if he was living there during all the seven times). He plugs the book he's written about Vesuvius, its history and its relation to his family. His daughter runs the shop and she gives Lottie a sliver of glittering carbon silicate apparently from the centre of the volcano.

The walk up to the volcanic crater is steep and windy, over grainy ash and lava. Lucky it is only 10.30 am – coming down three hours later it is boiling and we pass scarlet, over-heated faces struggling up. I can imagine the view should be stunning over the Bay of Naples, but it is shrouded in cloud/mist/haze. Vesuvius is extraordinary. The new (1944) cone emerges from the centre of the old (79 AD) crater where everyone now parks. It's pinky-grey and barren (there is just some lichen and a few struggling trees) and rather ugly. It is easy to imagine the eruption though, and the lava paths and flow angles are plain to see. Lottie buys a bracelet made of lava ash and pearly stones from one of the many trashy little shack-shops, and spends endless time searching for pieces of well-shaped lava (hardly difficult, there is nothing but!) to bring home, constrained only by my vocalised thoughts on having to carry it for the next three weeks.

The paths are edged first with wooden rails and later chain links. It all seems rather shenzi – corrugated iron shacks selling ice cream and souvenirs – but in an odd way it doesn't detract from its ugly charm. One is only allowed to walk half way around the crater (600m diameter, 200 m deep) but there aren't great crowds, so we stop for ages at various places and try to imagine the centre of the crater filled with bubbling lava and steam. It looks extinct now; the slopes undisturbed.

We decide not to explore the ruins at Herculaneum today because it is so hot and we are tired by 2 pm. We return by train (the wrong one to start with but everyone is friendly and helpful) and head back to the cool of our rooms. We hope to buy fruit and yoghurt for lunch but nothing is open until 5 pm, so Lottie smears marmite with her finger on biscuits saved from supper last night. I am hungry but it will do me no harm I guess. I should have eaten more at breakfast but the rolls were hard and heavy – I wish I'd chosen the soft sweet brioche like Lottie.

Great discovery! We are allowed to use a swimming pool belonging to 'The Green Garden', a complex of holiday chalets up the road. We spend a lovely couple of hours under lush green banana and lemon trees, flanked by bright pink geraniums and deep blue plumbago. Nice pool, nice rest. They charge for hire of chairs and towels, both of which I discover are compulsory even though I am happy to lie on my sarong on the tiled floor. Maybe we look rather untidy littering the ground. There is a bonus in the Thompson rep. at the reception office who gives useful tips (oh joy, in English).Tomorrow, she informs me, is Assumption Day, a major Italian holiday, so it is not a good idea to rely on trains or buses. So we'll 'do' Capri, if the ferries are running, which it is thought they will. We buy huge crispy rolls, butter, tomatoes, yoghurt and peaches from the supermarket for supper. We are ravenous by 6.30 pm – so it all tastes extra delicious. (Nota bene: the best item we brought out was the MARMITE!) I bet we'll need more insect repellent. We smear it on liberally, but still they bite: Lottie's feet, my legs. And Lottie's bites are right under where her flip flops rub which makes them worse. I expect we'll run out of plasters too. Not scratching is an unpleasant exercise in self restraint.

Later we wander into the old town. It is not yet dark. Our goal is to get to the Marina Piccolo which has been recommended to us as pretty. We go a 'lost' way round! Sorrento is buzzing alive at this time of the evening, everyone doing their 'passegio'. There are alluring shops and cafes, and extraordinary people sights – particularly the women. There are horse drawn carts (and even a blacksmith at work by the pavement edge: much thicker shoes are used for these cobbled streets and the hooves are cut away smaller than the shoe and a rubber pad fixed over the frog in the base of the horse's foot; to reduce bruising I suppose). There is black sand at the Marina Piccolo when we eventually find it, having meandered through a rather ugly, industrial part of Sorrento's edge. It is a pretty place with twinkling lights and a high overlooking Virgin Mary statue in a hollowed arch. We share a fanta, paddle, wander, and come back a better way up cobbled streets, past a stunningly beautiful old hotel (Bellevue Syrene) – all cream paint, palm treed gardens, enchanting lights at ankle height, perching on a cliff top. It would be a lovely place to go for a pampered treat. It is dark by now and Sorrento is still buzzing. I would have liked to buy a tiny oil painting I discover in a shabby little back alley studio – but the prices are far too high. We go back to the hotel exhausted.

Friday 15th August.

I am woken at 6 am by Lottie whimpering in desperation to scratch mosquito bites. We eat sugary soft rolls for breakfast. The little dining room has more people in it now at the little round pink and green tables. The owners' children – plump dark haired girl and boy – play on a sofa in a corner of the room by the door. They have a kitten which leaps everywhere and takes a fancy to the straps of Lottie's back pack which I use as a pack to carry water, maps and things we might need for the day such as sarongs and suntan cream. Lottie takes a fancy to the kitten and plays with it far more than she eats breakfast. She doesn't seem very hungry, but drinks hot chocolate happily with her roll. We set off, rather short of time inevitably, to the Marina Grande to catch the 9.25 am ferry. It is a big hydrofoil with gunky pollution from its funnel. It is only a twenty five minute run in the heat haze, and there is no outside deck so sadly views are limited anyway. Capri is enchanting – just what I'd imagined Sorrento would look like. Ice cream colour houses perch on the hill, flanked by two mountains. Beautiful houses, with lovely little courtyard gardens tumbling down the slope to the harbour. After a diversion to the chemist to buy plasters for Lottie's flip-flop rubs, we book tickets for a boat trip round the island. It turns out to be packed with Japanese Italians – rather rowdy ones. It is an excellent trip to make; a really good way to get the feeling of the place. There is a long wait at the Blue Grotto for a rowing boat to take us inside – but it is worth it; it is so beautiful and peaceful, and enhanced by other boatmen singing good tenor (great acoustics). It is high tide, so it is difficult to get into the grotto through the little cave opening – we have to lie flat in the boat and wait for exactly the right wave swell. I am impressed by the limestone stalactites in huge arches and hollows everywhere. A harsh but bejewelled green and rock island.

We take the funicular up to Piazza Umberto (lovely clock tower) and eat apples for lunch on the church steps in the shade. A disgusting aged dog, with over prominent genitals, lifts its leg on a sacred pillar. Then we find our way to the other side of the island down stepped alleys to the smaller marina; finding our way is thanks to some Ceylonese Italians from Naples. They are rather too friendly towards Lottie, and give us too much information about themselves in a mix of Italian and English. I feel wary. Is this the reserved Englishwoman in me, or am I right to be cautious? It's a sad state of affairs when one is suspicious of innocent friendliness, but surely naïve not to be. We find pretty pebble beaches where we stay for a couple of hours, and swim in semi-clean water across the harbour to a little quay above deep water which we dive into. I lie lazily in the sun listening to a group a Australian backpackers comparing, not altogether favourably, the coast here to the Croatian coast. Lottie is amazed and hugely amused by the large numbers of shamelessly snogging Italians in the sea.

We catch a bus back up to the piazza as the sun begins to slant behind the mountains, and walk down another path of endless steps back to the main harbour. I buy a slice of water melon for us to share, and we fill our water bottles from the fountain – only one between us because of the weight to carry. It is hot and we prickle with salt and heat. Waiting for the hydrofoil back to Sorrento I sit on metal gridwork watching the sea swirl darkly beneath. It makes me feel slightly seasick.

We are so tired by the time we get back to the hotel that we are showered and ready for bed by 8.30 pm. It's been quite an expensive day travel-wise, so once again we just spread marmite on a couple of crackers saved from breakfast, and share a peach left over from yesterday. We don't feel very hungry now, but I bet we will by breakfast tomorrow. The supermarket is shut anyway because of the public holiday.

Saturday 16th August

I am not that hungry this morning, oddly. We catch a 9.20 am train to Herculaneum. A day of Roman exploration today. We walk down towards the sea to the 'Scavi'. The sea used to come right up to the walls of the old Roman town until Vesuvius added 400m of land when it erupted. It is a brilliant place. I'd like to bring the whole school (that I teach at; a prep school for four to thirteen year olds) here on a day trip. It is worth coming to Italy for just on its own. Although it is so hot it is so interesting we hardly notice our dripping sweat. The town is so well preserved, so real, so accessible. There is a lovely note in the guide book stating (roughly speaking) that the site comes outside health and safety rules – so please can visitors be sensible and on their heads be it. (We so hope not literally!) One can go anywhere, touch anything. A brilliant place for children to play sardines! My favourite part is the suburban baths – they are absolutely perfect; they really make the concept of public baths in Roman times vivid. The reason it is so well preserved is because Herculaneum is covered in liquid lava mud instead of ash like Pompeii. So there was no looting. It was hard to excavate but not much has collapsed. Even the wood has fossilised and is still there. So, the buildings mostly have two stories, and even roofs. The mosaics and frescoes are mostly nearly perfect. There's an enchanting statue of a drunken Hercules holding a diminutive penis and apparently peeing. We saw a photo of the statue in a guide book and spent ages looking for it, searching every room. Eventually we found him tucked beside a box hedge in a courtyard garden; he is tiny, not the life size statue we expect. We sit on an ancient marble bench in a 'domus' to admire a wooden screen used by the owner to give him some privacy in his study from the hall. Surely they can't let tourists wander and touch so freely forever? It will all erode and people will abuse the freedom. We love the mosaics on the floors (that we can walk over), especially the pictures rather than the geometric designs, and the way they used shells to decorate some of their wall mosaics. We love the colours of the frescoes – terracotta, creams and pale blues. We see a sad entwined skeleton of mother and child embracing in the death meted out by Vesuvius's lava. It is very moving.

We go back to the pool for an afternoon sunbathe and cool swim. Lottie has ace time diving for coins with gang of collected 'friends'. Lying in the sun, Lottie happy in the pool, I people watch. A foursome of Italians is playing cards nearby – two girls, two boys. In their early twenties maybe. Handsome lean stomached young men with long wet look eye lashes and seal sleek dark hair. The girls, one fair, one dark, are studiedly casual and bikinied. I'm not sure the fair one can really be Italian though she speaks it. I imagine that she must work in Italy. Perhaps in the art world – she wouldn't look out of place at the front desk of Christie's in London. She's quieter and more serious than the dark girl, and not so good at the game – whatever it is. I start a conversation with an English couple, Jim and Helen, who turn out to be on honeymoon. She's in the middle of health and safety qualification exams. I'm interested and we talk about the job opportunities it offers. It seems to me that one would end up insisting on a great deal that one didn't believe was necessary just because it was the law. They are an easy couple and I can imagine them coming back to 'The Green Garden' with children in years to come. People are impressed by our adventure, and surprised Lottie is enjoying it. Another couple, David and Caroline, parents of boys in Lottie's diving gang, say that they found it hard to persuade their boys to want to do interesting things. Their excursions are accompanied by complaints and whingeing. Maybe that's because there are two of them; two children and two adults. Lottie's got my undivided attention and me hers, and nothing to do except to be interested. And her mind set is geared to exploring and looking.

We eat bread, marmite, tomatoes and yoghurt for supper for 2.50 Euros, sitting on our balcony in dying sunshine. Above us on a higher balcony a woman shrieks a conversation with someone on the pavement below. Traffic passes infrequently but comfortingly. Crickets zither invisibly. We mull over our favourite bits of the day. Lying in bed, we watch Italian television with contented pleasure.

Sunday 17th August

We have a totally exhausting day – but one that is filled with prettiness. We catch an 8.20 am bus to Positano after an early (for us) breakfast of our usual soft sweet rolls. It is an enchanting village with ice-cream coloured houses holding onto the cliff by their toenails. We walk down twisty alleys to the sea, past gloriously tempting and vastly expensive little shops. One – 'Louise' – is like a cottage garden of colour and floaty materials. Once more there are beaches of grey grit and parasols - Lottie and I persuade a mafia like group of swarthy Italian males to let us onto the paying beach for free while we wait for the ferry to Amalfi. It is a lovely boat ride; gorgeous to see both Positano and Amalfi from the outside in. Amalfi's pretty too, but built in the valley and so flatter. We go through an arch into the main square from the harbour to St Andrew's church and go down to the crypt where he is buried. His body had been rescued from Turkey during the Crusades. The crypt is very ornate with dark heavy wood carvings. Great artwork in the church, especially above the altar of St. Andrew being kiss cross crucified. Lottie is disappointed that one can't see more of or inside his tomb - the altar in the crypt is built over the top of the tomb which one can only see the top of through little grilles. The cloisters are Arabic and surrounded by Roman sarcophagi. An odd mix. After buying a sun hat of cheap straw and another film for the camera (at extortionate cost) we catch a bus up the winding hill to Ravello. The bus journeys today are dramatic. The road runs along the coast on the outside edge of the mountain and cliffs, supported either by rock outcrop or stone arches. There's hardly anything except a centimetre of road before the cliff plunges to the shimmering expanse of blue sea. The guide book recommends 'The Garden' to eat at - and when the bus stops right outside it, and I see the staggering view from the tables on the shaded balcony, I throw budgets to the winds and we have lunch there: utterly delicious spaghetti with cherry tomatoes and basil. Lottie has plain spaghetti with some parmesan and butter which she thinks is delicious too. We play cards afterwards (10 card gin rummy). Wasps strum busily near other tables, though luckily not ours. Then, hot, and since Ravello is asleep in the heat, we ask a hotel which is conveniently next door to the restaurant if we can use their pool (which I have seen from the bus). They charge us, but not a great deal since their poolside is fairly empty. We meet Patrick and Gemma; he from New Zealand, she in the Royal Ballet just back from dancing Swan Lake in Moscow. Lottie creates these passing friendships by getting them to throw coins into the pool for her to dive for. I stub my little toe rather badly - fractured? – there's lots of blood anyway. Later we explore Ravello, a short limp from the restaurant through a tunnel into a broad and airy square above the sea, perched rather like a vast veranda on the cliff. There is a lovely square and the church houses the tomb of St. Pantaleone whose blood liquefies like St Gennara of Naples, three times a year. Disaster follows failure of liquefaction apparently. (Last time St Gennara's failed Naples lost a big football match against Milan!) I long to come to a concert at Villa Rufulo sometime – it is such a dramatic setting. The bus journey back is long but Lottie sleeps through most of it. The bus is crammed tight with bodies standing as well as sitting. When a bus in front of us, on a steep corner of the hill, breaks down leaving no space for passing it, everyone is patient and chatty. A bonding experience. Lottie sleeps on. I meet an Austrian teacher with a heart as huge as her bosom, and Cliff, an American chiropractor, who is back packing round Europe, who gives helpful tips about cheap places to stay in Rome, and flatteringly expresses some hope that he might be back there by the time we get there. (I might have used his tip – the hostel sounded cheap and friendly – but it was such a long trek from the station). We are late - 9.30pm - back, so rather supperless to bed. I fall asleep while Lottie is still watching James Bond film in Italian on TV!

Monday 18th August.

We take the hydrofoil to Naples. We have been lengthily warned about the dangers (of Naples, not the hydrofoil). Rosemaria who owns the Hotel Savoia says she has never been there and never will! One woman I talked to while waiting for the Sorrento bus from the airport said it is her favourite city – but everyone else I ask says it's dirty and full of criminals. I carefully remove all my rings etc and take no bag except for a plastic carrier bag for the water bottle and guide book. So, I feel safe. The hydrofoil winds its way round the bay in forty five minutes and docks beside a huge tanker. The sun is hot even from the crowded inside of the hydrofoil. First impressions are good even from the edge of the harbour, with a multi-laned main road running across the front of us. It turns out to be a wonderful city; full of character. Lottie and I feel the same way; we are captivated and excited by the atmosphere. We go first to St Francesco di Paulo's church - like the Pantheon, domed and beautiful. A huge fascist marching square outside it sports scarlet banners and is surrounded by government buildings. Then we walk through the poor Quartiere Spagniole: Narrow cobbled alleys, washing lines spanning the width, buckets on ropes from little balconies. It is full of chatter, mopeds and little dark stairways. Exciting. We walk and walk. We pass beggars – mostly women, often with children or babies. Lottie feels sorry for them. Are they genuine? Naples is renowned for its poverty apparently, but I am sceptical.

"Why do they beg then?" Lottie asks. "Can't they get jobs?"

"Maybe not, if they are drug addicts," I say, hoping she's not too young to learn about this side of life. Still, here we are seeing it, so she might as well.

"Are they?" she questions. I don't know but they look somehow different from just poor. Their eyes are dull, these women, and they mutter to themselves as they hold out supplicating hands. They are skinny and dirty, but Lottie and I agree there's no point in giving them money even if they are poor too, just for them to spend it on drugs. And the babies look plump and happy. "Maybe they're borrowing them from friends," says Lottie thoughtfully, "to make us feel sorrier for them." And do we? Does a girl and a baby tug, as is intended, on the heartstrings more? Well, we agreed that it actually made us feel indignant that they were 'using' a baby in this way. If they were. Or is this affluent cynicism?

Emerging from the narrowest little alleys we pause and buy fruit from a stall – a pear for Lottie and a fig for me. At the corner, on a door step, two little girls are playing. Near them, leaning against a wall is a film-style Italian youth – jeans, T-shirt, shades, cigarette in mouth, hands in pockets, one leg lifted, his trainered foot flat behind against the wall. An Alsatian lies at his feet. A teenage girl dressed identically except for the addition of scarlet lipstick stands beside him chewing gum and talking on a mobile. As we pass, the youngest of the little girls dances from her game to prance beside us. She holds out an arm badly wrapped in loo roll and liberally painted with red felt tip. She chatters away – so easily understandable in any language – with her hand held out. Lottie and I laugh but I feel it impolitic to give her anything. She touches my arm engagingly, her brown eyes twinkling. Lottie is fascinated. She knows she would be so shy if she tried to act like this. I shake my head at the child, laughing. She is insistent. I say,

"I suppose you'd even like a bite of my fig?" Who knows what she thinks I've said, but she nods eagerly,

"Si, si," she trills. I finish my fig in one mouthful, feeling rather selfish and ungenerous, and, holding Lottie's hand, fearful in case anything suddenly turned nasty, we walk out of the darkness of the alley into sunshine. The child dances, laughing, back to her doorstep, loo paper unravelling in the air from her arm.

In Piazza Gesu Nuovo we stop for an ice-lolly and sit and rest for a while. Then we go next door into the Norman arched and stone sculptured church of St Chiara (lovely stained glass). I take especial note of it in order to be able to describe it in detail to a pupil I have this year who is called Chiara. We peer into the nuns' cloisters – a beautiful, light, airy, mosaiced, walled and columned oasis, and admire the prickly lava rock facade of the Gesu Nuovo church. It looks like the surface of a dinosaur made with egg boxes at nursery school. We walk on up the street where they make intricate Christmas cribs out of bark and palm hair – they are strangely naff in spite of the artistic skill that has gone into them

- and go into the church of St Georgio Armeni with its gliding white robed nuns. We gawp at the unbelievable over-the-top gold beauty of the pair of gilded organs in their lofts that dwarf this tiny pretty church dedicated to St Patricia. We walk down more cobbled streets - sadly the Duomo is shut - and negotiate the vicious traffic of the Piazza Garibaldi to the station. We haggle with African stall holder for Lottie to buy a small wooden giraffe (idiotic given the travelling), which though excellent value turns out on closer inspection to have a broken leg and is earless! She calls him Invalido (Italian for disabled). He is of course endearing in his inadequacy and Lottie weaves a whole background story for him, her imagination flying high. Yet another item, I think cynically, to carry around in the back pack.

We queue for ages at Naples station to get our Trenitalia tickets validated and to suss it all out for when we go to Rome. Naples station is huge and crowded and confusing. Queues stretch lengthily from every counter. Train information is well displayed – they seem to leave on time and delays are posted airport fashion. I know we have to get our Trenitalia tickets validated – once we leave the South, we'll start to use them – and so I join a queue (of course the wrong one!) and we work out which platform the train for Rome will leave from, and how often. We have been told you always have to reserve seats because trains get so full and they don't always let you stand. This is an odd idea to get used to – the great thing about trains as opposed to planes is that you can catch or miss them at will. You have to be so specific and organised if you have to book seats. (As our journeying goes by I discover that the booking part doesn't really matter very much so long as you don't mind being moved from your seat by people who have booked).

We catch the Circumvesuviana train back to Sorrento, and spend a couple of hours at the pool. Then we eat crusty rolls, tomatoes and yogurt from the supermarket for supper, again sitting on cast iron chairs on our balcony. Delicious. Talking about our day, we agree that we'd like to come back to Naples some day. Maybe for a long weekend with an empty suitcase for shopping. I want to buy packets of the stripy pasta; it's so pretty - rainbow colours and every shape and twist. Lottie wants street traders' goods – designer bags as presents for her sisters, sunglasses. She has fallen for the way they lay them out on rugs or sheets at the side of the road, all so cheap. "Even if they are only copies," she sighs yearningly…."or stolen," I add. The sales pitch is unaggressive and good humoured. Maybe they can tell (our scruffy clothes, the plastic carrier bag?) that we aren't going to be good buyers. Naples has such grimy charm. We had only walked from the harbour to the station – but we'd like to see more and spend more time there. The Rough Guide extols restaurants and shopping arcades, both of which we have missed – deliberately – and I'd like to climb the coastal hills on a clear day and see that famous bay unmisted and un-heat hazed.

I wish we'd brought scissors for Lottie's diary (for cutting out pictures to stick in. We've brought the glue, but of course scissors aren't allowed in hand luggage on aeroplanes) and our fingernails which seem to be growing so fast!

Tuesday 19th August.

It is the hottest of days - and we probably do too much. We catch the train to Naples, the metro to Pozzuoli, and then trudge 15 minutes uphill to the volcanic crater of Sulfatara. We walk through a camp site – campers seem to have a nationality of their own - round the white crusty crater base; we are blinded by the stark whiteness, and amazed by jets of sulphuric steam, by the smell of rotten eggs, by the heat of patches of ground under our feet. The Romans called this area Campi Flegrei (Fiery Fields) and thought of it as the entry to Hades. I shall now always think of hell as blindingly white. A brick sauna had been built by the Romans (and more recently restored) over some of the steam holes - the steam emerges at a temperature of 160 degrees - and as we put our heads under the brick arch to see what it is like, a drop of boiling condensation falls from the arch of the sauna entry onto Lottie's shoulder and sizzles the skin away, even through her t-shirt. Fearsome. It is very painful (the only time she cries in the three weeks), but she says she is in a way glad it has happened because it is quite something to be burnt by a volcano, and live to tell the tale. She hopes the scar will last forever. (Sadly for her it fades after three months). The ammonia sulphate in the steam turns the surrounding stones red and yellow eventually, and we pick some up to bring home. A very bright and dazzling crater which we leave with gladness, both that we've come and that we've left. It is a downhill walk back, past a supermarket that is open and cool where we buy a box of biscuits for lunch (the only thing they sell that Lottie would consider eating), and then we catch a train to Pompeii.

I try to book at the tourist shop at the entrance of Pompeii for tonight's Son et Lumiere. An English version is on Tuesdays. I buy a phone card to do so, but number on the information sheet doesn't work. Hassle and time later I get through - eureka! Then off we set round Pompeii having gulped down a mug of iced fresh orange juice from a stall. It is midday by now - and so hot. We attach ourselves briefly to a guide (until we discover he charges each person 100 euros at the end of the tour) and learn about Roman sewage disposal and stepping stones and cats' eyes before we peel off. We like knowing about the cats' eyes especially – tiny little pieces of white stone set at the edge of the Roman roads to reflect the moonlight so that the carts could 'see' where to go at night. I'd never have known about them without over-hearing the guide. He is affectedly urbane and professional in flannels, striped shirt, Panama hat and an umbrella which he leans on, furled, like a walking stick when he stands in the shade. He has a neat black moustache and makes me think he should be in an Agatha Christie film. Most buildings are only half a storey high - but the big public places are impressive: the forum, the theatres, the baths (and loos!), the amphitheatre (so well preserved). So we ignore endless identical stone rooms and walk the endless cobbles to the things we haven't seen at Herculaneum. As a reminder of the devastation that swept through Pompeii, there are sad casts of dead bodies, most with the skeleton and bones peeking through. The expressions of pain and the contorted limbs are moving. Lottie stands for a long while in silence by a child's body.

Four hours of walking and exploring later we come back to the hotel for cool respite before the late night Son et Lumiere. It has been so hot that we can feel our T-shirts wet against our backs and tummies. Thank goodness for ancient Roman fountains and water troughs with modern piped/tapped water. Another 2 euro supermarket supper, but Lottie says she likes them better anyway. How economic! Now that we've been living this adventure for a few days I recognise that accommodation is definitely the greatest cost (and I've well underestimated the amount it will be, even though we are heading for the cheapest possible options), followed by travel - though we have done a great deal; it's over an hour to Naples, and Puzzuoli is 45 minutes on again, for instance. Sorrento is an excellent central base however. Some time I'd like to see more of the Campi Flegrei such as Curra with its Sybil's cave.

The train journeys on this Circumvesuviana line are very familiar by now. The busker saxophonist (keys held with elastic hair ties) knows us well already, and doesn't ask us for money but smiles and plays for a little while near us because he can see we enjoy it. Someone is pickpocketted on the train today resulting in the miraculous appearance of train officials and a party atmosphere as every Italian male joins in with his twopennyworth. The women treat the men like indulged children; certainly they aren't on a pedestal. They're very tactile, often grooming each other, and very chatty as family groups, pairs or friends. Less attractive is a great deal of nose picking, and one man who spends 40 minutes wiping his sweaty armpits with increasingly soggy wads of tissue. A gay couple lovingly wipe each other with baby wipes on Naples station. The Circumvesuviana meanders from Sorrento to Naples, and Vesuvius broods over every one of the 30 plus stops. Often you glimpse the sea but mostly the line runs between high rise blocks adorned with washing. We are both coping well with the heat and are now used to dripping sweat all over us. But today is our first midday exposure - and I wouldn't want many of them. Hats are vital.

By 9.30pm we are back in Pompeii for the Son et Lumiere. It is ace: brilliantly lit - and in English. It is set mainly in the forum and round the temples. We meander, hand in hand, near the edges of the group. I try to imagine myself back 2000 years ago. Would I have been outside in the night? But the sky, the same sky as then (not an original thought I know), is huge and high and velvet-dark above us, the stars pinprick bright. The recorded drama unfolds; the guides are quiet and polite. Lottie squeezes my hand. She doesn't listen to the recording – the information washes over her. I whisper important bits in her ear, hoping that it doesn't annoy the others of the group – like seeing a film at the cinema when the plot is being explained nearby rather less than sotto voce. We walk over rough ground at set moments in the tape, the lights illuminating certain buildings ahead of us. At the end a huge film projection of the volcanic destruction of Pompeii is shown on an ancient wall at full volume: ash, falling rubble, terror, flight, death, flowing lava. There is one funny moment: the voice over is talking about how the emperors began to be worshipped as Gods and is explaining that Emperor Augustus had a temple built for just this purpose: the lights rise and spotlight a stray dog standing in said temple. We instantly christen him Augustus!

We go back by train, having waited for half an hour on the platform. We sit on the steps uncaring of the dirt. It is late and we are tired. I expect Sorrento to be throbbing with late night life as we walk back to the hotel – but the streets, anyway, are quiet.

Wednesday 20th August.

We have a blissful day. We take a boat to Ischia – an island bigger than Capri, dominated by huge castle on a mound by the harbour entrance. I go to a little tourist office which gives us a free map of the island. We would like to have explored it all, but one could spend too much time travelling and waiting for transport and not enough just enjoying some of it. So we catch a bus to Ciera which is on the far side of the island, which means I can look out at the scenery of the island as we drive, and then we spend the rest of the day in the sea swimming. The beaches are, as usual, crowded, but at least there are some free beaches (so often the beaches are paying beaches and are expensive), and there is lovely clear warm water apparently ionised and full of minerals. The sand, rubbed in, makes our skins so soft. Sadly we aren't allowed in the spa baths at Poseidon's Garden because Lottie is too young. So we blow some euros on a delicious lunch at a rather scruffy cafe which is full of Italians, including an extraordinary body builder with a hugely spotty back. We eat delicious spaghetti in tomato sauce, and chips for Lottie. Lottie sleeps on the boat back, well sunned and sea-ed out. I watch her sleeping, her cheeks pink, her hair wild and tousled, tiny pieces of grit in her eyelashes, and I feel an enormous sense of contentment in her existence and in our mutual adventure.

We have to change rooms at the hotel, because we decide to stay in Sorrento one last night and our smaller double bedded old fashioned room at the back, with its balcony overlooking lemon trees, is delightful. There's a strange arrangement whereby a cupboard holds the loo, basin and shower taps. The floor slopes (inadequately) towards the middle for drainage.

I leave Lottie to shower and walk into the middle of Sorrento to a travel agent's to reserve train seats for tomorrow. I am horrified to discover there are no seats on any train before 12.30pm. And a 6 euro booking fee. Ah well. Although I do not want to leave Lottie for too long, I am not worried. She isn't! She has settled into the travel-and-explore routine so well – and the Italians are so warm and friendly towards her. Rosemarie is always pinching her cheek (which annoys her, while at the same time she is pleased by the affection it implies) and admiring her hair. And so I take my time getting back. The first moments alone. I drift along narrow alleys breathing Italy and the evening heat and feeling sad that we are leaving Sorrento. I love it here and could happily linger on. However - Rome tomorrow. Hope we find somewhere to stay! From now on it is all unknown, unplanned, uncharted.

Thursday 21st August.

Easy! Two streets way from the station, 4th hotel we ask at, 50 euros for our room which is fine - balcony, bed, bathroom, fan and breakfast: Hotel Rom Antica. Seems good value, hope no catch. First hotel said 55 euros, second full up, 3rd 60 euros - so maybe on a par. (An Australian friend of Sophie (my eldest daughter) whom we coincidentally bump into at the Trevi fountain of all places is paying 16 euros a head to be in a dorm of 13.) It is an extraordinary meeting. I only met her once when she came to stay for a local agricultural show which Sophie thought would give her a feel for the English countryside. Lottie and I were talking about the myth of throwing a coin into the Trevi Fountain to ensure that one returns to Rome someday. I give Lottie a coin and try to watch her carefully from the top of the steps as she weaves her way through the teeming crowds that are flocking round the fountain, talking, taking photographs, just milling about. I lose sight of her for a moment too long for comfort and call out her name, quite loudly. Lottie doesn't reply, wherever she is (later she says she never heard me call anyway; she is entranced by the wealth of coins in the bottom of the fountain, and makes her way back to where she has left me in her own time). Instead I hear my name, called out in an Australian accent tinged with disbelief. "There can only be one Lottie in the world," she says, "so I knew it must be you." We greet each other warmly. She is still travelling round the world as she was when I had met her, but this isn't a working stop in the way England was. I think it was clever of her to recognise me, and tell her so. We part happily, with none of those false assurances that we would meet up later.

But to go back to earlier. There is no hurry, nothing we want to do with the day before we catch our train and so we have an idle start and leave with warm embraces from Rosemarie of the Savoia. The train to Naples is hot and crowded. We cross the station to platform 14 and a wonderfully deluxe intercity whisks us through fertile plains at the foot of hills (Formia, Latina etc). Mostly we play cards and argue about whether to play (Lottie) or whether to look at the scenery (me). And then this easy arrival. The hotel is run by a man from Mauritius and a girl from the Philippines. The room is high up and has a tiny balcony looking onto roofs, skylights and windows, and other balconies. The buildings rise up above us as well as below, but we can see enough blue sky to know that it is hot and sunny. Pigeons land on the balcony rails, but we tend to keep the heat out by closing the curtains. We waste no time, but unpack fast, determined to see something of Rome before bed-time (I know that these cheap hotels we find near the stations in the cities are in pretty seedy insalubrious areas, but they really only become seedy and insalubrious after dark, by which time we expect to be safely ensconced in bed!). We are hungry too and want an ice cream at least. So, glad of the street map given to us by the hotel, and armed with the Rough Guide, we set off quickly into the city at about 3.30 pm and end up exploring for four and half hours! Our hotel is near the church of St Maria Maggiore (and its loud bells) so we go past there and past the Coliseum and the Forum and the Wedding Cake up onto the Capitol and down to the River Tiber, across the Isola Tiberina (all set up for a gigantic outdoor cinema: tonight's showing is The Hours) into the Trastavere. All Rome seems to be asleep; shops are shut and the pavements are empty. I expect a more villagy atmosphere, more arty and bohemian. I am disappointed. We stop at a booth where a charming Italian talks to us volubly in a mixture of Italian and rather good English about all the things that are going on in Rome that we might enjoy visiting or exploring. Back over the river to Campo Fiori (just waking up), we have a drink and peanuts beside poor old Bruno (bronze statue of, burned at the stake) and several hundred pigeons, one with chewing gum stuck to his foot which gives him a very odd limp! Then, rather accidentally, we wander on to Piazza Navone, and then the Trevi Fountain via the Parthenon (I LOVE that building). We go to the wonderful ice cream place on the corner of the square and Lottie has meringue and wild strawberry. Delicious. I fall in love with a white linen skirt, seen while window shopping, and with Lottie's encouragement, buy it. Disgraceful indulgence! Such a silly colour for back packing, and linen a daft material for stuffing into a back pack – hardly crumple free - and not good for the budget!

Friday 22nd August.

We have a very full day, mostly on the hoof. We walk briskly to Piazza Berberini, filling the water bottle at the fountain (a regular and necessary activity not least because the water in the bottle warms up fast) and find the Cappuchin church. A little old woman in black is begging on the steps, a Macdonald's cup held out for coins - Lottie decides she is too old to be a drug addict and therefore deserves charity. We give her some coins, the amount decided upon by Lottie who wrestles with the twin desires for generosity and economy. The 'cemetery' - where over 4000 Cappuchin friars have their bones and skeletons, some in hooded habits, is quite extraordinary. Vertebrae and ribs are arranged in flower and star patterns on walls and ceilings; even the lanterns are made of bones. Quite how some of the skeletons still have parchment dry flesh on hands and faces, I have no idea. Macabre and yet art, gruesome and yet oddly moving. We have to go into the (rather plain) church afterwards to pray. It just gets us like that. (Back in England, talking about this experience, Lottie denied being moved:

"It was only Mummy who felt like that," she said dismissively to a friend – but she was moved at the time, unless she was pretending). We go briskly on to the commercial secularity of the Piazza Spagna. Lottie decides to use some of her own money to have her portrait drawn - rather well too, though it makes her look about 16. I wait while it is done – it takes about forty minutes – leaning on the balustrade at the top of the Spanish steps looking at Rome spreading away below and to each side. Terracotta roofs against hazy blue skies, straight streets, wooded skylines. I listen to tourist conversations about shoe shops and sales bargains. I try to think about what it would feel like to be Italian, to live in Rome. I can't. I'm too much me. But I like the atmosphere, like the idea of living abroad. England feels very far away. I don't feel homesick at all. Strange how quickly one can feel at home somewhere else. And I feel at home in Rome. Yet I have heard that Italians are not great to be married to, because however successful, suave and sophisticated they may appear, they are hooked into their all-controlling mothers. Once you have children, if you are living in Italy, the Italian mother-in-law expects to have, and is expected by her son to have, open access to your home, your children, your life.

Clutching our paper roll we walk down the Spanish Steps, past trash touts (well, what they are trying to sell is trash), and over the St Angelo bridge (I love those angels lining it). We pause briefly to admire the castle and decide against going in (because it is rather expensive and we have to have priorities), and wander on to St Peter's Church. Suitably shrouding our shoulders with our sarongs (many people are being turned away; bare shoulders and thighs are not allowed) we join the queue to enter. Lottie is amazed by its hugeness, by the dome, the 4 poster bed of an altar, by the size of the statues, by Michaelangelo's La Pieta, by St Peter's sepulchre in the crypt. I love La Pieta. The marble gleams so softly. And Mary looks far too young to have body of the dying Jesus-the-man in her arms; almost younger than him. It is the most beautiful face of Mary that I know. We sit through part of a service in a side chapel - funny how catholic priests conduct so much of the service with their backs to their congregation, sort of fiddling at the altar - and enjoy the sung chant of a group of visiting French priests who kneel in an arched line by the altar,

semi oblivious to the gawping tourists. We then choose to climb
the 400 steps to the cupola (disdaining the lift and its long queue)
and tittup up the tiny narrow steps leaning inwards. So high we
climb and then all Rome is spread away beneath us. Wonderful.
There are good loos at the second level too – it feels odd to be
peeing on top of St Peter's church. We have spaghetti Bolognese
for lunch at a café in view of the branched arm columns of St
Peter's square. It is cheap and good.

Then we move on to rather a muddle of an afternoon. We have
decided to explore Lake Bracciano. The guide book says Romans
escape there at weekends to avoid the heat of the city, and seems
to imply it is accessible from the train station. It takes us ages to
find F.S. San Pietro (the station the guidebook says we should use
for this local line, which is supposed to be close to St Peter's) - no-
one seems to know where it is, and it doesn't help that the first
person we ask is undoubtedly drunk. Then we have to wait nearly
an hour for a train to Bracciano and when we arrive there (a super
triple decker of a train) an Italian says Anguillera is closer to the
lake so we leap on a train back the way we have come. When we
get to Anguillera the bus driver laughs at us, says it is a long way
to the lake shore from here, and sends us back to Bracciano. On
that train the first and only ticket inspector that we ever see on
that line, comes to check our tickets. I hand over the Trenitalia
pass, and carry on playing cards with Lottie, leaning on the table
between us. When, after some time, my pass is not returned, I
look up to see if there is a problem, and catch the guard trying to
look down the front of my T-shirt.

"Is there a problem?" I ask in my best and politest Italian.
He shakes his head.

"Non." I stretch out my hand for the pass, but he holds it
closer to himself and continues to try to peer down my front. I
would have liked to have got up and moved into another carriage,
(Lottie and I are the only passengers in this carriage and I feel
marginally nervous and vulnerable), but I really need my pass
back, so don't want to leave it. I decide confrontation would

be an error, and that it is best to ignore him. I firmly carry on playing cards, Lottie shooting me anxious glances but perceptively knowing not to say anything. Eventually the guard hands back the pass and moves off down the train. When he is out of sight Lottie and I giggle and whisper in nervous relief.

In Bracciano at last we get lost trying to find the right road down from the town to the lakeside - so it takes us ages to walk there (steeply downhill; I am dreading the walk back). Anything would have been pleasant, we are so hot - but actually the lake and its strips of beaches are really lovely. The water is clear, cool, fresh and clean. When we are swimming we look back at the shore from the lake and see, rising, the battlements of the castle (very medieval) in the town. We have a very happy couple of hours AND there is a bus back to the station. Bliss. We determine to come here tomorrow and have a day off cities. The journey back however is a mistake. I should have paid 1.50 euros for the tube from San Pietro instead of which, to avoid the tube altogether, just to save money, we head to Roma Ostiense, a main line station, and have to wait ages for a train to Roma Termini, the main line station near our hotel. It takes 2 hours to get home. How silly. Not surprisingly Lottie falls asleep with her head on my lap at the Jazz concert we go to that night. We walk a long way to Villa Celiamontana - very pretty and attractively floodlit - and then picnic in the park while listening to a memorial concert for a well-known Italian nightclub jazz singer/player/composer called Bruno Martino. There lots of little candlelit tables, bars and a happy atmosphere. It is funny the way all the Italians take their dogs with them to things like this. Terriers on laps seem to be quite enjoying the jazz, and larger dogs doze at people's feet. One Jack Russell howls along with each song gently and tunelessly. Since Lottie is asleep anyway, and I am weary, I decide to leave in the interval. I half feel it is a waste of money, but I have absorbed what I want to from the evening already. Lottie walks most of the way holding my hand with her eyes shut! We get back to our hotel room at 12.30 am. Luckily nothing too insalubrious or seedy is going on in the streets round the station area round our hotel.

Saturday 23rd August

We have a switch off day. We take the Metro to the FS station, then a train to Bracciano, and back to the lake. It feels familiar now, the walk down the hill from the town. Familiarity breeds a sense of possessiveness; it feels like *our* lake. We are trying to keep our spending down, but succumb to the allure of renting a pedalo, just for half an hour, for diving off and playing. We pedal out quite far in towards the middle of the lake, although when we don't pedal, the breeze tends to blow us sideways. It is lovely looking back at the shore from the water, everything there rather blurred and small. We have great fun. We invent monsters of the deep and scare ourselves on purpose so that diving in is a bold and daring thing to do. Lottie teases me by pretending to pedal away after I have dived in. It's quite an effort heaving oneself up the little ladder on the back of the pedalo to get on board again. The water is wonderfully clear and cool. It is a gloriously sunny day but with a breeze and little puffy white clouds. We eat chips for lunch and the best ever creme caramel ice-cream. Lottie particularly has lots of swimming, and we have card games and stone skimming. Lottie, unprompted, says she feels so happy. I am so glad - indeed it is all most relaxing - and the lake water is nicer to swim in than the sea, because there is no sticky salt residue. Lovely!

We witness a dramatic scene between two families. One small three or four year old boy is throwing stones. Mostly at other children. Mostly missing them. His parents don't seem to notice or care much. Then he wings a largish one with some force and it hits a woman under the eye; quite badly, it is cut and bleeding. There is a typical Italian argument with everyone joining in, but the interesting thing is that no-one seem to get cross with the boy. The general attitude from his parents is 'e bambino'. While the row rages volubly round him, the boy sits in the water still chucking stones! I'm not over impressed by the discipline of their children. They are pretty spoilt and indulged, especially the boys. Much adored and cosseted, and the moment a tantrum is thrown, Italian parents seem to give in. Pity. The husband of the woman with the cut eye is trying to dab lemonade on her wound. It's presumably the only liquid to hand. She brushes him away angrily and tearfully. Lottie and I take them our bottle of water (which is kind of us because it is precious stuff). They are grateful.

There are downsides to the day however. We leave Bracciano at 6.15pm and catch a bus to station. We then catch a train into Rome to the metro – I panic because I can't find anywhere to buy a ticket. Booths are closed, no newsagent is in sight (newsagents sell metro tickets). So I travel without a ticket, terrified of being caught all for the sake of 1.60 euros. It is a horrid feeling. We make the long walk to the Pantheon at Lottie's request to buy ice cream and sweets from the amazing gelataria and then the long walk back to the hotel – we arrive at 9.15pm, hot, hungry and tired. There are no supermarkets or little food shops that I can find in Rome. Lottie has saved breakfast toast and marmite and an apple. Luckily our hunger is less in the heat. I am worried too about travel tomorrow. Do we go to Florence leaving in good time? Or leave very late and sleep on overnight train to Venice thereby saving the cost of a hotel night too? Lottie has wild solutions that turn every night into a train journey and involve spending the day at Lake Bracciano, which she loves. The guide book says accommodation in Florence and Venice is both expensive and non existent unless booked months in advance - so I guess we'll have to find somewhere outside and bus/train in. But where I wonder? One could spend a whole day just looking I fear. It's moments like this that it would be good to share with another adult - on the other hand there is a certain ease in just making unilateral decisions.

I have found Lottie just old enough to involve in some of the decision making. She has a good notion of what she might like to do and where she might like to go, and given a decent handful of adult facts, either from guide book or knowledge, she can make sensible decisions. I like giving her choices as much as possible: where and what and when to eat; what priorities to give the money we have; whether to go into this or that museum, church, castle or whatever; even where to go next.

So she chooses the overnight train to Venice!

Sunday 24th August

I think today will be tricky, hanging around waiting for the night train, but actually it works out fine. Leaving Lottie to watch TV (she loves Italian TV - proving that language is no barrier if the plot is clear or the acting good) I walk to the station to sort trains. Several queues later I have reserved seats to Venice leaving Roma Tiburtina at 22.30. I should have reserved a couchette - and later I wished I had - but I mishear/misunderstand the man to say they were 60 euros each when they are actually 16 euros each. The Hotel Roma Antica lets us leave all our luggage in an empty room and are friendly with their farewells. We walk to the Coliseum. On the way down the road, just past the St Maria, we are, mildly, mugged. Two Albanian girls in their late teens stop us. One is holding a map and pushes in front of me thrusting it under my nose. The other attaches herself to my arm to hold me back. They are aggressive and practised. At the same moment that I can (just) feel a hand sliding to the zip of my money belt, I clamp my free hand over it and shout, angrily, in English. I can feel the smoothness of the canvas and at the same time the faintly sticky warmth of a stranger's skin. Lottie says later that I shouted in best teacherly fury. It is effective. They pull back and move away fast. Their expressions are startled but not contrite. Lottie says I was so scary it wasn't surprising that they ran away. She and I are luckily more amused than frightened by their attempt – since we are safe and unharmed and nothing has been stolen. I am rather proud of my swift reactions – but there is really nothing to be proud of since I didn't decide my actions, they just happened.

Arriving at the Coliseum we marvel at its size. I have now sussed out that with a UK passport one can get some entries cheaper, and children either half price or free. We join a guided group because it bypasses the two hour queue, and because as a teacher with a UK passport I get our tickets cheap. The guide we are allocated speaks too fast and is too heavily accented for Lottie to understand, so I spend quite a time interpreting what she is saying for Lottie. The thing that interests Lottie most is that ordinary women weren't allowed to watch the gladiators. Such sexism horrifies her and she is most indignant. There is an excellent exhibition of the athletic Roman composed of statues rescued from the Coliseum and dispersed round various museums and now gathered together. Wonderful statues (all the willies broken off, Lottie is gripped to notice) and trophies with wrestling and boxing scenes silhouetted on them. Oddly (since I presume it is easier to paint the human form accurately than to sculpt it in stone) the statues are far more beautiful examples of the human body; the black pictures of athletes on the trophies are rather strangely shaped and stick legged. Eventually we walk off to the Circus Maximus – which is disappointing in that there's hardly anything left except the shape. Gone are the stands, the spina, the meta, the dolphins to mark the laps. Only dry grass, rather litter strewn, remains. We eat watermelon in the shade of a cypress tree and try to imagine the chariot races. You need a good imagination. Then - and it is hot - we mooch into the Palatine Hill complex and stare rather blankly, due to heat and weariness, at the ruins of Caesar Augustus's palace. We are feeling so tired and hot – lethargic really – that we lay out our sarongs on marble slab seats under some cypress trees – and try to doze. Lottie sees large purple ants crawling up the marble and refuses to lie down. I do, regardless of ants, but find I can't shut my eyes in case anything happens (what for heaven's sake?) to Lottie.

Rather a long walk later through the Forum and up onto the Capitol and down again, we find a restaurant which is a scruffy noisy little room packed with plastic flowers and Italians, and slide into the welcome darkness for lunch. What's that idea that if you eat where the locals eat you will eat well? Sadly not always true - the food here isn't that good, and everyone seems to be locals – those that aren't somewhere else on the ubiquitous Italian August holiday. They refuse to cook spaghetti carbonara for one - we have to both have it or both have Bolognese. So, of course we have Bolognese (no way Lottie will agree to eat carbonara! goodness me, it is new and untried!) and it is far too salty. Still, the proprietor, small, moustached and funny, is larger than life and good value. His side kick, a large woman well suited to the cast list of a James Bond film, is rude to everyone and bossy in turn. We linger, playing cards happily in the cool, long after we have finished eating (it is the only time we leave food on our plates).

Moving on (or rather kicked out as they empty), mid afternoon, we explore alleys and wander blindly (or at least aimlessly) until we find recent excavation work which has uncovered three temples, the oldest in Rome. Camped in the caves, infuriating the archaeologists, is a cat sanctuary. 400 cats are draped everywhere. Not such a great smell, but interesting hearing how it started and how it is funded. It is manned by voluntary workers and funded by donations; there is apparently a problem with deserted and stray cats in Rome, so they manage to get some funding from local government too. Also people can buy kittens from the centre. Lottie wanders around while I talk (very good for my Italian practice) feeling soppy about the cats, especially the kittens which are mostly in cages.

We go back to the Pantheon for ice cream and some card playing, pigeon and people watching - and I drag Lottie back into the Pantheon again (much to her disappointment because she has thought the Pantheon was the name of the ice cream shop!) I make her sit in silence just gazing at the light pouring through the hole in the dome. I love that place. So plain, so simple, so rounded. And I love the way the light angles into the building through that hole, and love the way modern technology has sorted the problem of the rain coming in, with little drains on the floor.

Then, heading back to the station, we pause for ages in the Piazza Navone to watch portrait painters and a man who imitates pop singers and can-can dancers with finger glove puppets - he does an ace Michael Jackson. We sit on the ground to watch. It feels very studenty. The latter part of the evening drags however. We spend most of it sitting at Roma Tiburtina waiting for the train - which is delayed. I am bored and rather chilly. Lottie talks to two girls - Japanese students who are travelling round the world. They talk a mixture of French and English. Once on the train, I discover the seats pull out to meet in the centre of the carriage thereby making a sort of bed. Lottie crashes asleep almost immediately, but I find it cold and cramped and I hardly sleep. Guards are like nurses in hospitals - they always do their rounds just as you fall asleep. Fumbling under my clothes for my well hidden tickets makes for wakefulness. The train is packed - even the corridors - with dozing or talking bodies - most of them African. Our reservations are in the wrong part of the train; lucky we don't end up in Trieste. So we have to move up three carriages at 5am. Lottie is in stitches of laughter because I lose my balance and sit on what I think is a pile of luggage in the corridor, but which she can see, because she is behind me, is actually a sleeping body on top of a pile of luggage. I not only sit on him once but twice as I lose my footing, causing him to wake and sit up in horror. I never even notice. Poor man. It can have been no light weight since I had my back pack on as well.

We arrive in Venice in pouring rain, thunder and lightening. Weird but dramatic. We trudge wearily and wetly in the dark in search of a cheap hotel.

Monday 25th August.

I am so tired that I am glad that anyone is awake to tell us they have a room. We peer down dark alleys until we see a light. An elderly man agrees to a room and a price, and then lets us have it straight away, so we flop into bed and sleep until 10am. Bliss. It is still cloudy and cool when we emerge. The canal is turbulent and brown. We buy a 3 day water bus pass and take number 41 anti clockwise round Venice. It is interesting to see Venice from its outsides. It appears less quaint and more functional. Real life happening. Last night's storm has left a choppy sea. We stop at Morano to watch glass blowing in the factories. Each display in every factory is the same: horses. Only after we have visited St Mark's do I realise that they are supposed to be representative of the bronze horses on the top of St Mark's. A sort of Venetian logo. I spend most of the morning begging paper table napkins from cafes for Lottie's increasingly streaming cold. Prices are much higher here. Breakfast at a scruffy cafe costs 6.50 euros just for a croissant, a cup of coffee and a glass of milk. It is fun emerging from the hotel and seeing an alive and colourful Venice. In daylight, the hotel turns out to be in a tiny dark alley not far from the station on the way to the Jewish Ghetto. It is not particularly seedy, just rather run down and with a rather damp smell. Our window opens into a tiny little internal courtyard floored with green plastic grass, rather like the sort of stuff fishmongers put under their ice. But it is safe and practical and in the scheme of things hardly cheap. I read that without the tourists Venice would be a ghost town. It makes sense; there seems nothing for Italians to do in Venice except sell glass to tourists, or run restaurants for tourists, or show tourists round the beautiful places. But it's a shame for it is so pretty - the mix of water, cobbled alleys and pink houses is quite enchanting. I hope artists and writers and poets live here. I love the narrow pavements, canals with tiny arched bridges that you glimpse from side to side from the water bus. It doesn't seem very crowded really. Especially since it is the summer which the guide book says is the most crowded time of year. Perhaps more people come in the spring for the Festival of the Masks. I had heard that Venice smells in the summer – but it doesn't at all, unless we are just lucky after the great storms and rain the night we arrived.

We are ravenous by lunch time, so we eat back in our room - more rolls and marmite! - before heading off down the Grand Canal by water bus to the Rialto. There are wonderful market streets everywhere, and we watch a brilliant candle maker for hours. Exquisite craftsmanship. The candle maker has a mentally and physically disabled brother who sits on a chair by him and sometimes takes the money. He is greeted warmly and often by other stall holders as they pass. He has the most huge and beautiful eyes. It is a dreadful city for temptation; such a lovely place to buy presents. But we are tired so we come back to the hotel for more rolls and marmite and fruit and yogurt before having an early night.

I must find a bank tomorrow. The cash won't last and I'm not sure we can do an overnight train again unless we take it all the way back to Naples because we can't get from Roma Tibertina to Roma Termini at 5am since the metro is closed. Can we sit on a station at that time for a couple of hours? How safe would that be? Research needed.

Tuesday 26th August.

We have breakfast in a different part of the hotel in the street leading from the main station to the Ghetto, which turns out to be the bigger, grander sister hotel. We have a wonderful breakfast, the best ever: muesli and scrambled egg, fresh not powdered milk, fresh soft bread, nice coffee. But Lottie is not feeling too well so it is rather wasted on her. We wander gently off by water bus to St Marks Square. It is not too crowded (too early perhaps?). I am expecting something huger church wise, but I love the intricacy of the carvings and all the shimmering mosaics. It is all so shiningly gold. We climb to the Loggia and see the bronze horses hidden away and then their (larger) copies on the parapet. Lottie wants to climb on their backs - I would like to too! We look at the endless winged lions (chimeras?) of St Mark and hear an amusing story about St Mark's corpse popping out of a pillar during restoration work where it had been hidden earlier. I sit on the steps opposite the Doge's palace while Lottie feeds the pigeons. They leave red scratch marks on her arms from where they have perched on her. I am not impressed by the tacky rows of plastic and metal chairs and tables covering so much of the square, but I like the musicians (piano, double bass and violin) by one cafe. We catch a gondola across the canal for not more than a few cents (Lottie wants to go back and forth many times, but they won't let her – I don't blame her, it is lovely being so close to the water) and then we explore back streets (buying nectarines for lunch on the way) vaguely in the direction of the Galleria del Academia. The rooms are full of huge religious pictures - one or two gorgeous ones: 'Feast at the House of Levi' over which there was a scandal because of its lack of reverence; 'Young man in his Study'; a lovely small picture of a very old woman with a wooden bowl. Lottie enjoys 'Death of 10,000 Martyrs' and anything with St Sebastian (all those arrows). She's mighty good on whose being crucified too if it's Andrew or Peter. But she is tired sooner than normal and not feeling brilliant so I take her back to the hotel and leave her there to shower, rest and watch TV while I slope off to find somewhere to get more cash.

Oddly enough, I don't feel worried about leaving her. The hotel feels safe and friendly and the teenage girl on the desk can speak English. But it does feel different without her. I feel as if I am being looked at differently, not so affectionately, by men and women. On the water taxi, an ornate, brash Italian woman elbows me hard out of her way so she can take photographs from the rail where I am standing. It rather hurts. I mutter something rather less than under my breath about courtesy and manners and in a second there is voluble and aggressive shouting. I shut up but she is now in full spate. I move away. A man shrugs his shoulders consolingly and points at the sun, miming that it is the heat that makes people bad tempered. I smile cautiously at him. I don't dare be too friendly without Lottie in case it is misinterpreted.

I have to go to the Rialto having discovered that Italians work on cash machines for which you need a pin number which I don't have. It is quite hard to find a bank that will give me cash from my MasterCard. Eventually I find a Bureau de Change. Walking past the school of St Theodore I see that there is a Baroque and Opera concert that night - a sort of concert mix of music and arias from the eighteenth century in eighteenth century costume. The pamphlet shows a programme of some Mozart, Rossini, Donizetti (fun) and Bellini and Offenbach. I reckon Lottie will probably be well enough for it and so I book seats. Then I potter about for a while enjoying the sunshine and the water and the pink walls and the odd feeling of being alone. I buy some Venetian pastries for tea (not that nice, rather heavy and stodgy) and return to the hotel to collect Lottie, and we walk a little way to sit on the steps by the Grand Canal for a picnic tea. She does indeed feel better and she climbs a nearby fig tree and picks ripe figs for me - delicious! It doesn't feel illicit; an elderly woman sitting on a bench under the trees offers encouragement, and the ground is littered with the pink splashes of fallen burst figs. We feed sparrows on crumbs and watch boats. High tide later nearly covers where we have been sitting - apparently St Mark's Square is submerged 250 times a year, but that part of Venice is the lowest. We go back to the hotel to write diaries and stick in postcards (Lottie). Mostly they are better than photos and more immediate, but the one of St Mark's altar panel with its thousands of jewels set into gold does not do the real thing justice. It is well lit in the postcard admittedly, better than it is in St Mark's, but gosh what wealth the Catholic Church has. I slightly wonder why it didn't get dispersed to the poor more over the centuries, given their creed. And all our two and four euro gawping fees head in the same direction, wherever that may be, I guess.

The concert is lovely. Small enough for a perfect view even from the cheap seats, very glamorous (beautiful costumes), a wonderful water bus journey through the dark, lovely music and singing. The 'cellist is particularly young and pretty and we even see her on the water bus back. It reminds Lottie that she's done no 'cello practice for a month. Well, there are some things we are not backpacking with, and a 'cello is one of them! Having said which Lottie has eyed the buskers with a keen mercenary eye and wondered how much she could earn playing at street corners. On the way back that night we watch gondolas with lit candles on their prows and agreed it is wonderfully romantic.

I am not altogether sure how to play the next few days. I lie in bed worrying and planning, half listening to Lottie's measured breathing beside me. We could stay tomorrow in Venice and then catch the night train. In the morning I offer her all the options. In the end we decide we will spend the day in Verona and catch the night train from there to Rome, which, unlike the trains from Venice, actually takes us to the right station for catching a train northwards again in the morning to Florence. Lottie is keen on travelling overnight by train; she enjoys the excitement and the novelty and actually seems to sleep well. She also spreads all the remaining cash out on the bed, and spends a long time shuffling it into piles for the number of days that are left. She calculates, accurately, that there isn't enough money for the requisite number of nights in hotels. I know nothing about Verona; it just seems somewhere I'd like to explore. It also has in my mind some strong Shakespearean connections which I am intrigued by. Bit of a worry about the backpacks - we must find somewhere in Verona to dump them early on for the day - they're too heavy to explore with.

Wednesday 27th August

After another delicious breakfast we catch the 9.22am to Verona. It is ridiculously close from our hotel to the station - such an advantage when one is lugging heavy packs. We have the whole carriage to ourselves. I am glad to see some more Italian countryside and (rather plain) towns. Lottie's cold is better/gone and miraculously most of the presents we have bought in Venice seem to fit in the backpacks. We feel well and happy. I surprise myself this holiday by not really planning more than a day or two ahead except in very vague terms. Not like me usually. And it has worked so far. Lottie's contributions to decisions are still sensible - even though she's so keen on overnight train travel. Mind you, though one misses the scenic views it is a good way of not wasting long hours of daytime.

Padua (passing through by train) looks disappointing. No doubt it's changed since Shakespeare's day. Apparently it was obliterated by bombing during the war, and then rebuilt.

Verona is lovely. Quiet and pretty with its fabulous Arena set over to opera. Lots of Egyptian set pieces for Aida (huge and glorious) litter the piazza. Thinking we might see Carmen on Friday night (a better introduction to opera for Lottie than Verdi I thought) we tramp the streets in search of a cheap hotel - a good way to explore - but the cheap ones won't let us book in advance. We manage to leave our backpacks at the left luggage in Verona station for the day, for not too many euros. We climb the Lamberti tower - great view of the city - and visit Juliet's balcony. She may be fictional, but the family Capello (Capulet) wasn't, and her house is sweet. Horrible tacky commercialism elsewhere though; love notes stuck to the walls around the balcony courtyard with chewing gum.

We walk along the river side to the duomo, and while we are waiting for it to open for free, one of those neat chances of fate occurs. The new bell is delivered with great pomp and ritual, mixed with farce. It is lowered from a lorry by crane, shining gold and well inscribed, by a sort of radio controlled 'mover'. There is some difficulty in getting it placed accurately over its stand, where it is going to sit for two months on display before it is hoisted into the bell tower. Various elderly citizens wish to input, and there is a degree of ineffectual pushing of the bell and a great deal of voluble chat. The bell is struck some ritual number of times by a wooden pole, the priests look on, and it is all a lovely vignette of local untouristy life. Inside the duomo is a beautiful pair of organ lofts with baroque screens.

We catch the 23.00 overnight to Rome. Couchettes this time.

Thursday 28th August.

We catch an early (6.47 am) train back from Rome to Florence. We have had much better night's sleep. Almost instantly we find a very cheap dour hotel. It smells of sick. We walk into the centre of Florence grabbing a croissant on the way – we have learned the value of eating standing up – it is much cheaper. Florence is horrible - dull, dirty, lacklustre and ugly. A horrible place with absolutely nothing, least of all the Ponte Veccio, to recommend it. I wish we hadn't come; I wish we'd gone to Sienna instead, which now we won't have time to go to. (Later, back in England, I was told it was the light that ruined it. It is a little grey and cloudy today, and apparently the beauty of Florence is much affected by the angles of light). The only joy is bumping into the Fentons (friends from Gloucestershire) when we are choosing a 'cheer-us-up' ice cream. They sweetly buy us lunch in the first smart restaurant we've been in - and a glass of wine! We see Michaelangelo's David. He seems to have been moved from the Galleria to the Palazzo Veccio and is outside, encased in scaffolding - rather a surprise just to come across him like that round a corner. (I suppose he is the real one?) I'm sure he's better outside than in, but I hope they find him a more attractive resting place. Perhaps they are frightened that without stringent security, vandals will remove his willie like all the Colosseum statues. The queue for the Uffizi is three hours long, so we ignore that. Ghastly place. (Someone else said that most of Florence's joys are indoors). I try to cheer myself up with a Florentine haircut - only Lottie and I reckon that was a mistake too. Oh dear! We are early to bed - no choice: it is the seediest area and a grotty hotel.

Friday 24th August

We have a better day. We are glad to leave Florence and the trains go like clockwork. We nearly have time to explore Bologna when we change there, but Lottie isn't so keen, so we don't. She thinks we'll miss our train if we go off Piazza hunting!

It is nice to be back in Verona. The little 1 star Auberge Catullo has a (lovely) room for us; we buy cheap tickets for Carmen from ticket touts, and we catch a train to Pesciera on Lake Garda to spend the afternoon there. We swim in clear water, but the bottom is muddy and the beach stony and we get back in time to shower and change. We feel very underdressed - most of the rest of the opera crowd are so glamorous. Still, it's hard to pack glamorous in a backpack. Even the white linen skirt I bought in southern Italy now looks like a piece of crumpled tissue. I remember that the Romans found the stone seats hard to sit on when they were watching the gladiators, and rich Romans always got their slaves to carry cushions to the amphitheatres for them to sit on. So Lottie and filch the inside of a pillow from our bed and put it into her backpack and take it to sit on. A good move. We arrive an hour before the performance started, and it is far too late! The unnumbered seats on the old Roman marble seats get filled up at 7pm. Even so we have a good position and are beside a sweet Scottish couple who offer to share their wine with me and give Lottie tiny little candles to light in the overture (a tradition, I gather). Carmen is amazing - and still amazing 3 intervals and 4 hours later at the end. There is a cast of over 200 with horses (picadors, pulling carts etc) and donkeys (for the smugglers) and a troupe of flamenco dancers (all scarlet and black dresses, long swinging hair, tap shoes and castanets). The orchestra includes 11 double basses, 12 'cellos, 4 harps, 3 bassoons etc. Lucky us - opera on an indoor stage palls in comparison. Lottie is gripped, totally happy to stay awake until one in the morning. We are astonished by how hot the stones remain even when we leave. We duck under the ropes in one interval and go down to the orchestra pit; no one seems to mind, and we step over the broken champagne glasses and agree that we have a much better view of the stage from our 'gods'.

We are tired by the time we got back to our auberge - lucky our room is so close to the Arena.

Saturday 30th August.

We sleep late - but catch a train to the lakes again, having succumbed to Lottie's pleading to go to Gardaland, Italy's largest amusement park. Well, she offers to use her money, so fair enough. All the trains go wrong. We catch a eurostar train to Milan by mistake, which is almost non-stop. We get out at its only stop - Brescia - having been admonished by the female guard for 'not paying attention'. Well, at least we don't have to pay the large eurostar supplement. The next train back to Pesceira, however, is an hour later - and that gets cancelled - so it is ages before we are at the free Gardaland bus stop outside the Pesceira station. I am convinced nothing would happen then either, but eventually a bus turns up.

Gardaland is everything Lottie and I expect - just as ghastly or just as wonderful depending on which of us! 6 hours later and I am more exhausted than by any Roman ruin, large city, steep volcano etc. There are endless long queues, but some good rides though. I feel I have to go with Lottie on them so I have to be rather brave and undergo terror I wouldn't otherwise have opted for - which I suppose is good for me. By 6pm we are starving and shattered - reduced to going to Macdonald's of all places, which has the only advantage of being cheap. And I suppose the atmospheres are similar. We are both sad that we have spent so long queuing for rides; that we have missed some of the tented shows we would have enjoyed - like the dolphins, the ice show, the laser light show and the magician. All the same I think Lottie does not feel her money has been wasted.

The trains back worked blessedly well and we are glad to be back in our hotel (they each begin to feel like 'home' quite quickly) to shower and write diaries. I note that the train pass has been a real blessing - it makes even mistaken travel so anxiety and hassle free.

Sunday 31st August

There are long - but with clockwork changes - train journeys to Pisa. We play cards ad nauseam! We haven't really got enough money left so we find a hotel that takes credit cards for this our last night. It is a super hotel in the Campo dei Miracoli, with every possible luxury especially as Lottie gleefully points out, TOWELS. (Not all the cheaper hotels do). She makes quite a potion in the basin with all their shampoos etc. Then I have a short panic when, checking that our flight tickets are still intact after all the travelling I discover that, all the way back in England on the morning we flew out to Naples, BA had taken Lottie's Pisa to Gatwick ticket in error and left us with her Gatwick to Naples one instead. I hope it will be OK tomorrow - at least I have mine, and our customer receipts.

The leaning tower is wonderful. Although it is very expensive to climb, we do (old hands at towers now), and we love the lean as we circle the climb, the indented marble steps, the view. I am terrified by the stiff wind at the top, scared that Lottie will get blown under the iron railings and away. She of course finds this amusing. While we are up there the bells ring which is lovely. We can't afford to go into the Duomo and the baptistry as well, but I love Pisano's wonderful 3D 700 year old bronze doors fronting the Duomo. Another treat for Lottie is that she drives a horse and carriage on a tour of the medieval parts of Pisa (such a university town). It is a lovely last day, and we even treat ourselves to a proper lunch/supper at the restaurant outside the hotel. (I am able to order spaghetti carbonara for one; I have been longing for it ever since we arrived, and especially so after the salty mistake in Rome).

So, time to come home. I can see the leaning tower from our bedroom window; the top layer, its pie crust hat of a top is lit. It is our last night of sleeping under a single sheet; our last day of lugging the marmite pot around; our last day of heat. Italy has become so unforeign in these eighteen days. I feel as if I know most of its bus and train time tables rather well. I can read the headlines on a newspaper (they made a wonderful crisis/drama out of the power cut on the London tubes). And there are places that we haven't been able to explore in the time: I want to see Sienna and Sicily and the coastline between Pisa and Rome. The Rough Guide has whetted my appetite for them; it has proved a remarkably accurate guide book, and since it has been my only reading matter for three weeks, I know most of everything it says about Italy. I'd like maybe to go to Elba again (I went there once for a family camping holiday as a teenager). I'd like to revisit Ischia and Venice and Positano. It's been a success. No dramas. No accidents. Good health (except for Lottie's 24 hour cold). We've lost weight without meaning to or noticing, except our clothes are loose. None of the hassle of normal life -no make up, or alcohol, or arguments or pressure. And I expect we are rather fit with all the walking. Lottie points out that she wouldn't have enjoyed it (got as much out of it) as much if she'd been with a friend because they'd have played around. In parallel I'd say she wouldn't have enjoyed it as much, or at least in the same way, if there had been two parents or two adults with her, because she'd just have tagged along behind more. I'd do it again. Maybe Spain (Seville, Barcelona, Madrid) next time?

Monday 1st September.

A new month today. We have to make an early start to the airport - by taxi since the buses haven't started at that time in the morning. I sort the ticket problem. I have a last croissant, and buy

a glass of cold milk for Lottie. The flight leaves on time. Lottie
sleeps. England eventually curves under the belly of the plane.
We catch the Gatwick Express to Victoria. England is greener
than I remember, and the roofs slope, and the houses are such a
different colour. And there are all those little rectangular gardens
neatly sloping out behind the houses. And it's cooler. Ah well,
home sweet home.

SPAIN – 2004

NOT MANY weeks after we had returned from Italy, Lottie and I were already talking about our next adventure: not whether but where. It had taken us both quite a while to reacclimatise ourselves back home, and Lottie especially, back at school only a few days later, found it hard to be a child in a peer group again, so I decided we would go for a shorter time, and return with a longer chunk of the school holidays left. It was also still necessary to adventure in Europe where it was cheap to get to. It was a tiny thing that decided us. Lottie, now nearly ten years old, was asking about holidays I'd had in my childhood. Mostly I had spent long idyllic weeks at home with my pony, but one year we had all gone to a rocky coast in Spain, and in the mists of my memories I remember I had been taken to a bullfight. One of Lottie's favourite small child books had been 'Ferdinand the Bull', and it was also the time of the great 'anti-hunting' debate. We talked about bullfights and hunting for days (she had always wanted to go hunting to see what the thrill some of her friends talk of is all about). It seemed as if it might not exist for much longer – the call for a ban was gathering momentum. If hunting was banned in England, how much longer could bull fighting last in Spain? Then in December we were invited to join the Warwickshire Hunt for a day when they were meeting within hacking distance. She loved it. It was the best fast day's riding she'd ever had. (God only knows if the hounds killed; if they did we never knew about it). We agreed that you can't be anti something you don't know about, and that maybe you can't properly know about something you haven't experienced. We decided that we wanted to go to a bull fight.

It looked as if Spain was our next adventure. I bought another Rough Guide.

In fact, confident after the ease of last year, this year's adventure was less carefully planned or considered in advance than our Italian adventure had been, apart from booking flights at £11.99 each, each way from Coventry airport, using the new airline Thompsonfly – and that was a finger-crossing risk since at that time (February) they hadn't started operating and hadn't even got planning permission for any airport buildings. I decided that we wanted to explore Southern Spain – Andalucia mainly – and so we flew to Malaga. I realised I knew nothing about the geography of Spain at all, but Malaga looked south enough on the map, and Thompsonfly went there. Then, on a brief flick through the Rough Guide, I read about La Tomatina, a tomato festival near Valencia on the last Wednesday of August (just about the right time), and Lottie had thought that sounded great fun. Thompsonfly had flights there too, and so we booked flights back from Valencia – wherever that was; I hadn't even looked to find it on the map. The other thing I discovered was that trains were expensive in Spain compared with Italy, but car hire wasn't, so I decided that we would hire a car and use it like a suitcase and hotel all in one, and sleep in it. Ultra economy!

And then, once again, we forgot about the whole thing until a week or so before we left, when I started reading the Rough Guide and bought a Spanish dictionary and phrase book. A kind and generous friend, worried about my over-relaxed attitude, booked us a car with air-conditioning, the luxury of which I hadn't thought I could afford, and a hotel for the night at either end of the trip.

Thursday 12th August

Suddenly it is Thursday morning. Not a red eye flight this time, so a relaxed start – or it should have been. Odd how much there suddenly seems to be still to do. I check that I have all the documents – passports, the e-mail confirmation for the hotels (the first one in a village ten minutes drive from Malaga airport), the voucher for the Renault Kangoo from Europa Gold Rentacar. The idea is that this particular car, which is more like a van, has enough space in the boot once the seats are folded down flat for Lottie and me to sleep in comfort.

Lottie and I pack in a remarkably last minute way. A pair of my shorts are still wet from the wash and go in a carrier bag. We take a case with towels and sleeping bags, and then a backpack each. And of course the ubiquitous marmite!

The flight leaves at 16.40. It feels strange having so much time to hang around, and it certainly means we should have forgotten nothing. (As it turned out I forgot my toothbrush; luckily an easy thing to buy). Thanks to a man driving into me in the Countrywide Stores carpark a week earlier, Saga Insurance funded the taxi from Pudlicott to Coventry airport (as a cheaper option for them than me hiring a car for a fortnight). The taxi is late arriving, but not flight-missingly so. Coventry airport is tiny at the moment, tucked into an industrial estate beside Walker's Crisps, with a portacabin for check in and departures. Instant check in is followed by instant departure security, followed by a comfortable half hour wait beside a coffee machine, and then we are strolling across the tarmac to our little plane. It all feels so calm and low key compared to international airports like Gatwick. An airport official is being ticked off for not wearing his security necklace; limited building works are gently taking place; it's only ten steps from the taxi drop off point to the check in desk; you can watch your luggage being loaded (very reassuring); there never seem to be more than two or three flights leaving an hour – if that!

There are smiley, friendly hostesses on board; we have three seats for the pair of us; and the tea is good: big cups, and I get a second fill up of hot water on my tea bag for my £1.00 – good value. The flight takes two and a half hours. The last forty five minutes over Spain, from Madrid onwards, is beautiful. We are flying low enough to see the land: dry, brown, and then suddenly awesomely mountainous. The low sun slashes orange metallic light on splattered shapes of water – one looks like a running rabbit. Then we are above Malaga and circling over the sea. Long grey gritty beaches and endless high rise buildings – how could they fit in more? But there are cranes and building sites in profusion.

Landing and luggage is quick and easy. It is 8.30pm Spanish (or as Lottie calls it 'Spaniel') time. (I suppose, in her book, that makes the Spaniards, 'Spaniels'). It is still hot: 35 degrees apparently. There is a short queue at the car hire place (easy to find and to get to) and a very short walk to the car, easily found in its numbered bay. We have quite a nerve racking drive in the dusk to Bedalmedina and La Fonda Hotel. I realise that nearly all my driving in France has been in my own right hand drive car – it takes a bit of habit breaking to get used to changing gear with a different hand. And where are the headlights? Luckily I don't read until later that this stretch of road from Malaga to Marbella is the most dangerous and death-ridden in Spain. Anyway, Lottie sorts out the air conditioning technology, and the road numbers tally with the road map (later they don't), so much to my surprise, though much later than the 10 minutes suggested on the hotel print out (probably due to me driving at about 35 mph) we reach Bedalmedina Pueblo. Winding up the hill just before the village (which actually doesn't seem to be physically separate from Malaga) we pass a bullring – decorated, circular, floodlit. Our first bullring. Lottie says the ring is full of red suited matadors – 'training' she says wisely. I nearly stop, but lose my nerve in the heavy traffic. Later that night we see posters – a bullfight – 'La Corrida' – is on Sunday. We don't want to hang around until then – but we can always come back.

Luckily La Fonda is signed off the road – or its parking is. The reception entrance is a hefty hike uphill into the village centre up a pedestrian incline and into the main square. We have too much luggage and I quickly wish we had left most of it in the car – not an action recommended by the guide book; apparently rental cars are prime targets. La Fonda is behind vast wooden doors: cool and modern within Arabic structures. We are taken down the street under lights and tangerine shaped paper lantern bunting to an 'overflow' apartment block. It is a huge cool apartment; bedroom, bathroom and sitting room. We dump our stuff, admire the twinkle light views from the (two) balconies, and go to explore. It is fiesta time. Music throbs from the end of every street. The main square has a huge stage and amplifiers: flamenco dancers/singers are performing (Lottie calls them 'flamingos'). The cherub spitting water into the fountain is swarmed over by small children. A beautiful elderly woman in a glorious Spanish costume of yellows and golds and rusts sits in a plastic chair, feet tapping, all her bracelets slightly jangling. It is a very Spanish occasion – I hear no English voices. Police hover, unwatchfully chatting up pretty girls. Orange shirted police with Alsatian dogs stroll past. Lottie and I stand and watch until the volume of music (the Spanish female singing voice sounds very harsh and screechy) gets too much for us and we go back to the hotel to have supper. It is about 10pm. The restaurant is almost empty – we are obviously far too early; it does begin to fill up over the next half hour. The only other English people are two couples who provide good people watching entertainment. One girl – bubbly and fun, rather like an older version of our neighbour's 12 year old daughter Amy – has a cocky boyfriend with quite an eye for the duller but probably sexier other girl who is wearing what looks like a black crocheted tea cosy halterneck. Her boyfriend is a large lad in a shiny football shirt that says 'GOATS' on the back. Perhaps his name is Billy.

We have fun with the menu, eventually choosing two starters each. I have fish soup and then aubergine gratine (recommended as an Andalucian speciality) and Lottie has melon and then lasagne – and eats it (!) even quite liking both the white sauce and the spinachy meat sauce. Not bad value for a total of 23 euros. After supper we wander back to the flamenco singers in their white spotted and scarlet dresses for a while. There is quite a good guitarist. Then we walk to another square by a white washed church where there are pop singers on their stage. The view over the roof tops from here over Malaga to the sea is lovely – all lights but no buildings (in the dark). We wander the streets for a while until Lottie says she is tired and I realise it is nearly midnight. It doesn't feel like it – socially the night is just beginning.

I sleep quickly but not well. The music pounds until dawn. Lottie says she recognises Brittney Spears songs and more. I only hear pulsating Spanish guitar and Spanish songs. At some point in the heat and noise I realise our balcony windows are open. Closing them makes it quieter and cooler as the cir conditioner works properly. In fact we then sleep until 9.30am.

Friday 13th August

We wake up to a hot blue sky. Breakfast is by the pool and already it is stifling. The hotel is prettier by daylight: courtyard gardens and mosaiced floors and steps everywhere – it is built as the whole village is, on the side of a hill. Milk was UHT, the juice disgusting (until we realise that it is undiluted orange squash: so that is what the jug of water is for). We eat a little of everything: rolls, cereal, yoghurt, boiled eggs. Then we swim in the pool, but I feel fidgety. I feel we should be off to explore. In the event we take full advantage of the hotel bathroom before we leave (forgetting our shampoo, left on the side of the bath, bother it) at about 11 am.

Where to go? I thought we'd head for El Chorro, a gorge in the mountains. We take a white (on the map) road, in the recommended direction. There is no road number so we get lost a few times. We are soon climbing high. We stop in V. de Concepsiones for an ice-cream and (useless) directions. It is absolutely infuriating not speaking fluent Spanish: they really speak no English out of the main tourist centres. We stop again later at a café with the most enormous car park in the middle of nowhere (and it is almost the last building of any sort we see for a while) and the barman draws us a map. God bless the international language of art. The driving then becomes scary. There are bits of rubber tyres from blow outs all over the road. In one lay-by is a water trough where cars are drawn up. Drivers are filling water containers. The road is increasingly twisty, top speed 25 kph. We stop to look at a flock of brown goats at a watering hole. (The first time you see something is always the most exciting. We screech to a halt on a dusty corner and run clutching the camera). Bells are round glossy necks; there is a sleepy eyed shepherd and two dogs. Later a different flock cross the road; later still another flock lies sleeping (shepherd too) under olive trees. The ground is brown and stony with occasional swoops of dark yellow oat stubble. There are intermittent horses and ranches – low white buildings – but what do the horses eat? – and bull warning triangles – but no bulls or bull farms that we can see; only a huge black metal bull sculpture on a sky line. I keep mistaking horses (or goats) for bulls from a distance. Lottie corrects me scathingly. It is boiling hot. We are in the best place in the air conditioning of the car.

El Chorro is hardly signposted. We drive through El Torcal national park – weird limestone rock mountains – and arrive at about 2.30pm. The campsite is near a tiny railway line that disappears into a mountain tunnel hole. Reception is closed (as it always is apparently). We park outside under trees and go to the pool – bliss. An idiot German boy old enough to know better does a back flip and cracks his head hard enough to cut it open and draw blood. There are no signs about the depth – and it is very shallow; health and safety would have had a field day.

Later, eating cheese and ham on toast and drinking coke at the little camp site bar, we hear a blonde English family chatting, and with relief ask their advice. The father, luckily Spanish speaking, tells us that the girl behind the bar will book us in and he sorts it out for us. He has a 5 year old and a 2 year old in tow and they are celebrating the older child, Josh's, birthday. Balloons are strung on their tent. Josh offers Lottie some of his birthday cake but she doesn't like cake much, so refuses (nicely!). They are kind and tell us all about the Gorge walks, near and far.

It is so hot. We swim all afternoon until about 6pm when I think perhaps it will be cool enough to walk. I can't have been more wrong. We are soon scarlet with heat. It is still and airless. We walk along a dirt track beside the gorge, past a vast aquaduct – now the railway line – and start the climb uphill. The track is stony and steep. After about a kilometre we see a huge concrete pipe disappear into a tunnel. We follow it for a while, glad of the coolness inside the rock, but it gets too dark to see where we are going – does the tunnel ever end? So we turn back, reluctantly hitting the heat again. We pass a bronzed German artist – gold tooth and bandana and sketching easel; rather sexy – who suggests we should cross the Gorge on the railway line. We edge our way over boulders, a vast drop beside us, and down onto the tracks. They stretch across the Gorge on metal girders and disappear into the mountain. On the cliff – dangling – is a catwalk, half demolished. The guide book says it is unsafe – a British woman had fallen to her death in 1998. A rusting sign near the path we are on warns us that it is a grave risk to go further. Round the corner of the cliff the railway line shoots out of one mountain, crosses the gap on a metal line, and shoots back into the next. Gingerly Lottie and I set off to cross the gorge on the narrow metal path beside the tracks. A train chugs past. We look anxiously to see how much space there is on either side of the train. Not much. The air floats down to the river at the bottom of the gorge through the girder struts which are painted green. Half way along, we lose our nerve and turn back. Lottie is frightened by the thought of the next train; me by the height. An adrenalin moment.

It is still boiling hot. We pause under eucalyptus trees, faces scarlet. We find a gushing stream of water and drink and splash. It tastes earthy.

When we get back at 8pm it feels as if we have been walking in a desert for twice the time. We go to the bar and drink 3 bottles of iced drinks each – at 1 euro each, not an extravagance. Then we swim again. The pool may be small but it has an amazing view of the hydroelectric plant and the mountains.

Later we find the tiny supermarket behind a bougainvillea tree near the station. (And the ticket office doubles as a bar). We buy bread and fruit for supper. We spread our towels on the grass by the pool – we are the only people there – and play chess while we eat. I have a tiny penknife for the butter and for peeling the peaches. I lose it that night, but find it the next morning wrapped in the peach peelings and bread paper I had put in the bin. A lucky refind.

When it is dark we go back to our car, now parked under eucalyptus trees – it was a hard task to get it there: its engine is not keen on steep up hills, and the camping grove is terraced. We are still picking prickly pear thorns from our fingers. (Earlier, on the way to El Chorro we had stopped to look at some huge cactus plants. Lottie picked a ripe fruit, and thinking it felt like velvet, stroked it. It took me half an hour to get the worst of the prickles (softly vicious gold fur) out of her hands. They linger though.)

We try to fold the Kangoo seats to make one flat place at the back, but sadly it doesn't work like that. The back verticals fold down over the back seats rather than into a hole left by the back seats pulling up. So Lottie sleeps in the boot space and I sleep along the back seats. It isn't as uncomfortable as it sounds as we can both (almost) stretch out. It feels odd wearing nighties in the car. I thought we would read but the lights fade out after five minutes. Every now and then I turn on the engine for a blast of air conditioning. Eventually we decide to risk mosquitoes and open the windows. It is a quiet night and we don't wake up until 8.30 am.

Saturday 14th August

There are good showers and loos – and of course this morning I find the penknife. I am determined not to lose more than the shampoo this holiday. I thought we would have breakfast at the bar but nothing has been delivered: yesterday's croissants are rock hard. Lottie has hot milk and I have bitter coffee, and then we set off.

I want to drive along the other side of the Gorge on the way to Antequera (to see ancient caves) and try and find the guide book path to the catwalk we had seen this side yesterday. We cross the huge greeny dam by the hydroelectric plant and wind our way around the gorge to a bar called El Miramar at the foot of the dirt track mentioned in the guide book. We stop for – breakfast? We eat pistachios and drink orange juice – fresh in cartons. Lottie notices it is 5% carrot juice. The view is stupendous over a vast expanse of manmade lakes, reservoirs, dams, islands, rock outcrops and beaches, with mountains heaving up behind them. The bar is terraced, its bamboo ceilings covered in purple bougainvillea and raffia baskets. Leaving the car further up the track way up the mountain in a woodland glade, we get out and walk. It feels quite off the beaten track but there is a litter bin – symbol of civilisation! – so we aren't the first. We find a ledge overlooking the river far below. There is dappled sunshine with a brisk breeze, so we lay out a towel, and to the tune of the loudest cacophony of crickets, we play chess. This is clearly the game of the holiday. I play without my queen which gives Lottie a decent chance – which is added to by my not being easily able to tell the difference between bishops and pawns in the miniature pieced travelling chess set. This game is a stale mate.

We then take (accidentally) the scenic route to Antequera. More of a dirt track than a road (though it crosses the huge beginnings of a main road under construction), it bumps over stones in narrow zigzags. The only other vehicle for 42 kilometres is a motorbike. I pray again that our tyres will hold up. It's scary being so at the mercy of ones car. It is beautiful though. Olive trees and oat stubble, jagged cliffs, patches of water, a huge expanse of wilderness stretching everywhere, hardly a house in sight – just occasional little while blobs of farms.

Parking in Antequera is easy. Lunch first: we walk to Plaza San Sebastian with its lovely church tower, stop in the tourist office for leaflets, sit in a café and eat chips. Not very nourishing, but nearly everything else on the menu is fish. (Lottie still hates fish). We get lost going back to the car (I haven't taken enough note of where I parked it, just a photographic mental shot of the area). We end up retracing our steps to the café, cross and hot. Lottie's sense of direction proves better than mine and, after some arguing (Lottie would say I got stressy), we find the car with relief.

It isn't the last time we have to retrace our steps though. Finding the caves is a nightmare. And hardly worth it in the end either. There are just two signs on the way, whereupon we are left on the road to Grenada or Malaga with no more indication of their presence. The guide book says the caves are 1 kilometre outside Antequera so I know the dual carriageway is the wrong place to be. We drive back into the town and I ask at a bar and at a garage. We nearly miss them. |Nothing indicates their existence. I ask at another garage and a girl points at some huge rusty gates – padlocked and chained. Then we see an old man – gnarled stick and straw hat – inside the gates. He gestures past an articulated lorry parked at the roadside. We have to climb a sandy bank and duck through a hole torn in the fence. The old man leads us round a hummock: the caves are behind locked iron gates. He has no key but we can look through the bars. The old man talks fast and mostly incomprehensibly, but I catch the odd familiar word. The roof is made of a 180 tonne monolith; they are prehistoric; one was used as a tomb. On the entry stones are primitive carvings of stars and a moon.

It is a brief moment for such effort. We do not pay the guide despite his best attempts to encourage us – we feel he might have been an imposter: locked gates, holes in fences – not the marks of bona fide guiding.

We drive, a flat, fast, main road way to Ronda, without stopping, heading for camping El Sur just 2kms out of Ronda. This site is much more touristy – reception, shop, pool, and double the price. Great loos and showers.

We spend the last of the afternoon by the pool. Lottie makes friends with a seven year old German girl called Arleena. She tries to teach her chess but gives up and teaches her Snap instead. A success, and someone to swim with. Later we sit in the boot of the car with the doors all open, (bay 22) under our olive tree, and write our diaries. As dusk falls we walk to the campsite restaurant and eat garlic bread, tiny broad beans with palma ham and spaghetti (for Lottie) and share an odd tasting crème caramel. We start to play chess but are told not to by the waiter – "It's a proper restaurant, no games" – he ticks us off. The mountains in front of us turn pinky grey and then black. When we start being bitten by mosquitoes, we leave. 20 euros – not bad.

Sleeping in the car is something one gets used to. Lottie says she's comfortable. And I do sleep quite well. The sky is starry black through the windows.

Sunday 15th August.

Today and tomorrow are Spanish holidays, so supermarkets are shut (and shops too, but we don't mind about that). We wake at about 8.30 am – the campsite has been quiet except that our bay is beside the path to the loos so the morning is punctuated by the sound of passing flip flops. We are supposed to check out by midday (return of passport and pay) but the pool doesn't open until 11 am.

Perusing the guidebook I decide to drive immediately to a nearby village called Setinel for breakfast (will such a thing be possible?) and come back to the campsite for a last swim. Going through Ariatne on the way one has to negotiate vertical narrow streets by way of mirrors at either end – hairy, but it works. Setinel is carved into the mountains, the houses fronted onto caves – once cave dwellings without the modern frontage – on either side of a narrow river. We sit at a plastic table outside a cave bar. The barman makes Lottie hot chocolate – the coffee so bitter it is only drinkable with sugar in it – and the only food is crisps. Beside us, elderly male villagers drink brandy and aniseed liqueurs and eat slabs of white bread that they have brought with them, liberally covered in olive oil. Breakfast a la Setinel! Ivy dangles from the rocks above and the ceilings/roves of the rock overhang are covered in glutinous star shaped spider webs.

We wander a bit and then drive back to Ronda, stopping by the bridge to admire the vast gorge below. It is hot by now (though the mornings are much more pleasant than the evenings) but today there is a breeze. We spend a couple of hours by the pool before heading into Ronda again to visit the bullfighting museum – Ronda's bullfights all happen in September.

It is annoying that to find out about when and where there are fights one has to visit the towns. Antequera's helpful tourist office, for instance, has no idea of when there are/aren't fights in Ronda. Ronda can tell me there is a fight in Seville tonight but not about the one I have a leaflet for in Belamedina. Perhaps they keep information low key because of the antis – rather like hunting in England.

Lying by the pool leaves me time to think about journey plans (in between giving Lottie the marks out of 10 that she demands for various swimming routines).We should have left by noon, but although we have checked out I thought another hour's relaxation wouldn't hurt and the car is parked in shade outside the campsite. Planning is hard to do much in advance because, in a car, there is more chance of coming upon a distraction. But it is sensible to have some idea of direction or one ends up retracing ones path – awful when the distances are long – and two hours in the car feels like such a long time. Wasteful too, because unlike the train one can't multi task. If we want to go to the bullfight in Antequera we'll have to go back there – for instance – but at least it's on the way from Seville to Grenada. It's a pain having to go back to Bedalmedina and I wonder if we made the right decision. Perhaps we should drive to Seville where there is also a fight tonight, but I gather tickets are harder to get there and I'm concerned we'd arrive in Seville only to find that the fight is sold out – and I have no number to ring to reserve seats and not enough Spanish to do it in. Reception at this campsite kindly reserve us seats in Bedalmedina – perhaps I wish I'd asked them to do it for Seville instead, but that was before I knew there was a fight in Seville. Oh well, we'll explore flamenco dancing in Seville instead.

Driving feels less tense making today too as I get used to it here, and in fact I suppose there is less travel time than there was last year in Italy because we're not waiting at stations. The hardest thing is ridding my head of preconceptions about Spain – it's so different from the Marbella/Torremolinos sort of trashy Spain. I had never realised it was so mountainous – Carmen country I suppose. There is so little English spoken here – more so in the north I bet – so I wonder what other language they learn at school. I've learnt to ask teenagers for directions; they are more likely to speak a little English. Old men and women are USELESS – presumably if they ever learnt any English at school, they've forgotten it. But that's small town 'white road' stuff. Big towns – more touristy – it's easier.

Ronda is lovely. We park by the bullring – expensive but worth it; there are no other places in the centre and we are the last car in before it is full. We walk round the edge of the gorge to the Paradores Café: canopied tables overlooking the harsh drop – wooded hills and mountains stretch away. A slim ringletted youth has climbed the railings and is sitting precariously on the crumbling stone edge, eyes shut. A slightly Jesus look-alike. We hope he isn't listening to devils' voices suggesting angels will catch him if he leaps. Lottie is fascinated – and keeps going back to check on his existence.

I eat delicious roasted peppers with parma ham for 5 Euros. What a view. The colour of the oat stubble is like sand – it looks like a desert everywhere. Lottie's hair is almost the same colour now too.

On the way to the bullfighting museum we find a wonderful poster showing all the bullfighting moves – perfect for Lottie's Oral English exam. talk next year. The museum itself is great and includes looking round the bull pens and stockades and the bullring. The gallery of pictures, costumes and information is interesting. The bull pen system reminds me of the Roman amphitheatres – the principle of narrow corridors with doors lifted and lowered into place from above, is the same. Even the bull stable doors are opened by ropes from above. There are stables for the horses – picadors and mules or even the rondehereos. The ring itself is brilliantly smart, painted in red and white. One can see blood stains under the sand though, and gouge marks in the wooden barricades around the perimeter.

It is so hot now. We leave for Bedalmedina excited by our day. The road is almost empty and the drive only takes an hour and a half, including a stop at Ardales for an ice-cream. We decide to drive to Colin, near Cadiz, after tonight's bullfight, where the guide book tells us there is flamenco dancing on the beach – and there's a campsite too but I bet we arrive too late and have to park near the beach. The Atlantic is calm there apparently and waist deep for miles. It's renowned for its windsurfing. The journey approaching Malaga is depressingly ghastly. Civilisation is at its ugliest where poverty meets tourism.

We park outside the bullring in Bedalmedina and buy our tickets – ridiculously expensive at 90 euros each (front row in the shade) from Veronica who speaks good English. Her mother, she says, was one of the first female matadors. Only men can be picadors or banderilleros still, she explains. Her family own a bull farm near El Chorro (typical that we'd just come back from there!) and she says it is like herding sheep on horseback. She says the bulls were calm and docile (I knew they were like goats!).

She says her father is the boss of this area's matadors – and the matadors we saw here on Thursday night were at their annual matador fiesta party where young bulls were toyed with – by anyone who cared to try their hand with a cape; even children. I wish we'd known. She is sweet and friendly and we learn a great deal about the dance and art of bullfighting. We even discover that one of tonight's matadors is an (the only) Englishman.

We walk into the village and go back to La Fonda to see if they had our shampoo – no chance! But it is nice to see the square cleaned and pretty. We sit at a café until it is time to go back to the bullring – there's nothing Lottie can eat except bread – ah well.

By 6.45 pm there is a large crowd outside the bullring queuing for tickets. The ticket sales now take place (sun or shade) through tiny square holes cut in the outside of the wooden ring. We take our towels to pad our bums for the stone seats, find our places and discover that

we are right above where all the matadors are preparing. Leather cases, wide at the top for hilts, hold swords; pink and yellow capes are being cleaned; scarlet capes set up with the sticks to stiffen the top where they are held: - all is movement and colour. We can see the ornate costumes so close up – the detail, the embroidery, the pearls and gold, the bowed ballet shoes, the pink tights, the purple silk trousers (so thin and tight, nothing much left to the imagination), the black knots tied to the back of the hair, the black hats. Such good looking matadors – dark-haired, golden skinned, narrow hipped, slim, small men; two or three of them very young and long eye lashed and handsome. There is an older man instantly identifiable by his gingery hair and freckles and thicker shape as the only English matador in Spain at the moment – Fran Evans (Welsh?). Older, fatter men in brown trousers and ordinary shirts, with cigarettes in their mouths and less hair, fuss about folding capes, opening cases, bossing matadors. Managers, I think. There are boxed seats for vets, doctors and the president of the fight. We hear and see only Spanish voices all around us – all in the shade; very few people are on the sunny side – indeed all the fighting takes place in the shade too.

There is a small band – guitars and brass – and they herald the entry of every performer except the bull, in a formal procession to the President, marching and then bowing. The matadors come over to the side, immediately underneath where we are sitting in the front row, and one of the ornate shoulder capes is tossed – apparently a sign of appreciation – up to Lottie and me. I fold it neatly on my lap, but Lottie nudges me and points to where the other two capes are being displayed on the bars in front of our seats, so I hurriedly open ours out and Lottie arranges it proudly. What an honour! The ring empties and with some mooing and a bit of hat waving over by the bull gate, the first bull enters at a trot, black and sharp-horned. The first matador – the Englishman – and his assistants play the bull with their large pink capes, ducking behind barriers when the bull charges. More music heralds the arrival of the two picadors on horses, hugely padded. The picadors themselves have metal stirrups and have their legs encased in metal armour – we can see why as the bull charges the side of the horse with a clash of horn on metal nearly unseating the picador. Three thrusts of the pike are apparently the regulation before the picadors exit to more music and the two banderilleros receive their pairs of banderillos, spiked like harpoons. The ring is still full of matador assistants; the matador himself has come back to the barriers to drink water from a silver stirrup cup, to exchange his large cape for the small, scarlet cloak. But once the banderilleros have been placed – an act of skill and accuracy rather like close quarter long dart throwing (and dangerous too; one of the banderilleros has to vault the barrier, horns at his heels) - the ring clears to more music and the matador is on his own.

At this point the difference in skill and artistic levels are obvious in the movement of the matador's body – at best arched and almost tip-toed, fluid and balletic; in the swirl of the cloak around the matador's body or over the bull's back; by the toss of the matador's head; by his voice; by his ability to hold the bull's attention. We see extremes – clumsiness and beauty. This English matador dressed in gold and white has stiff awkward movements, learned not natural. His bulls lose interest and wander curiously round the ring while he tries vainly to attract their attention. He loses confidence, lacks accuracy, takes many thrusts of his sword to kill his bull, is booed and whistled at. The second matador dressed in gold and silver and scarlet is beautiful: cocky, very young, flamboyant and fluid. He plays his bull as if they are united. He mesmerises his bull, bringing it in tight circles round his body, touching it, his hip to its shoulder, making passes from one knee, praising his bull aloud, asking for more music (it stops when the President indicates that the bull is tired enough for the kill), walking away from his panting bull with a laugh. His dark hair becomes ringletted with sweat, his eyes dance with his feet. He is awarded one and then two ears for his performances.

But his accuracy is less perfect than that of the third matador dressed in purple and pearls, who is so boyishly young and handsome, and whom we notice shifting with nerves before his first bull.

"A bit of nervousness is a good thing," says Lottie, ever-wise. And it is. He is less flamboyant, more serious than the second matador, his movements neater. He catches the love of the crowd, the cheers are louder than the music. He is utterly accurate and clean with his killing thrusts and is awarded first two ears and then, to whoops of admiration from the crowd and a huge grin of pleasure from him, two ears and tail. After his victorious circuit of the ring he is borne out on the shoulders of his assistant. The second matador follows him, buoyant. The inadequate Englishman trails out through a different gate, alone.

It all gives us so much to talk about, to muse over, to relive. We had been so close so we could of course see all the gore, all the blood. We could see the bull's eyes, his eyelashes even, and the battered tips of his horns where he'd rammed the wooden barriers. So too could we see every movement of each matador – the sweat above his eyebrows, the expression on his face, the set of his jaw, even the tiny cut – or smear of blood – on one finger. We could see the dust on his shoes, the wisps of sand on the pink tights. So we were very close to the cruelty and the art. And at its worst there was no art, and at its best there was an illusion that there was no cruelty. In the end we had a problem with the fact that these bulls were deliberately bred to fight. They had done nothing harmful – indeed their eyes looked kind and they had to be goaded into their charges; unlike foxes they were not vermin destructive to a farmer's livelihood or needing their numbers to be kept down. We both admired the skill and beauty of the matador, but we did feel sorry for the bull. We wished the play, the dance, the art, the skill, could all take place without picador or banderilleros or sword – just man and cape. Lottie said she didn't want to see another bull fight for a while – "not until I'm 20," and when she did it would have to be the best matadors only. So we won't go to the fight at Antequera – and only if the timing's right in Seville of Madrid – and I'll be quite happy if the timing doesn't work out given the prohibitive cost: it makes The Royal Opera House look cheap!

We drive through dusk into darkness for over an hour until I am tired. We go to the loo in a service station and then pull off the main road towards the port that services Gibralter, park by a hotel and flake out in the car for the night.

Monday 16th August.

When we wake at 8 am we discover we are parked a foot from the sea – calm and barely rippling. We drive straight off and stop for breakfast at the first open café we come to, beside traffic lights. Locals only. We have milk and sponge cake. We drive on to Tarifa, past wind farms perched on the damp green hillsides, through thick grey cloud. Tarifa is the most southerly part of all Europe, famous for its windsurfing beaches. We play in the sand below an island military zone. People are fishing from the rocks. We walk a long way down a nearly empty wide sandy beach – but no-one is windsurfing today; the waves are small. Lottie does cartwheels. Two plump-thighed women walk past briskly, chatting. A dog barks in the seaweed. Tarifa looks flat roofed and plain from here. We discuss catching a ferry to Africa from here (one can) but although Lottie is keen, I think we should concentrate on one country at a time. We drive on to Conil passing pretty campsites tucked into pine trees along the beach, which we later regret not stopping at.

The tourist office in Conil tells us there is no flamenco dancing tonight on the beach (which the guide book had indicated) – only a cinema and music. We by-pass the town beach (probably a mistake) and go to a campsite that boasts both beach and pool. It is full. We park outside on an uneven stony track, take our towels, and set off to walk through the campsite to the beach. It is so far we nearly turn back. The campsite is packed (with Spaniards); noisy, chaotic and not at all my cup of tea. We trudge past a compost heap, through rusty gates, car parks, sand dunes, more car parks, and finally, hot and rather fed up, we slide down a sandy hillock to a small golden cove. It is popular but never becomes unbearably crowded. The water is clear and blue. There is a big fishing boat nearby at anchor, a delicious little restaurant where Lottie and I share delicious paella (yes! But she only eats the rice, picking everything else out), a bar for ice-creams, and the grey clouds have gone. Best of all it is local – not a French, German, Italian, American or English accent around. It is banded by orange cliffs and protected on the right side the arm of a sea wall. Conil shimmers low and white in the distance on the left. We have a beach day; playing chess, writing diaries, swimming, dozing, lazy. A breeze keeps us cool.

The landscape is so different on this coastline. Softer, lower hills – and rather windy. The ridges are covered with wind farms – armies of them marching along the road. It's greener too but not as beautiful. We pass acres of bull farms and see fields full of bulls. But they are fenced in here; no bull warning triangles. The atmosphere is very different, the houses and villages not so white.

Mind you the coast itself is not developed like Marbella etc and so preferable.

We mooch up from the beach mid afternoon, once again the journey back seeming shorter, and are tempted by the campsite pool for an hour. We eventually leave for Seville at 5pm – my least favourite part of the day; hot and airless, so a good time to be in the car. The route curves away from Cadiz with boggy marshland on either side, leaving the umbrella shape for trees behind, and bends north through flat dull plains. Jerez is white and attractive on the hillside; vines take the place of arable farms. Time passes to the sound of Maroon Five on the CD player. Lottie eats a bag of pistachios. 12kms short of Seville we angle off to Dos Hermanos where our guide book says we will find the nearest campsite to Seville. It is unsigned and hard to find. My Spanish improves through necessity. But it is worth the time spent finding it. It's 300m from a bus stop to Seville – half an hour away. Surely that beats trying to park in the city centre. It's cheap, it has a pool, it's friendly, and they speak English. Best of all they can book us to see some Flamenco dancing in Seville tomorrow night. Couldn't be better. We'll spend the whole day in Seville – but can always come back after lunch for a swim if we want. (Hope we don't want, I expect Seville to be too interesting).

Thank goodness the Spanish holiday ends today – shops will open again and everything will be more normal.

Is it really only our fourth full day? It's hard to remember what day it is at all. We have good showers tonight. The best thing to have brought was our loo roll. Campsite loos don't seem to have any – except for El Sur at Ronda where the loo rolls were on a wall outside the loos. I reckon that encourages extravagance. We buy yoghurts and mini croissants at the little campsite shop (everything else for sale needed cooking), and put a towel on the red dust beside the car in the dying sun. This campsite (Vilsom) is quiet and orderly. A friendly Scottish couple next door lends us spoons for the yoghurt which Lottie carefully washes and dries with tissue afterwards to return to them. We discover that what we had thought earlier might be an oil leak round the door of the car is actually melted butter from the El Chorro picnic. I'd put the plastic carton in the door pocket on its side and as it had melted it had drizzled out. If I was Europa Cars I wouldn't want this one back much. It's only got 3,000kms on the clock too. We've added about 800kms to it so far.

The weirdest thing about this campsite is that, actually, it's beside a dual carriageway. Opposite is a shopping complex – Carrefour, Nike, Macdonalds. And one is unaware of it all. High walls with inner hedges surround an oasis of hibiscus and cobbled paths. Citrus trees provide shade and the pool is glorious: big, deep, curved and surrounded by chairs, grass, palm trees and huge monkey puzzle trees. The atmosphere is upmarket and elegant. Very different from the noisy chaos of Conil's El Faro site that we didn't stay in.

Tuesday 17TH August.

Going to sleep when it gets dark seems totally natural now. I wake at 7.30 am and the sun is hardly up. There is a little wind and some cloud. There are little black plastic pipes sticking up beside the fruit trees which dribble water into hollows by their trunks. The campsite café is great for breakfast: red plastic chairs and tables under what looks like a wisteria tree. A sweet green-aproned girl toasts French bread for us and makes us hot chocolate. A heavily made-up, surly looking, elderly woman sits near the counter in a wheel chair. Bread is on her plate but it has to be put in her hand – she takes one bite, puts it down and it has to be put back in her hand later for the next bite. I never see what happens with her coffee. People walk past us to the showers – an interesting assortment of nightwear, the least attractive being the older European man, large of belly, only in too small swimming trunks and sandals. He could do with leaving more, all even, to the imagination. Lottie and I agree that we only like boxers – as knickers and swimwear. For girls, cute is better than seductive at that time in the morning – in a campsite anyway – but immodesty and unbrushed hair seem to go hand in hand.

The children we have seen (Spanish) are well-behaved. They stay up late with their parents but are not overly spoiled. There has been much less crying and temper tantrum behaviour than we witnessed in Italy. Grandmothers are much in evidence but not bossily so. At Conil we walk with a Spanish family, chatting a bit. The parents, carrying the beach kit, stride off ahead, very 'together'. Behind waddles (operative word for both) a small baby boy in nappies, hand in hand with his plump elderly granny; both content to go slowly. A comfortable arrangement. In the El Faro campsite the children tumble about without too much attention from the adults – and yet there's lots of southern European tactile affection too.

We catch the 10.30am bus to Seville. I realise as we reach the bus stop that I've forgotten my camera, damn it. We don't go back. We poke about in a cheap shop opposite until the bus comes, and see enormous and horrifying cockroaches scurry across the floor under a clothes rail and under the crack at the bottom of the wall. 2 euros and a painless half hour later we get out in Seville opposite the old tobacco factory that Bizet based 'Carmen' on. It is huge and grey beside orange Moorish palaces. A friendly German couple on the bus tell us which way to go for the cathedral. In a fountained square on the way we see a line of horse drawn carriages. We give in to the expensive temptation. It is the skewbald first in the line that does it. Phillippe, he is called. Anyway it feels like a romantic way to see Seville. And so on we hop, Lottie beside the driver, and we spend a happy 45 minutes clip clopping down streets, through plazas, past grand houses, now often museums, into the beautiful Marie Louisa gardens: all places we wouldn't have walked to and are glad to see. The driver stops Philippe in Plaza de Espagna – huge curved government buildings arched round a vast fountain – for a drink from the fountain pools. The wind is in the wrong direction and we are liberally sprayed with fine misty water. Cool. The ceramic mosaics on the terracotta plaster make the beauty. Moorish castellations, spinarets and arches intersperse with modern buildings. Our driver chats happily to other drivers – and to us as we pass places of 'interest'. I understand more and more – and I hope I've got it right when Lottie says,

"What was that, what did he say?" and I translate. I am just a bit further on than that stage when one doesn't really understand a word but know exactly what has been said. At the end Lottie feeds Philippe – and the driver who holds out his hand for one – with polo mints.

"He was older than the other horses," she says kindly afterwards. "That's why his trot wasn't so high. And his eyes were smaller."

We walk to the Cathedral passing the Alcazar (the ruler's palace). Apparently the Cathedral, built on the site of the old mosque, covers more square feet than St Peter's, Rome or St Paul's, London. It is indeed huge, but size alone does not make beauty. Three aspects are interesting. Firstly, Christopher Columbus's tomb. His remains seem to have travelled a bit – from Havana to the monastery in Seville where he spent several years, to this cathedral in the twentieth century. It is dark and gloomy, held up by four knights representing four regions of Spain – Castile and Leon in the front, Aragon and Navarra behind. Secondly, and most spectacularly, is the altarpiece; a vast gothic 'tablo', the largest and richest in the world, a carving on wood depicting 45 scenes of Jesus's life, covered in gold. The lifetime's work of Flemish Pieter Doncart. Staggering. Finally, the bell tower, the Giralda, left over from the mosque. We climb it (of course; we like towers), to see the view of Seville from above where the modern buildings seem to crowd out the Moorish. It gives us a good view of the Alcazar though, with its old castellated walls and arches. I look at a pictorial guidebook in a souvenir shops to see if it is worth going into – and feel that Lottie anyway could do with just pottering in the streets around: the Alcazar's interest appeared to lie mainly in more Arabic ceramic mosaics and arches. The Giralda is easy to climb being ramped as it spirals round each of seven floors each with seven central chambers filled with treasures and artefacts explained in English as well as Spanish on information sheets pinned by the doorways. It seems odd to me to discover that the architect who designed the cathedral was French.

It is starting to get hot; the clouds have cleared. We explore a couple of little streets leading away from the Cathedral to the river and find a café – chosen because it has something Lottie can eat: chicken. As it turns out, it is perfectly lovely. An old Moorish house filled with mosaiced wood, with low ceilings, brass lamps and mirrors. We sit at a table on the pavement, the waiter is charming, the food delicious and fairly cheap (I eat paella), and we are serenaded by two Spanish guitarists. They wear black velvet knickerbockers and scholars gowns – buskers from the University, maybe. Opposite, crumbling stonework is held up by coarse rope netting. Window boxes front open windows that show rooms in a complete state of dilapidation.

We sit for a while. An Australian tout comes selling tickets for an open roofed hop-on-hop-off bus tour. We buy one (children are free) because it goes round the other part of Seville (as it turns out, the miserable part). Eventually we say goodbye to our friendly waiter – who gives Lottie a skipping rope as a present – and wander the shady narrow cobbles of Santa Cruz behind the Alcazar. We buy a red and black bull T-shirt for Lottie, presents of miniature fans for my class at school, and wish the little mosaic wood boxes were cheaper. We potter in and out of shops, round curved Moorish walls all around the Alcazar, and peer through iron gateways into lush citrus gardens, until we are hot and tired. Then we head for the river and the bus tour.

It is hot in spite of the breeze – especially at traffic lights which we learn to dread. The audio headphones work intermittently which makes for odd disconnected snippets of information – but good enough. The longest part of the tour is round the old Expo '92 Trade Fair site, now eerily mostly deserted. (It makes one wonder: all that money spent on buildings for a single occasion.)

There is a theme park of sorts still operating but it seems empty too. The best sight is the futuristic bridge Puento Nuevo – a white structure built by the balance of the road and one angle curved white arm poking into the air. It is built without supports – just mathematical balance and wires.

Still hot, we walk in the wisteria covered shade of a pavement path along the river edge, to the bullring, buying ice-lollies on the way. We like Solero shots – lime and lemon; Icy little balls of flavoured coldness that melt on the tongue as you shake them into your mouth. The bullring museum has cheap guided tours in English. This bullring is the second largest and the second oldest in Spain (Ronda is bigger and older though it seats fewer, and Madrid, a modern ring, seats more but is smaller). It is in fact slightly oval in shape, and brightly white and orange – the plaster outside painted the colour of the arena sand. The president's balcony is grand and pillared. The tour is fascinating and we learn so much about the history of bullfighting:

In the middle-ages young noblemen needed to be trained for war. Two games were developed for this purpose – both on horseback, both with long spears/pikes. In one they had to charge at papier-mache heads hanging from chains. In the other they had to fight bulls – four or five at a time in a square arena. The horses had no protection and so were often killed. The officers too, I expect. Pictures in the museum dating from then show riders, horses, bulls and spectators in the throes of bloody death – not to mention a bull leaping the barricades. The officers wore decorative uniforms because the thick embroidery helped pad them against some injury. From these beginnings modern bullfighting developed. Matadors fought on horses for a long time, and when they began to fight on foot with swords it was part still military training, part exhibitionism. Not until the twentieth century were horses padded, so between ten and twenty picador horses were killed in each fight. Now they are very seldom even injured. Few matadors have died recently, although this season four were seriously injured. The dangerous moment is the kill.

The bull is tired; his head is down and kept down by the flick of the cape. The matador stands between the horns and has to be close in order to plunge the sword to the hilt in the neck in front of the withers. Timing and speed is all – and predicting the bull's movements. If the bull lifts his head and twists it sideways when the matador is arched above it, he will gore the matador, probably in the stomach. No wonder Fran Evans was scared and messed up killing his bulls. We see the infirmary where wounds are treated in a fully equipped small operating theatre.

In the last room of the museum are two interesting things. Firstly, a painting of a matador with a wicker chair. One of the twentieth century greats, he was considered eccentric or even mad because he fought sitting down – even killed sitting down. Actually he was lame and could hardly walk. He died in old age of a heart attack, while every direct male descendent of his that has been a matador has been killed by a bull. Secondly, amongst the bulls heads on display as a mark of respect for their bravery, is a sharp horned cow's head – Iselda. She was killed by her breeder after her son killed a master matador in a fit of vicious unpredictability. Bulls get their strength and size from their fathers and their characters from their mothers. The breeder didn't want another mad bad bull bred from that cow. Apparently matadors often train with cows not bulls because they are nastier!

It is a super museum – full of bullfighting paintings, costumes and history. We enjoy it. Afterwards we sit in a café mulling it all over until it is 7pm. We have booked, through the campsite, to see a patio tableau of flamenco and Spanish guitar. A bit hit and miss and I would so much rather have just come across it in a tapas bar (though I think it starts later in the night than we are usually up) – but I wanted to make sure that Lottie saw it somewhere, sometime. We make our way to the low dark room with a theatre stage at one end, laid up with seats and tables. We are the first to arrive. We eat salted almonds and I have a glass of ice cold, very dry, sherry from Jerez taken from a wooden cask. It is delicious. The dancing is flamboyant and energetic. A cast of 4 men and 5 women with castanets, fans, sleeked back hair with bright combs, and an array of wonderful, ever changing costumes, stamp and writhe and sing. Great fun. One of the men though looks very unSpanish – Sean Beanish in fact; a Sheffield lad?! He lacks the black oily curls. Sadly the place is rather empty; only the first five or six rows are filled with tourists like us, and most them are a large group of Japanese, one of whom climbs up on the stage and makes a fairly decent stab at flamenco dancing, encouraged by the professionals and cheered by his friends. Although I think Lottie doesn't really notice, it is somewhat tacky, and appallingly touristy.

It is still warm when we walk back through Seville to catch the bus back. Darkness falls quickly. On the bus are the friendly German couple again. We make friends – he is a teacher and they ski in Meribel as we like to. A daughter has worked in Lincolnshire for a year so they've been to England. There is a standing joke that nowhere is better than Munich (where they live). We laugh about the superstition of bad luck in seeing a new moon through glass, groping our way through language difficulties. They have, it turns out, a camper van beside us at the campsite. They thought we were Spanish because our hire car has a Spanish number plate. I am impressed by the bikes on the back of their van (they are older than me), and say so. They laugh – they've driven 4,000kms and biked 4kms. All for show!

We are tired but fall asleep talking about flamenco dancing. The moon gleams in a starry sky that we can see through the car windows.

Wednesday 18th August

We spend a happy morning by the pool – more luxurious than many a hotel. It is quiet and restful. We set off for Cordoba at 2 pm after an incident.

A fierce and aggressive lime tree – not that one wishes to disparage Spanish trees in general – wished to delay or even prevent our departure and so thrust a wooden fist through the window of the back door as we were reversing out of the campsite bay. I am sure it hadn't been growing there when we arrived! There was a ghastly noise, a sort of crunching scrunching noise, and a large amount of broken glass which I sweep up with my flip flop – and we thought only the bulls were unpredictable and dangerous! Oh dear – and so the locking system doesn't now work. Still, on the bright side the car is still driveable – an open back instead of an open top! It makes driving sound odd – cars coming up behind sound as if they are in the boot. It takes a little getting used to. I ring Europa Car who, thank God, speak English. We can exchange our damaged Citroen for a new car but only from branch offices in Cadiz, Malaga, Almeria, Alicante or Valencia – all three or four hours plus away. Only our possessions are at risk – and I think a thief would grab a bag not knickers, so if we take out our kit and strew it about the car…..one case is ripped anyway, and nothing is worth much. I'll carry papers, money, phone, camera – and of course Milli, the only thing Lottie minds about being stolen.

However, I feel a bit tense and shaky for a while. Luckily the drive to Cordoba is uneventful – Lottie says we've had the bad luck visited on us by looking at that new moon through glass – and we buy fruit and yoghurt in a supermarket for lunch. I feel hungry - hungrier than last year in Italy where we seemed to eat little. The broken window has exacerbated other discomforts: - my cracked heel is bleeding; Lottie's damaged fingernail is flaking off painfully; money seems to last such a short time, even though I thought we were living cheaply by being in campsites at about 15 euros on average a night (which given the good comforts of loos, showers, cafes, pool, on site shops, is truly excellent value. Most of the hotels we stayed in Italy offered much less in the way of comfortable facilities).

I drive badly in Cordoba – trying to look for traffic lights and campsite signs and other traffic all at once. A bus narrowly misses me – my fault. Cars drive hard at my bumper and hoot if I go too slowly. I get ratty.

Mind set is all. I think the campsite is horrid on sight, and the receptionist cross and rude. It is probably me. I am irritated that there is an extra charge for using the pool which I think looks crowded and suburban – well, it is the municipal campsite: what does one expect, 1km from the city centre?

Lottie clearly wants to mess about in the pool and since I reckon hot and bothered is not the way to see Cordoba's Mesquita, Spain's grandest and richest Moorish mosque (a visual gem apparently), I settle by the pool to unwind. At least everyone is Spanish. Two hours later I feel better.

I muse as I lie in the sun. I think I don't want to drive the six or seven hours to Madrid. The guidebook says the landscape between Cordoba and Madrid is dull and it doesn't look as if there is anywhere particular to stop except for tiny mountain villages way off the beaten track where they are surprised to see visitors. Which has its attraction. But a fast AVE train takes 2 hours. I think that's the answer: a day trip. If it's a success we could even do it twice and go to Toledo from Madrid – but that might be too much. The plan could be then to drive after that to Granada and then take the road to Valencia through Almeira and along that coastline. A better plan!

After a laze in the hot evening sun, we set off by bus into Cordoba at about 7.30pm. The bus takes us to the station from where we walk through palm treed gardens, through a tented market, past an open air blues concert towards the Juderia (the Jewish quarter) and (oddly) the Mesquita. We wander through tiny white cobbled alleys and into dead ends; then, hungry, we find a tapas bar. Casa Pepe. Glorious. Low, dark wooden ceilings, a tiny open courtyard strung with plants and vines. We sit in a little tapas room off the restaurant and, since we are early by Spanish standards at 9pm, have the undivided attention of a lovely waiter who makes helpful suggestions about the tapas. Why isn't there the equivalent of tapas in England? It's brilliant. Half starter sized amounts of everything for about £1. We have prawns in a sauce, a sort of tomato and garlic mush with bits of bacon, a sort of cheese and garlic mush with hardboiled egg, chunks of aubergine fried in batter with cane honey dressing, a pudding of nougat mousse and caramel ice-cream, and Lottie drinks fanta and I have a huge glass of icy dry sherry – and all for 14 euros. It is great fun. We half chat to people eating different tapas near us – such as bull's tail. It looks like chunks of meaty vertebrae which I suppose it is. It is a good atmosphere and is soon vibrantly busy and popular. Our waiter soon has no time for us and we leave after 10pm, anxious about missing the last bus back.

On the way back we feed sleepy horses waiting with equally sleepy drivers for late night hire, with polos. We admire the bell tower and doorways of the Mesquita, floodlit and golden. We find our way; we don't get lost. Life is mellow.

Thursday 19th August.

I toss and turn a bit in the night, trying to make decisions. Nothing the guidebook says about Madrid inspires a visit except the Prada to see Goya and Velasquez. It doesn't seem worth the 120 euro train fare for us both (or the six hour drive). Just another big (rather modern) city it would seem. I'd rather go to Toledo, the medieval capital city nearby. In sleep, as the best decisions often happen, it comes to me. We'd go, if we had time, from Valencia, and go today in the early afternoon heat, straight to Granada. I don't like this campsite much anyway, although Lottie who has made friends with a Spanish girl and plays bullfight diving games with her, likes this pool the best.

So we have breakfast in our nighties by the car, sitting on a sleeping bag, of water, peaches, yoghurt and pistachios. Quite nutritious even if odd. Then we drive into Cordoba to go inside the Mesquita. The traffic is fine, though I miss a few signs and go more than once round roundabouts, and we park in the main avenue, beckoned to a place by a keen attendant for 60 cents.

Hard to tell whether that is the official parking fee or his keen personal collection.

We walk easily, retracing some of last night's steps, to the Mesquita and enter the orange grove inside its huge metal doors. From the orange grove one enters through one of the original 19 doors – the rest are now sealed – into the mosque.

It is amazing. It is my favourite interior of everything I have ever seen. The pillars and arches just disappear, around and away – 2,900 of them. The brick and stone stripes, the marble floors, the upturned urn lighting – it's so beautiful. And then, in the middle, suddenly, sombre and tall, soaring from the double arches, is the beige stone of a cathedral, built in the 16th century in the middle of the mosque by Carlos V. The history is interesting – the guide book fulsome in the telling – but the visual impact needs no knowledge.

We wander for ages. Coincidentally Lottie sees her swimming pool friend with her family there and says a pleased hello. Eventually we emerge the other side of the orangery and sit in wicker chairs for freshly squeezed orange juice and a cup of coffee.

I think Lottie is bored so we drift in and out of souvenir shops (all of them much of a muchness) and buy some presents. She cheers up quickly and we meander through the alleys and courtyards of the Juderia and find the bullfight museum. It is interesting because the skin of the cow Iselda whose head was in Seville's museum is hung on the wall beside a marble effigy of Manolite, the matador who was killed in 1945 by her son. Everything to do with this apparently horrific 'in arena' death is on display: Manolite's photos, clothes, cape, the banderilleros, sword, bloody shirt; photos from the newspapers about the goring, tickets from that day. There are more paintings, photos, costumes – to do with Manchaquita and Cordobes particularly. We are good now at telling the era of the painting by whether the picadors' horses are padded or not.

The courtyard is enchanting – full of scented jasmine and bright blue plumbago, with the sound of guitar music drifting from somewhere. I tell Lottie the Mesquita is my favourite interior. She says home is hers.

We walk up a side alley and found the synagogue. A small, simple, square room with white carved walls. Quite a contrast with the Mesquita.

It takes us a couple of hours to drive to Grenada – but on the way we make a detour to a ruined Caliph's palace and city which housed, originally, his harem of 800 wives. It is like exploring a Moorish version of Pompeii on a small scale – except that it is built with terraces and ramps on the side of the hills above Cordoba (what a view!). The Grand Hall – striped curved arches and columns with the flavour of the Mesquita – is lovely.

The road to Grenada travels through hillsides striped like Pharaoh's headdresses with olive groves – as far as the eye can see. As we near Granada the mountains of Sierra Nevada, pocketed with snow, rears high. On the way a handful of white hilltop villages breaks the road. Wealth must be increasing; all have extensive building taking place on their outskirts.

We find the city campsite, near the bus station (which is <u>not</u> very near the centre). Camping Sierra Nevada: very luxurious. 20 euros, but probably worth it. We head for the pool (it is 5pm by now and much to Lottie's delight she finds an Australian chap who she'd talked to in the pool at Cordoba is also here. He had taught her a new swimming stroke and they while away an hour or two here creating synchronized routines. Mark (he likes the inside of St Mark's, Venice best) is travelling the world before he starts his own business. He's been in advertising for 6 years – so he must be in his late 20s. He's very tolerant of Lottie – hope his motives are OK. Perhaps it's more fun swimming with someone else than not – even a ten year old.

The pool is lovely – the whole set up is. There's no doubt that this extensive travelling and exploring is well broken up by poolside relaxation. A lunch or supper or two in a lovely place has a similar effect – better perhaps because it gives one a feel for a place.

We are getting used to our open/broken back window. It does mean the air conditioning isn't so effective though. I found the hardest habit to break was changing gear with the left hand – but I now feel more confident even in cities.

Mark spends so much time playing with Lottie that I buy him a drink to thank him. We sit under an umbrella at the pool café drinking milk shakes and talking about his two year travels, about bullfights, about Howard the Australian Prime Minister ('a little man in every way'), about the value of the Australian dollar, the meaning of his Chinese Jade necklace ('all will go well'), about his plans to help disadvantaged teenagers realise their potential, about his parents (German father, Hungarian mother). Funny how meeting people works. It's always through Lottie. Once is an acquaintance. Twice, I tend to say hello too.

Lottie and I come back to the poolside bar for supper. I have Tortilla (Spanish omelette) and Lottie has chips. Not the cheapest option but the supermarket is shut and Lottie is hungry. We write our diaries under the stars until we get anxious about the mosquitoes and go to bed.

One week gone.

Friday 20th August

A good, even excellent, day. We head for the Alhambra, the Moorish fortress/palace on the hillside in Granada (for which Grenada is famed). Now this place is hard to get into. You can reserve tickets by telephone; the first available yesterday were for Sunday. Or you can queue for the 1,000 or so that they sell on the day at the entrance. Queues start at 6am. Ticket offices open at 8am, gates at 8.30 am. One is awarded a time slot for the palace.

Well, aren't we lucky that Mark is going early to queue and says he'll queue for us too. We arrange to meet by the entrance – or in the queue – at 8.30am. I have turned on the mobile phone and set the alarm for 7.30am so this morning I haul a sleepy eyed

Lottie from the car (bed!) and catch a bus at 8am for the centre. I feed Lottie on pistachios and the last peach for breakfast on the bus, which drops us by the cathedral, a short walk from Plaza Nuevo at the foot of the hill.

Granada from the bus isn't beautiful: a large modern city full of shop fronts and traffic lights. But once we've set off in the little minibus from the square which takes us through the castellated archway up the hill (we could have walked), the whole feeling changes.

There is an excitement in the air around La Alhambra, even given the tourists and the litter bins. Can one breathe the fierce magic of 2,000 years ago when Mohammed 1 built it? The reddish walls push up out of the hillside, thick and strong.

We find Mark well back in the queue – he's been there since 7am. But it is moving slowly and by 9.30am we have a ticket – for three people, which means poor Mark is stuck with us for the day. He then remembers he's forgotten his camera and wants to go back to the campsite by taxi to get it – our ticket slot is for 12.30pm, so there is lots of time. Lottie says that she wants to get her camera too, so off they go together, arranging to meet back at 10am. I go to the tiny café by the entrance and buy a cup of coffee and settle down to read up about La Alhambra.

At 10 o'clock, I suddenly panic. What have I done? Allowed my rather too beautiful blonde10 year old to go off with a nearly strange man – I don't know his surname or his car registration, or really anything much about him. It is silly to worry, I tell myself; I can judge character well enough, can't I? He is an ordinary, decent Aussie guy. Everything will be fine; the campsite will have his name, his registration number, even his passport. He's just paid for his ticket into la Alhumbra; he's queued for three hours, he won't want to miss seeing it. Everything is perfectly normal. Isn't it?

And it is. They turn up, cameras in hand, just after 10am. I rent two audio guides – and it is money well spent. They are particularly good ones. Various places around La Alhumbra are numbered. One presses the number on the guide – rather like dialling on a telephone – and listen to the relevant information. So one can hear it out of order, again, or even not at all.

La Alhumbra is divided into three areas. The Generalife, where we explore first, is the Sultan's summer palace and gardens up on the hillside with a wonderful view of Grenada, the mountains of Sierra Nevada, and of his fortress. It is a series of patios, pools, gardens and a simple Moorish palace. It includes a garden with a (now dead) cypress tree where the Sultan's favourite wife met her lover, chief of the Abencerrajes, 16 of whose prices were murdered by the Sultan Hasan in revenge. I like the wooden lattice windows in the summer palace. Everything is well preserved except that the plaster would have been brightly painted. There are clever fountains and water systems including an open handrail on steep steps in the garden that has a flowing stream in the gully. We potter slowly. One garden is divided into squares by high myrtle and cypress hedges and arches. It is like a maze for one can't see out of the flowered squares except through the arches. It is wonderfully cool. The advantage of the strict limitation of numbers is that once inside – in the morning anyway – it feels quite empty. Since one can stay in as long as one likes, by the afternoon it is more crowded.

We walk over a bridge, down from the hillside, over the palace fruit gardens, and along the ramparts to the Alcazabar – the fortress. The path takes us past the ruins of a government city of houses, baths, schools, barracks and gardens – even a monastery which has been converted into a hotel.

For a ruin the Alcazabar is wonderfully complete. What a place, what a fortress! Huge and repressively strong – vast thick walls. We climb towers high above Grenada and look at the snow at the top of the Sierra Nevada. We potter amongst the ruins of the barracks, and see cannon balls in the alcoves of the old armoury. We stand on the bell tower; we see the Islam key carved into the stone as a symbol of Islamic faith above the gateway;

we sit under wisteria trees and eat cheese rolls; we fill our water bottles from the fountains.

In the road between the fortress proper and the palace are a few artisan shops. In one we stop and watch the marquetry of inlaid wood. Intricate and Arabic in design, using star shapes and geometric patterns in different woods and cow bone. It must take ages to complete, all done by hand using veneer wood, a sharp cutter, powder and warm glue. There is a lovely hotel – Hotel America – beside the palace – I go in to see how much it was for the night (170 Euros) and see an enchanting courtyard restaurant through an arch. It would be a wonderful weekend visit.

At 12.30 we enter the Nasarid Palace - or we think we do. We go through large imposing doors set in a vast white palace façade – oh no, this is the palace of King Carlos V who destroyed some of the Moorish palace to throw up his huge ostentatious edifice. The great circular open roofed hall was even used for bullfights. We retreat and find a sign directing us to the side. Round the corner, hidden away, is a simple carved door: the entry gate to a jewel of light and fairy architecture. It is, in places, gasp making. Photographs hardly do it justice – and anyway the effect is emotional as well as visual. Water reflects columns like mirrors, white marble reflects white light, ceramic mosaics cover walls, frothy meringue stalactites (mockarabic) cover ceilings. The plaster work is like lace; intricate, delicate, ornate – a weaving of Arabic poetry and geometric design especially stars. Windows are arched and latticed. I could have visited and revisited these rooms and halls and courtyards. Exquisite. I can see why people queue for four hours. It is worth it.

The way leads us, suddenly, into plainer rooms once lived in by protestant monarchs and briefly by Washington Irving whose book 'Tales of Alhambra' I buy and am reading with pleasure at the imaginative revisiting. And from there into water gardens and a meandering circuitous route to the entrance gate again.

It is 4pm. Time has passed without length. We wander up the other side of the hill from La Alhambra, over the river, into the shabby cobbled streets of the old Muslim quarters and, hungry, find a café and eat Spanish pancakes filled with spinach, cheese and mushrooms. Delicious.

Mark's mother, it transpires, is much like mine: determined and adventurous, and a psychiatrist (mine is a psychological counsellor). She took her two sons to India when Mark was eleven. It's given him a meditational mind set: he spent a month in an Ashram a few years ago. Lottie is appalled at his stories of sitting silent and without moving <u>at all</u>, for three hours. Mark reminds me of Andrew (Lottie's half brother) – dark, kind, spiritual, calm but a little tortured, full of wander-lust.

The café has a view from below of the Alcazabar of La Alhambra, and is beside a river full of geese – so we sit and stare and recover our energy for a while, and Lottie tries on (and then wears) Mark's Crocodile Dundee hat, and then we set off into the Alcacabin to wander steep cobbles at random, past a white walled monastery, window boxes, dilapidated doors, a church, ceramic street names and into a square where a guitarist sits on a wall and locals eat and drink in a square beside a dentist's and a Moorish arch. Glorious.

We are so tired when we got back at nearly 7pm – and hot too, so we leap in the pool until it shuts at 8pm, Lottie and Mark do flips and somersaults endlessly. I nip into the campsite supermarket and buy peaches and yoghurt and cereal bars and drink for supper which Lottie and I have sitting on the ground by the car on my sleeping bag. We play cards until sleepiness overcomes us and brush out some more broken glass from the back of the car, arrange our sleeping bags and go to sleep.

Saturday 21st August

I have the worst night's sleep. The seat belts poke into my sides, I just can't get comfy, my bones ache. Infuriating. Maybe nine days of sleeping on a back seat is enough.

We have a cup of coffee/chocolate and toasted rolls at the poolside café and then set off walking to find the bullring. On the way we find a huge shopping complex so I can buy another film for my digital camera – my spare has fallen out of its carrying case and is lost. We have been told the bullring is 700 metres away but it feels like more – already it is a boiling day. Granada's bullring is large like Cordoba's, but stone, so less ugly. We wander round, find a bar inside open, go in and see the arena. It is closed, says a notice, for repairs, and the bullfight advertised is from today for three days in a village called Martos near Jaen. Jaen is on our way to Toledo – I have decided it is worth the drive and I don't like the sound of the coast from Almeria to Valencia – so we decide to go to one more bullfight especially since they are comparatively cheap – 50 euros for the best seats.

Back at the campsite we swim and read and drink milkshakes until about 2.30pm when, in the heat of the day, we set off for Martos to book tickets for Monday on the way to Toledo.

Back in the rugged mountains, striped with dark olive lines, under the vast blue skies, it is an easy drive; there is hardly a car on the road at this hot time.

Martos is tucked away in a fold of the hills to the west of Jaen, white housed with a great hill covered in fortress ruins (or huge monoliths; we don't climb the slope to discover) behind it. We seem to be the only non-Spanish there and no one speaks any English. The Andalucian dialect, I discover, is lisping and uses the palate and throat rather than the lips. Words are pronounced slightly differently from the dictionary: adios for instance leaves off the 's'.

Waiting to buy our tickets we watch vans arrive to unload roses for sale (to throw at brilliant matadors) and I learn from them that tonight's 'corrida' is different – it is with horses not on foot: cabillos (the 'b' is pronounced 'v' – so that's where we get cavalry from). Lottie and I look at each other: we are in complete agreement. This is what Veronica at Bedalmedina had talked about, this is what the guide book said was the exciting and brilliant bullfight to see if one got the chance – and we have the chance.

So our plans change: we will stay tonight in Martos.

Unfortunately, waiting, a nasty old man sours our happiness for a while. I don't see but Lottie does and is distressed by his repulsive down-the-front-of-his-trousers gestures. A sad old geezer but disgusting and horrid for Lottie. Another learning curve I guess.

We go to a café to console her and, discovering there wasn't a campsite for miles, decide we might treat ourselves to a hotel tonight after the 'corrida'. Beside the café (ah fate!) a hotel is signposted up the road near the bullring. I am dubious about what it will cost, being 3 star, but we trudge up there to find out.

Hotel Hidalgo is a gift. The large entry hall is cool – marbled, glamorously furnished, filled with bullfighting posters, models, sculptures, bulls' heads. And they have just one room left at 65 euros. We take it, of course, and find it wonderful. Cool marble floors, great bathroom and an enchanting curved white balcony that overlooks the bullring and looks out over the mountains. It is bliss to be in comfort but after an hour or so, we leave to take our seats in the ring.

The seats are packed. Spaniards smoking fat cigars, wave, shout at friends and whistle, argue over their places, buy crisps from a girls with a basket and drinks from a boy with iced buckets. The man in front of us sits on a lacy hanky far too small for his spreading bottom. The atmosphere is noisy and exuberant.

The President arrives, the large brass band strikes up, the procession enters. Oh, the beautiful Andalucian stallions, long maned, muscled, gleaming and branded. Their caballeros are dressed in bull herding clothes – felt hat, leather chaps, short jackets. The side metal stirrups and high pomelled saddles are presumably for safety and long day rising comfort. The caballeros perform a dressage dance of high trot steps, cantering on the spot – Lipizzaner stuff. Beautiful.

The structure of the 'corrida' is the same – three caballeros with two bulls each. The first cabellos with his bull is terrifying until we get used to it. Lottie and I are embarrassed to discover that we mind far more about the horses (unpadded and unprotected, reliant only on the riding skills of their cabellos and their own speed and flexibility) getting hurt than the men. We hold our breath and each others hands. Little by little we begin to recognise the moves of the dance: - when the cabellos throw the banderillos into the bull's neck the shaft breaks off leaving a brightly coloured flag which is held low and to the side to attract the bull so he doesn't attack the close moving flank of the horse. The hard learned dressage steps mean the horse can move his hindquarters away from the bull leaving the cabellos still close enough to strike. The speed of the lance charge is necessary to enable the horse to move away fast too after the strike. In between movements and attacks the cabellos perform wonderful feats of horsemanship – leaps into the air, rears, slow high trots, even making the horse kneel on one and then two front legs. These are a form of showmanship and bravado since if the bull had charged in the middle it would have been harder to escape. The flexibility and strength of the cabellos is considerable for they often place the banderillos from across their bodies almost lying backwards on the horse. A stick is stuck in the middle of the arena presumably to orient themselves during their dizzying turns and twists.

There is no time or space to feel sorry for the bull. The kills seem to be quicker (the cabellos dismount if the first sword thrust fails and use the cross sword on foot. The cross sword severs the spinal cord causing instant death) and the movement is faster. All one can see, really, in ones scope of vision, is the cabellos and the caballeros. Even the change of horses is fast, the fresh horse visibly waiting just outside the gate. Each bull is fought with three horses so that there is no question of the horse tiring. It is exciting and awe inspiring for the riding skill is phenomenal.

There is even high comedy. The horse (the only horse) used to drag off the dead bulls creates a major scene. He kicks his way out of the traces, goes backwards, sideways, bucks, kicks, breaks the yoke, and adamantly refuses to carry out the task. The crows go wild with laughter – cheering and whistling and whooping. Eventually a 4x4 has to drive in and yoke up to the bull's horns; the crowd is convulsed.

Emotions run strong. They wave their white hankies vehemently at the President to state their opinions on each cabellos' merit. We have a good view of the President's box and it is interesting to watch him confer with colleagues, deliberate (on skill, accuracy: like a dressage test?) and finally throw his white handkerchief over the balcony. Once for one ear, twice for two, and thrice for a tail. The last cabellos (Montes), with his last bull, receives that highest accolade with fantastic riding and clean fighting skills.

Afterwards we spend some time by the huge horseboxes watching the stallions being unplaited and untacked. There are streaks of blood on their sides from the spurs, the sweat is still wet on their necks. Equipment is packed into soft old leather cases. Their headcollars are tied tight to the lorry with chains. Patches of bull blood on a shoulder show how close they have fought. Beautiful horses, that somehow look a lot smaller out of the arena. And to cap it all, our hotel is being used by all the matadors and cabellos. We walk down the hotel passages with dark olive skinned men in green, purple, pink costumes, and pass open doorways and see leather hat cases, costumes flung on a chair, shoes by a table, a matador wrapped in a white towel. It is all utterly thrilling.

It is festival time in Martos, but Lottie and I go to bed. The sheets are cool and soft. It feels good to lie flat on my back with my toes stretched out. We fall asleep to the sound of a band playing and loud fireworks which light up the walls of the hotel.

Sunday 22nd August.

We are woken early by whistles and shouts. I slip out of bed. The bullring is filling up, I see out of the window, mostly with young men. What could be happening? It is only 7.30am. Couples appear, the girls clearly still dressed for the parties from the night before: they haven't been to bed! I try to go back to sleep – Lottie still is. It is impossible. By 8.15am there is music to accompany the shouts and the arena is full of young men playing with pink capes and a football. I begin to get an inkling of what is going to happen – bull running.

What a great way for young men to work off testosterone and last night's excesses. Three young bulls, almost calves, sharp horned and feisty, have about forty minutes each in the ring chasing these young men. When the bull is tired he goes out – back, presumably, to his mountain grazing. The boys are suitably full of fear and bravado. They egg each other on, run, leap the barricades and practise passes with their capes. One or two fall and are pummelled by the bull; one is tossed high into the air by the bull's bony forehead.

Lottie sits on a chair on the balcony and watches until the end at 10.30am. I fetch her toast and hot chocolate from the bar downstairs.

The hotel is lovely. The heaven of sheets, a pillow, of being able to stretch and turn over, of having a bath, of using clean towels, of being able to wash ones hair in comfort.

We leave to the sound of a nearby Spanish guitarist whose singing is just far enough away to sound pleasant.

A drive on an unfamiliar road always feels long. When you have little idea of how long it will/should take, it feels even longer. Half way to Toledo, accompanied by Maroon Five as usual, I begin to regret the journey. It had better be worth it. We go the wrong way and get lost in the ugliest industrial estate I have ever seen. We have a nasty lunch in a café by a service station which is dirty, hot, smoky, noisy and where they are too busy to have time to try and understand my Spanish. The landscape is as dull as the guidebook has indicated. The plains are huge and eventually the hillsides are covered in vines instead of olives. Don Quixotic windmills are a brief and rare pleasure near Toledo; we see our

10ᵗʰ black metal bull sculpture and our 6ᵗʰ Spanish guitarist ditto. A bull farm with its own scruffy bullring is interesting and just outside Toledo is a magnificent ruined castle on a hill beneath which shelters a pretty village. Elsewhere castles on hills have been replaced by radio masts.

My first view of Toledo is not endearing. It feels dour and grey. But it is cloudy as we drive through and later, by the pool of El Greco camp site which has a good view of the river and the town above, when the sun came out, it begins to look pinker and creamier. The campsite is good too and again, once I have swum and unwound from the drive, I begin to have a happier view of our surroundings.

I telephone England for the first time which is a mistake. One has been away for far longer in ones own time scale than in the time scale of people at home who hardly notice you have left. One expects more delight from them at hearing your voice, and feels disgruntled by their matter of fact tones. It's probably better not to be in touch but then one feels out of contact altogether, Anyway, apparently it has been raining and grey all the time in England, so I'm glad we aren't there.

We have a (luckily) rare glimpse of the less pleasant side of the Spanish male on the way out of Martos. We have only driven a few hundred metres from the hotel when we see a pair of beautiful Andalusian mares being ridden by a couple dressed in bull herding clothes. They are so elegant. Lottie wants to photograph them, so I turn the car round and follow them up a lane where we discover, in a scruffy, sandy field, overlooked by a building site, a horse fair. I park and we walk in. It is an almost exclusively male affair, but we are so entranced by the horses we don't notice at first. There are stalls with wonderful tack – Andalucian saddles, high pommelled and wide, with metal stirrups; bull sticks, bull whips, bright headcollars. There are Andalucian foals, tiny ponies, mules, an enchanting grey donkey, colts and fillies. One gets loose and no one cares. Lottie's hair is stroked by a gypsy type who, before we could protest, lifts her into the saddle of a ribby bay gelding, and walks her round. We decline his offer of another circuit but at least Lottie sits in a bull breeder's saddle – very different from the one she has at home. Later I see the ribby bay being ridden by the gypsy type and rearing. It is hot and dry and very bright. Suddenly I take on board the nature of the chat and laughter around us – not so pleasant and aimed at us. They are simple Spanish farmers, toothless and wizened, but we stand out like aliens: female, young, blonde. It feels uncomfortable. We leave. I understand why Christina Sanchez, the top female matador (Veronica's mother I think) retired early: many male matadors refused to share a bill with her. There hasn't been a single girl in the arena for the bull running this morning. Most of the people in the bars are men. Catholic southern Spain is still a man's world, and women aren't always welcome.

We are lucky though to have stumbled on places off the tourist track. The Rough Guide for instance doesn't even mention Martos, and maybe why should it; it has nothing historical to offer. It's just a Spanish town. But the horse fair is an example of the surprising sort of thing that gives a feeling of a Spain that is as different from Marbella/Torremolinos Spain as a beach is from a mountain. It is also the advantage of a car – the flexibility makes for surprises. However, if I was starting again I'd never have tried to explore more than Andalucia in two weeks. Andalucia is full of variety and beauty and interest and could have happily been explored for longer. Still, a venture to Toledo gives a comparison, and Valencia (which we have to fly back from) will be different again. I feel though that my heart is in Andalucia – its mountains, its oat stubble, its olive groves, its Moorish influence and remnants. Pity about the high rise hotel and package tour strips along its coasts – but they can be ignored. Driving through the wide expanses can even be a joy now. The main roads are good and - except that Spanish drivers are fast and impatient, driving terrifyingly close to ones bumpers, and hooting and flashing – easy. Maybe all the hooting flashing has more to do with me overtaking too slowly for their liking. Lottie and I play Maroon Five tracks on the CD player: our favourite, about hitting the highway, a mixture of jazz and blues with great lyrics, has become track-of-Spain, and we sing along, alternately, together, giving each other marks out of 10 for the rendering. Lottie is a critical judge; I am rarely given more than 5.

The El Greco is a lovely place to relax. The view of Toledo from the terrace is stunning. To one side runs the river – huge and dark with herons immobile on untidy islets. Vine covered verandas flank the pool with tables and chairs in the shade. The voices are mostly Spanish with some French and Germans, but the man in reception is able to speak some English which is useful for information. The campsite is also beside a large imposing castle – the notice on the gates makes me think it is a prison of some sort, but it turns out to be an insurance company!

That evening we drive the 3kms into Toledo, parking easily outside the old city gates. Walking in is uphill; steps, ramps – up and up until we are hot and panting. Lottie buys one of those leather flasks that are an art to drink from because you tip them into your mouth which means you have to swallow with your mouth open. Looking through a doorway I am given a tomato by a woman from a box overflowing with them. Delicious, eaten like an apple while walking.

We buy marzipan pastries in the main square; walk around the cathedral, the Alcazar, the mosque; explore endless narrow streets (up and down) and find a cheap restaurant where Lottie eats spaghetti fast and hungrily. It is delicious and while we eat we watch that night's bullfight at Malaga on television through the window of another café opposite. Although you get to see close ups of faces, and repeat action in slow motion, the excitement and therefore the bravery and skill relationship is lost. And the bull has no character on screen. No, definitely a bullfight should not be televised: the 'corrida' is a living event to be participated in, not watched.

It is dark by the time we get back to the car, and old Toledo is floodlit. A wonderful position for an old city that needed to guard against invaders. No wonder it was the erstwhile capital of Spain.

I am dog tired tonight and long to sleep. Lottie who has slept in the car on the drive to Toledo is in party mood! Eventually she stops chattering at about 11pm. In the distance is Spanish flamenco singing and the tinny jollity of loudspeakers from some street fiesta.

Monday 23rd August

It is a sunny day after yesterday's cloud. A kind French family near us, packing to leave, give us their milk. We wake late and eat a lovely breakfast of soft bread rolls and marmite on the terrace, writing our diaries until the pool opens at 11am. We will drive back to Jaen and try and find the campsite that is apparently 7kms away near a village that I can't find on the map(!) before going to our last bullfight at Martos, We both think that after the beauty and thrill of watching the caballeros it will be somehow less – but we came to Spain to see/understand/learn about bullfights: and we have. It has been expensive though. Three 'corrida' have cost a total of 365 euros, about £270. Quite a chunk out of the budget.

We leave at about 2pm, going to see the bullring in Toledo on the way – a low old crumbly stone circle – lovely. The journey back seems quick and it is a joy to drive back into the familiar beauty of olive stripes and oat stubble, white walled houses and castles on hills. We don't quite have long enough to find the campsite, but we are early for meeting Mark before the bullfight so we drive into Jaen and up above to the Castilla St Catalina – an old Moorish fortress perched on a craggy mountain top. Part of it has been turned into a (very expensive) hotel which we have a drink in so we can explore. Vast vaulted ceilings, tapestries, dark stoned castle corridors. We walk over the rocks – the view is stunning, an endless bird's eye vista stretching forever.

We meet Mark strolling down the main road in Martos. He's spent this afternoon dancing in the foam filled streets at the fiesta and is full of joy. The day before he'd crossed the sea over to Tangier – very Islamic and anti western, he says – on a five hour visit. He has bought picnic food for us all, so we find a shady piece of grass and eat fruit and crisps and biscuits and catch up on each others adventures – Lottie is pleased to see him again and determined that our adventures have been as fulsome as his. A pretty, sandy coloured dog adopts us (or our picnic food) and trots at our heels thereafter.

We are all excited by the bullfight tonight. Manuel Diaz 'El Cordobes' and El Fandi are all big names apparently and the arena is totally packed. The buzz is incredible – and we are used to it. Mark is thrilled and amazed – and yet also in considerable anxiety, not at all sure that the slaughter of bulls fits with his spiritual mind set. The crowds are in full fiesta mood, girls in multi coloured flamenco dresses, covered in flowers and spots and flounces, and they clutch white hankies and red roses. There is a big band and a pair of gorgeous bay Andalucian horses to lead the processional parade to open the 'corrida'. Cordobes fights first – fast. bold and daring. He presses his forehead against the bull's, passes the cape from down on one knee, kills swiftly and is awarded two ears. The lesser known Puerto fights next – neat and efficient, close to the bull's flanks, hand on the bull's rump. Then El Fandi – such a peacock, such a drama queen, such fun: he stamps in (mock?) fury to get rid of his over-helpful assistants. The art and skill makes it all seem so easy and the bull so unferocious. What flamboyance and flair. Great stuff, those first three bulls, and the crowd on their feet with cheering.

Sadly the fourth bull is a fiasco. The knowing crowd disparage the bull on its entry. It clearly isn't up to scratch and they rise to demand its exit. The president of the 'corrida' ignores them (maybe there weren't more than six bulls delivered and so there isn't a replacement). This bull turns and kicks rather than charging. Poor 'El Cordobes' who'd drawn that bull has to forego the fight and merely try and kill the bull functionally and without getting hurt. It is horrid, a disaster, and looks what it is: butchery. The crowd are cross that the President hasn't listened to their vociferous demands and the mood becomes sombre and quieter. They boo that bull as it is dragged out (poor thing, not its fault) and 'El Cordobes' is deflated and reserved. The 5th and 6th bulls are fine but the whole edge has gone and can't be recovered. Puerto and even El Fandi do their best to lift the mood – El Fandi even kneels down on both knees with his back to his bull, cape and sword on the ground, and leans back until the back of his head touches the bull's nose. It should have been phenomenal but somehow, sadly, the crowd just can't be lifted, and the bulls are badly killed and the crowd are silent, not asking for the accolade of any ears at all although in fact El Fandi does get one. And at the end the crowd chuck their padded cushions into the ring as a sign of their disappointment.

Well, it's good to get the mixed picture – and we learn more, even more, about this art. It has never crossed my mind that the bull has to be as good as the matador: the bull breeding game is as vital as the toreador's skill.

We wander the starry streets for a while, watching the fiesta bubble around us: cafes overflowing, music everywhere, market stalls, twinkly lights. The sandy dog finds us again, and again trots at our heels. Lottie is exhausted but scared of sleeping in the car outside the bullring (because we can't lock our car and she feels vumerable). Mark says the campsite will be shut by the time we find it (if we find it in the dark) and offers us the lower bed in his camper van (he has one in the uplift roof). Lottie is relieved and we accept. He locks us in and goes off to join in the fiesta properly. The bed is large and comfy and Lottie sleeps quickly and well. I listen to Spanish guitar, flamenco, pop and the guttural sound of voices passing. I lie awake feeling amazed at all our adventures – especially at myself sleeping in an Australian backpacker's camper van in the middle of Spain. Mark gets back somewhere near 3am – the unlocking system wakes me briefly – and then his alarm (mistakenly) rings at 7.30am.

Tuesday 24th August

Mark wants to go to the tomato festival too, when he hears about it, and then head north across the Pyrenees into France, so we agree that we will travel vaguely in convoy the long six hour plus haul to Valencia. We walk the litter strewn daylight streets of Martos looking for a café for breakfast and a loo, and find only an open air disco, music still throbbing, bodies still gyrating.

Back at the bullring crowds are pouring in for another session of bull running – 'Torilla Unguardiente'. We leave Mark contemplating whether or not to join in, arranging to meet at a dot on the map a four hour drive away; a little village called Banzerote.

The countryside gradually changes but attractively. It becomes greener and there are more and bigger trees, even poplars. The houses became yellow or pinky beige. We stop for the loo and a cup of coffee at Alcazar, a crumbly village dominated by a large castle (thus its name I suppose) on the hill. The Olympics is on the TV screen in the corner so we watch some gymnastics while we sip oranginas.

Banzerote, when we get there, is dead. I can't even see a café. There aren't even chairs or tables out on the pavements. Doors are locked. We thought we would give up and drive on and meet up with Mark at the campsite near Valencia, but as we head back towards the main road we see the glorious sign 'Piscina'. For 85 cents we leap at it. This municipal swimming pool is almost empty, but there is a bar, ice creams, loos, shady trees. As I am buying Lottie an ice cream forty five minutes later, we see Mark's van drive by so we leap in the car (wearing only our swim suits) and follow him. We drive round every tiny back street: no Mark. But we do eventually find his parked van and so we leave a note about the pool under his windscreen wipers. He joins us there half an hour later with great pleasure that we'd found a pool – his van has no air conditioning, and middle of the day driving, while lovely for us, is boiling tedium for him.

I buy chips for Lottie for lunch – they are so good, but come with what she thinks is ketchup and turns out to be chilli. It makes her mouth sore.

Mark has been bull running – so he is full of that. He and Lottie swim for a couple of hours and then we all head for Valencia and a campsite on the beach nearby; Mark on the longer dual carriageway, us on the shorter but ordinary road via Requera. We get 80 kms the other side of Albacete (we've been driving for over forty minutes), when, stopping for petrol, we realise we've left all our clothes by the pool. Dippy. We weigh up whether or not to just forget about them – but they include Lottie's new bull T shirt, so we go back. Tedious.

The drive through the mountains near Requera is stunning – fir tree covered mountains. But by the time we reach Bunol I am really tired. I've been driving for 7 hours that day and have had enough, so we decide to stay in Bunol – which is where the tomato festival is the next day anyway. We can't let Mark know but he rings my mobile phone from a coin box when he gets worried about us not turning up, and we arrange to meet in Bunol the next morning instead.

Being at Bunol the night before La Tomatina turns out to be a good move. The streets are full of music and fiesta. Lottie and I potter and buy candy floss. We also climb up to the old fortress on Bunol's hill and explore the museum that shows Neanderthal skeletons unearthed there. It's an enchanting town, a shack and shanty place, higgledy piggledy round its cream church with a pretty blue dome. Terracotta roof tiles top dishevelled roof gardens. Narrow streets slide down steps.

I thought we were going to sleep the night in the corner of the 24 hour garage, but because of the fiesta it not only closed but locked up and we are kicked out. We go to a stony lay-by opposite and sleep badly in the car – traffic hoots its way past all night, and

Lottie is freaked by the lorry driver changing into night clothes in his lorry cab in the lay-by behind us.

Wednesday 25ᵗʰ August

We wake up early. The garage has opened (noisily) and we stumble over to its loos and get coffee and hot chocolate from its machine. Although it is early, we decide to go into the centre and wait for all the excitement to start. We move the car nearer the centre, park, and walk down the hill to the main square – more of a roundabout around a non functioning fountain. Already quite a lot of people are around; maybe as in Martos they just haven't been to bed from the night before.

Occasional prone figures sleep on benches, pavements, plazas. Suddenly there are familiar words spoken – the village is full of Australians and New Zealanders. Everyone seems young. There are few children (even later) and few middle aged plus. In the street near the church three plump Spaniards stripped to the waist are covering a thick telegraph pole with grease from plastic buckets. It will be set in a hole in the tarmac, made solid with wood chunks and hung with a pig (actually a side of bacon) at the top. La Tomatina cannot start until the pole has been climbed and the pig taken down. There is considerable joshing between the greasers and the crowd. A TV presenter and his camera man, trying to interview the greasers, get chunks of grease chucked at them. It smells faintly antiseptic. Suddenly flecks of grease are flying everywhere. One lands on my arm – yes, definitely slightly antiseptic but with the consistency of Vaseline.

It is only 9am – La Tomatina starts at midday. We aren't in a hurry. We stand and stare. The TV crew are the butt of everyone's humour – the presenter even gets an early tomato thrown at him. Shops and houses lining the streets are being boarded up and covered in plastic sheeting as protection. There is lots of fancy dress: a man in a bikini with a pink hat and an umbrella; two men in red ballet tutus; a man in a wheel chair, flies done up with gaping safety pins with a huge homemade cardboard crown decorated with tomatoes; Superman is given the bumps, four Spidermen converge at once; an Arab sheikh chats to a pink wig with devils horns; several tomato costumes bounce along. Most people hold large plastic cups of beer, everyone is cheerful. We go to a café to eat some bread and play cards. A cross looking English woman barges past our table, sending Lottie's orangina flying, soaking the pack. She doesn't even look back – silly woman, what is the hurry at 10.30am? Young Spanish men rev car engines past us, windows open, music blaring. The civil protection units arrive, blue trousered and orange shirted, friendly and smiling. Roads are cordoned off with rails which are moved often to let various vehicles through: the ambulance; a Red Bull advertisement mini driven by a chic dark haired dark glassed girl, full of confidence and sass. Lottie and I walk back to the greasy pole. It is crowded now and everyone is so much taller than us. It takes us a while to get there and we hear huge cheering and laughter as some people nearly reach the pig, clambering on top of each other like human scaffolding. I lift Lottie up to see better and a Spaniard offers to put her on his shoulders – a great view for her. Then, amazingly, she sees Mark in the crowd. He makes his way over and takes her off the Spaniard onto his own shoulders. The crowd is thick and solid now. We reckon 10,000 thousand people are there and it is still only 11.30am. (The next day in the Spanish papers we read that it was 40,000 people and 130 tonnes of tomatoes. Later still in December of that year Lottie read in the Guinness Book of Records that it was the biggest food throwing festival ever). Mark (well over 6ft tall) strides through it all to a wall above a little plaza just back from the street – less of a crush and a great view point. Lottie sits on the wall. Below it has become a man's street. They are chucking T shirts at each other which they are ripping off each other. It is very good humoured. On the roof above is perched a TV crew. From the balconies, locals chuck buckets of water onto us all below. People have bought goggles – a hot sale from stalls along the way, as are waterproof cameras – which they later discover are useless. The minutes tick by.

Then a great roar and clapping go up – the pig/ham is captured! Ten impatient minutes later and a rocket explodes into the sky – the start of La Tomatina. Heads turn, somehow a path is made along the middle, and, accompanied by cheering, the first tomato lorry crawls through. It is an open tipping truck filled with yellow shirted Spaniards and tomatoes, with a flap back. Where the first tomato load is tipped is soon a scarlet mayhem. Sodden T-shirts are chucked along with tomatoes; some get caught on the wires of the overhead fiesta lights. Soon the street behind our wall is filled with squashed tomatoes. I pick some up for Lottie to throw. I get splattered with juice; Lottie is hit squishily on the head and leg. An elderly man beside us collapses, pale and still. Cold water is poured on him; the medics are nearby. There are five lorries in all and soon the square below is ankle deep in tomatoes and the air is full of juice and tomato flesh. Mark – who'd gone off to be part of the male melee, reappears covered from head to toe. Ten minutes before the end (the finishing rocket explodes at 1pm) he takes Lottie down into the mid-calf height soup of the road. She comes back with tomato covering every part of her, thick in her hair and on her legs, her Tomatina T shirt (9 euros) sodden with juice. She's loved it and Mark has looked after her more safely than I could have done, for it is slippy and chaotic in the road.

At 1pm after the final rocket, Tomatina rules decree that no more tomatoes are thrown. The crowds disperse quite fast, but a local woman on a first floor balcony, trying – too soon – to clean off her white walls with a broom, is too obvious a target, and some lads catch up handfuls of tomatoes from the road and chuck them at her broom. She clucks and squawks, they laugh and tease.

We are thirsty, sticky and wet. As we walk, locals aim hoses into the road. We catch a bit of water, but the best hose is wielded by a garage owner – at least our heads are cleaner. There are chunks of tomato in our ears. One man has very sore red eyes. We go to where Mark has parked his van and use his water to wash

our feet – it is too warm to drink – and set off with his empty
containers to find somewhere to refill them. Near where our car is
parked is another hose. We wash our hair and bodies and refill the
containers. Then we find a café for a drink. Failing to make the
(rather tipsy) barman understand in Spanish or mime about what
shandy is, I end up with two cans of beer, I can of orangina, I can
of lemonade, and three plastic cups. It is shady under plane trees
on the pavement and a relief to sit down in comparative peace.
Trains, coaches, taxis and cars leave Bunol all at once. Only the
Spanish seem to stay.

At about 4pm we walk back via the castle ramparts to see the
aftermath. The main streets have been hosed down and swept
clean by the fire brigade. The peripheral areas, streets, steps,
gardens, are awash with litter: cups, cans, shoes, goggles, tomato
soaked T shirts. Bunol is left deserted, calm. Almost back to
normal – they've kept the crowds out by closing every shop and
café or bar now.

We are tired. We say affectionate goodbyes to Mark who is
heading north into the Pyrenees and drive into Valencia, half an
hour away, deciding we are too tired to go to any beaches and
would rather go straight to the hotel that is booked for our last
night.

The Hotel Le Petit Bristol is a tiny High Tech hotel in an
alley behind the cathedral in the old pretty part of Valencia. The
parking – underground – is more expensive than some of our
campsites! The hotel is bliss, even if it is so high tech that it takes
us half an hour to discover how the lights and the air-conditioning
systems work – and we never really do conquer the multi jet
shower system. It is all chrome, glass, stainless steel and mirrors,
and has a huge balcony overlooking terracotta roofs – we are on
the 5th floor at the top. We wash Lottie's Tomatina T-shirt in the
basin and drape it over a chair back in the cloudy sun to dry. An
American woman leans round the bamboo divide on the balcony
and gives us a carton of thick Spanish peach juice. I leave Lottie

exploring the free internet access, and go back to repark the car. Valencia is attractive and elegant.

Later that evening, bathed clean of tomato pips, we stroll into the night. We eat spaghetti hungrily (lunch hasn't happened) while being serenaded by an accordion, and then sit on the steps outside the cathedral – floodlit - and watch skateboarders whiz around on the marble plaza round the fountain.

Bed – in blissful sheets and wonderful stretch out space – is a relief. No more sleeping in the broken Berlinger!

Thursday 26th August

We don't wake up until 10am! I wake in a panic that we are late for the flight home having had nightmares that Pudlicott (our home) was falling down in our absence. The sky outside the French windows is grey and we have missed the breakfast deadline. No matter, we have slept so well. I want to go into the cathedral and climb its tower to see Valencia from above. As it turns out there would have been time, but I am anxious about how long it will take to extract ourselves from Valencia and find the airport, so we dress, unpark the car and leave.

We're getting expert at spotting signs so we are at the airport in a trice – the first to check in when the desk opens. We hand the car keys back to the car rental company – we have driven 2 thousand 734kms: the Berlinger has her broken back windows, a graze where I think someone has kicked a can against her side, melted butter marks on her floor, and crumbs everywhere. But she has grown on us – and kept us safe. She has plodded along reliably, even if she struggled up hills, there was something tetchy about her gears by the end, and she (?!) tended to stall at traffic lights – but we are fond of her. Above all, not once has anything been taken from her even though we've never been able to lock her.

We sit in the airport café writing our diaries. Beside us is a group of three men: Lottie notices their waterproof camera and reckoning they've been at La Tomatina, goes over to ask. They have. They flew over on a 2/3 day trip specifically for it: David, the design guy from Sussex, Tim, the Londoner whose business is paper recycling and Paul, the Irish funeral director. Paul has been in the thick of it – one of the ones that battered the metal pulldown, covering a shop, so badly that the owner still couldn't straighten it enough to open it when we walked past at 4pm. It is interesting to talk to them: they are the types we'd have been scared of if we'd seen them at Bunol: big, loud, a bit drunk. But here they are big, funny, kind; just ordinary guys out for a good time and a new experience. Not that young either – they have children in their teens and twenties. Just big boys who haven't grown up much. Not poor either: Paul has a place in Spain near Malaga, Tim has a cottage in Ireland, David has just come back from a sailing trip to St Malo. An unexpected trio.

Anyway, chatting to them made the two hour wait fly by.

Back to Coventry airport and then home. Back to English rain. We will miss the Spanish sunshine. But it is good to leave before we really want to. I wish we had had a little longer – but we've been nearly everywhere we wanted to, and seen and learnt so much. What memories! Bullfights and fiestas, beaches and campsites, mosques and fortresses, white hill towns and deep gorges, mountains and olive groves, tapas and paella, hot sun and cold pools, horse fairs and tomato fights, long roads and cobbled streets, fountains and ceramics, new friends and new language. Another great adventure.

GREECE - 2005

ADVENTURING THIS year is hampered by the birth in June of eight black Labrador puppies. We can hardly bear to leave them but I have booked flights to Athens back in February before they were even conceived. We know we will miss these delicious bundles but we decide to continue with our plan to climb Mount Olympus, to reach the home of the ancient Greek Gods.

Not one mountain in fact, more of a range of mountains. 'Olymbos' itself – or rather its highest peak, Mytikas, - is 2917m high, the highest in Greece, the second highest in the Balkans. The Rough Guide says it 'regularly claims lives' – but only in the winter I believe. It will take two or three days to reach the summit: I must allow 6 days altogether.

Bearing cost and stamina and homesickness in mind, Lottie and I decide to be away about a fortnight. Once again I offer windows on either side of my preferred dates. Easyjet offer flights for about £100 each return – not too bad – travelling out on a Tuesday and back on a Wednesday. I look at a map of Greece. Where is Mount Olympus? (Does it really exist or is it as mythical as the Gods?) I find it in the north of Greece, much nearer Thessalonika than Athens, but search as I may I cannot find cheap flights, or really any flights at all to Thessalonika. (Later I learn that there are mostly German flights to there.)

The Rough Guide says that car hire in Greece is one of the most expensive in Europe, so I decide to train and ferry and bus our way around, but, casual now about travelling spontaneously, I don't even open The Rough Guide until a few days before we leave – and only then because friends holidaying in Zakynthos have invited us to stay. Where is Zakynthos (and how confusing that it is also called Zante)? I see the landmass splodge at the bottom of the Ionian Islands. Being fascinated by Odysseus I badly want to go to Ithaca – also, I see, an Ionian Island, a smaller splodge further north. Can we do it? Does it work? Probably. We say a tentative yes, for a couple of days only.

The flight is at 6.30 am – once again a tricky time in terms of travel arrangements, except that it's good to arrive in daylight in time to explore – so we stay the night before at a Gatwick hotel (the price for the night includes parking while we are away and works out in total cheaper than parking at Gatwick's own long stay car park). It all works fine except for an incompetent hotel wake up call an hour too early. Still, better than an hour too late.

Tuesday 9ᵗʰ August

Gatwick airport at 4.15 am is full of red-rimmed eyes: Thompson Air has had problems with aircraft last night and people have been waiting 12 hours or so for their flights. I worry that Easyjet will follow suit, but the EZ flights on the departure screens show boarding gate numbers. Lottie – eleven years old now - wanders off to case the shops. I mean to peruse The Rough Guide but my eyes ache with sleepiness. Opposite me a tired blonde toddler bawls. His father lifts him from his pushchair and the weight of the bags hanging on the handles makes it fall over. Eventually he falls asleep, scarlet and sweaty, in his mother's patient arms. Camaraderie has clearly sprung up between delayed passengers.

They chat cheerily together – and leap into action when at last their flight is on the screen, as if by moving fast they can ensure its departure.

Lottie returns and I go to the Bureau de Change to buy her Euros. I discover they will take (now outdated) drachmas. I have a 1,000 drachma note from twenty years ago so I send Lottie back with it. She is given £1.72 with which she buys sweets and lucozade. I consider buying coffee from MacDonald's but the queue is too long. The front page of the Mail declares that a revolutionary new cancer cure is banned by the government due to cost; the Telegraph reports nuclear production in Iran.

We board on time and taxi out only twenty minutes late. The Captain rambles inaudibly in a foreign accent – I suspect he may be trying to be funny. Lottie and I wonder if the bag with the shiny waterproof lining is a sick bag or a photo bag – the outside enables postage to Klick Photos for developing. Or both?

England seems sweet and green below us, but we are over the sea and then over France in minutes. We sleep, Lottie's head on my knees. The girl beside us in the aisle seat sleeps too, but more professionally: neck cushion, eye masks, ear plugs.

Landing in Athens we are told it is 27C and breezy. It is. We find the E95 bus recommended by The Rough Guide (now called the X95) to the centre of Athens – Syndagma – but knowing that the cheapest hotels are near stations I decide to lug the backpacks on the metro to Larissa Station to find a hotel to leave them at. The airport is 26 km outside Athens and the landscape, as we drive, reminds us of Spain – golden brown and dry. The big square at Syndagma is modern and light and attractive, and the Metro likewise. We are hugely impressed by how clean it is. 1.40 euros each buys us a ticket. Emerging at Larissa we head for the first hotel we can see, the Ariston, thinking that from the look of it, it will be far too expensive. It is simple but smart, stainless steel and glass. But – joy – it is an acceptable 55 euros for the two of us, with breakfast. The double bedroom is clean and comfortable; there is a bath as well as a shower in the bathroom. I open the French windows onto a tiny balcony and an ugly view of the station and tacky flats. But they speak English at the reception desk and are friendly. We dump our kit and set off again, back along the metro line the way we came, but one stop further to Acropolis, to climb the Acropolis. Getting out of the metro feeling tired, we pause at a café: Lottie has a truly delicious strawberry milkshake, and I succumb to the temptations of baklava, that filo pastry nut and honey concoction. Full, but even sleepier, we find the Acropolis entrance, pay our 12 euros and potter. It is disappointing after Pompeii. The view of Athens from the top is panoramic – but Athens itself is not really worth viewing panoramically.

Lottie stops to sketch marble slabs, stone carvings of lions, broken marble sculptures of horses. Her sketch book of Greece will be a form of diary, though I do wonder whether it will be as good a record in years to come as the written word.

Irritatingly my spare digital camera film drops out of the case by the amphitheatre. We retrace our steps to try and find it but with no luck.

It rains – little spatter drops – from a cloudy sky. We try and buy postcards but the ticket shops and the museum shop are closed. The museum itself is full of marble statues of priestesses and snakes and male torsos with very, very tiny penises. We peer closely to see if they are so small because they have been broken off – but no; intact and tiny.

There is scaffolding on all the ruins – massive reconstruction work is going on. Cats play amongst the metal poles.

We leave and meander into the Plaka district – little streets and shops and cafes lining them. The common tourist artefact is little pots and dishes with Greek heads etched on them. I am determined to buy nothing – our backpacks are heavy enough.

My knee hurts when I walk which bodes ill for climbing Mount Olympus. Maybe I'm just tired. We stop under what look like mulberry trees at a café and drink iced cappuccino and I order Tszaki hoping Lottie will like the cucumber and yoghurt mix.

She tastes only a little. It is rich and minty. Delicious I think. She eats only the bread.

We wander back to the metro and enter a church, drawn by the chanting. The black-robed, bearded priest sits in a chair near the altar where another priest, white robed, fiddles with altar items. Lottie says the chanting freaks her out. In glass fronted boxes there are ornate silver faced books, but the silver faces are carved out to show painted faces beneath – which I find 'freaky'.

Lottie looks at necklaces and bracelets with the Turkish 'eye' which she likes. She lingers over a pretty pink and white one for 2.5 euros. The shop-owner offers it to her for 1 euro. Easy bargain: it matches her pink skirt and white T-shirt. And easy to carry.

We head back to the Ariston. On the way I try and find the ticket office of the Pelopponese station to discover train times. I can't even find the station. A taxi driver from Patra tells me it's closed and tries to tell me where I go now. The Greek/English bit fails us. He offers to take us to Patra (which is where the ferries to the Ionian islands leave from) tonight for 50 euros – I'm not even tempted. Back in the hotel I try and work out from the manager where the station is. We have to find it: the only way by train to Patra is on this Pelopponese line. All the trains from the Larissa station go north. The manager doesn't have any answers but he has men staying from the railway depot whom he'll ask. He does, and writes it all down for me. It's up the road about 5 kms, and we agree that the best thing is for me to go there by taxi in the morning.

Lottie and I eat pistachios, the rest of the marmite sandwiches, a 'frube' yoghurt tube each and an orange. We play cards; a sort of concoction of whist and bridge. It's hard to play bridge with only two people, but it might be fun to give her a rough idea of what the game is about. I make us turn out the lights at 9.15 pm but we can't sleep for ages – either because it's only 7.15 pm in England or because of the coffee we drank. It's very hot – the air conditioning is inadequate (or I haven't got it to work properly) – and we are sweaty and sticky. I wonder how the puppies are, and wonder if Lottie is thinking of them too. I toss and turn thinking of family back home. I don't miss them particularly, but I worry about them and wonder what they are doing.

Wednesday 10th August

We have a lovely breakfast in the glass and pine area off reception: juice and coffee and hot chocolate and croissants. We pay the bill and book the hotel for our last night too.

Stepping outside, my wave secures an instant yellow taxi (I've had to ban Lottie's game of kisses for yellow cars; there are so many!) – but the driver doesn't have a clue about the station and stops to ask another driver. We do find it eventually – only 3 euros 50 for the fare anyway. A tiny crowded station with people spilling onto the lines and tracks. I buy tickets – 15 euros – and settle to wait for an hour. We play cards on the platform steps.

The train when it arrives (late) is old and dirty and full. It takes us 2 hours and forty five minutes to reach Dhiakofto where we have decided to go to on the way to Patra because it apparently has an unmissable rack and pinion track train journey into a gorge. Most of the journey is along the coast: out of one window we can see the sea, out of the other, scrubby hillsides. The white houses are red roofed; there are olive orchards and dry red earth. Corinth, I read, poor ancient Corinth, is still beset by earthquakes and has been rebuilt in breezeblock. But from round here, Jason gathered his Argonauts. Not far away Agamemnon had his fortress/palace. I can't picture it. The sea is as blue as the sky, but it seems too cosy, too neat. I see the land of heroes as bigger, somehow, harsher. Lottie and I play more cards. Somebody smokes even though it is a non smoking carriage.

At Dhiakofto the little rack and pinion train pulls out as we arrive. There are only four a day. I queue to book the next – at 14:30 – but am told the last one back is full. Fine: either we will walk back (two hours alongside the track) or we'll find somewhere to sleep in Zakhloro and catch the first one back tomorrow and then go on to Patra. Adventure!

We have nearly three hours to wait so we hitch up our packs and walk down to the sea. There, by the tiny port, is a straw shaded café on decking. We sit right beside the water: we can see tiny fish chasing a square of bread. Little fut-fut boats bob on their rusty moorings. A pebbly beach stretches under tamarisk trees round the curve of the bay. There is a brisk breeze but the sun is hot, the sky flecked with puffs of white cloud. Lovely. We eat spaghetti (Lottie) and Greek salad (me) and appreciate that in Greece they bring water and bread immediately – and free - to your table.

Nearby, there is a fishing boat pulled into dry dock painted like a gypsy caravan. The broad leaves of pollarded trees (I don't recognise what kind), growing through the café floor, rattle in the wind. There isn't an English voice in sight. Lottie tells me the sea is warm. She sits on the quay with her foot on a rope, sketching. It is peaceful and relaxing. Nobody clears our plates or makes us feel we should go. Bougainvillea and oleander flower pinkly on the stone walls. Everything is slower – as I have read I would find it – and it feels right and proper this pace. Lunch is 8 euros, but it has been more than just food we have found here. I begin to unwind. Lottie wears my sunglasses and looks very grown up and rather elegant. She says,

"How come I get bored with my friends after a while but I've been with you all my life and I never get bored with you?" Such a compliment. I want to remember that.

The narrow gauge train is magical. It effortfully chugs up a 1 in 7 gradient along the river through and up the gorge. The tunnels have windows cut in them, waterfalls bubble frothily, and the bridges are so narrow you hold your breath. We stop half way at Zakhloro. There is a room in the little wooden hotel for 20 euros. The village is only this hotel, the railway line, the river and a handful of hidden houses. We have a tiny balcony – two chairs and a table overlooking the gorge. Lovely. The room and the bathroom are tiny and primitive but utterly enchanting. And what a good price.

How can I be so stupid as to walk for two hours up a goat track to a monastery in flip flops? It is hot; the path is loose screed and pebbles, and it looks like a dry river bed. The views are stunning. We have shade stops, and it takes us twice the time that the guide book promises. The monastery is awful – burnt by the Nazi's in the war, it is now a modern monstrosity. Its saving grace is little water fountains of cold mountain stream water. We are freaked by the silver carved skulls and hands and bones – it's the little windows that are spooky. The chapel is thick with incense. Carved bronze hangs low, icons, paintings and velvet abound. I don't like it – the atmosphere is cloying. I have to wear a skirt over my shorts – Lottie, far sexier in sleeveless T shirt and mini skirt, is considered fine. The skirt is elasticated at the waist and gives me an enormous bottom. Lottie laughs at me.

It is worse coming down than going up and I fall three times – more scared of damaging myself than actually wounded. I am hot and exhausted by the time we get back.

I drink a huge bottle of beer at the hotel café to quench my thirst. Now I am sleepily tipsy. Lottie sketches, taking up the whole balcony table. Crickets shriek in the trees until the sun sinks behind the hills. The only sound now is the river.

I doze on the bed, sunlight filtering through the narrow shutters, until Lottie wakes me – "Mummy, do you like this sketch?"

We play cards again over supper. Our table is by the edge of the drop to the river, grey green in the dusk. The two waiters chat, smoke, drink, and serve us spaghetti and tomato salad and fanta for 8 euros. Lottie draws the Charmed sign (as in the TV series 'Charmed' about three witches, which she is passionate about) and our card game scores on the paper table cloth. I'm stiff (especially my ankles) and tired; we don't linger.

I have worn a long sleeved T shirt and knee length shorts, anxious as I get older about the drying and aging effects of the sun. My shoulders seem pale in contrast with my forearms. Never mind; it will be autumn and jersey time, back in England, all too soon.

It's lovely here. Clearly we like ramshackle rooms, water and hills. But I worry that I won't be up to climbing Mount Olympus. I'm longing to sleep but Lottie is begging for more cards.

Thursday 11ᵗʰ August

It is cool in the little dark room – even chilly in the morning, and dark with the canopy of trees and the sun rising behind the gorge. Our pants, washed and hanging to dry on the balcony, are still damp.

Downstairs everything is deserted. Someone is cooking in the kitchen though (lunch dishes by the look of it) and I point to the words 'yoghurt and honey' on the menu. She brings us two fried eggs. We try again. Two huge bowls of thick yoghurt and honey arrive – we only manage to eat half before I hear the rails rattle. I put the keys, and money for our food and stay, on the table, and we skip over the line as the train chugs round the corner. It is almost empty – but the driver won't allow a couple who have also stayed overnight (because last night's train back was full) to get on without tickets. There is nowhere to buy tickets; a tiny little ticket office is shut. I am relieved that I bought return tickets at Dhiakofto.

The journey down the gorge, while lacking the element of surprise, is just as exciting. The light is different and the journey – downhill – faster. The cliffs are etched in vertical grey and orange shapes and erosions that look like hieroglyphics. Corrugated iron shanty shacks are built into caves – who lives there, I wonder?

We have ten minutes to catch the train to Patra from Dhiakofto, but the short queue at the ticket office is so slow that we have to desert it when the train arrives, and buy tickets aboard. The ticket collector asks us if we have come from Zakhloro and is clearly then teased by the locals for his 'magical' insight.

The hour's journey is along the coast. In Patra I head for a travel agent's opposite the station and buy ferry tickets to Ithaca. There is a two hour wait so we go to a café by the port (close to the station). The Nescafe frappe is too bitter for Lottie so I drink both hers and mine and get her a strawberry milkshake. The coffee is too bitter for me too really, so I order a scoop of mocha ice-cream to go in it. Better. We write postcards, get stamps from a kiosk. I leave Lottie on her own in the café, in order to go and find a post-box, and end up trekking to the post office via directions from a nice man in a bank. I worry that Lottie will panic if I am away for too long - but this is the advantage of travelling in a pair – one person can look after the luggage during such treks. And that goes for the loo too – I always feel we should grab every opportunity in case there are none later.

It is hot now.

The 'Kefallonia' leaves on time. It is a big car ferry – but there is comfortable space, and chairs inside (where we dump backpacks) and on deck (where we watch the ropes being unhitched and wave at out shadows on the sea far below).

Lottie sleeps for most of the three hour journey to Kefallonia. I watch the foam on the sea swirl pale turquoise and stare at the rusty outline of mainland Greece and her outcrop islands. They are rimmed with gold but it is a band of stone between the water and the vegetation. I chat briefly at the rails to a man called Curtis – an American actor living in Prague on his way to Corfu because his Czech girlfriend can only get a visa for package holidays. We talk about roots – his were in North Dakota, but all dead or dissipated now – and the concept of destiny-less travel.

We slide past Ithaca and slip into the green curve of Kefallonia. The hilly slopes look as if a cloth of green has been flung over them. We dock at Sami. Cars and lorries unload and then we are off again arriving in Ithaca fifteen minutes later on the south west coast; just a quay at the foot of a vertical slope up which a simple zig-zag road is cut. This side of Ithaca is bare and steep. Stone, rock and scrub. For 2 euros a minibus takes 32 of us to the

capital – Vathy. Ithaca is shaped like a foot – the quay is at the foot
of a ridge which stretches between heel and ball; Vathy nestles on
the north of the heel, a deep bay within a bay. It is all instantly
enchanting. Vathy is like a quiet St Tropez. Ice-cream colour
houses, low beneath the hills, curving round the bay. Yachts slap
against their moorings. Out of the bay looms the hill of northern
Ithaca, apparently enclosing the bay into a lake.

We find a hotel – just. Everywhere is full, and there isn't
much of 'everywhere'. The hotel is far too expensive at 98 euros
but we need to sleep somewhere. I leave Lottie to enjoy the room
(she washes two pairs of her favourite pants and puts them on the
balcony to dry, from where, to her much repeated misery, they
blow away, lost forever). I head off round the quay to explore.
The sea is clean and clear, the quayside strewn with neat heaps of
fishing nets.

I retrieve Lottie and we eat – hungrily – spaghetti, at a café
in the square. I buy tickets for the 6.45 am ferry back to Sami in
the morning. I would like to stay in Ithaca and explore, but Lottie
wants to get to Zakynthos to stay with the Sloanes before we head
off for Mount Olympus. It will be tricky crossing Kefallonia to
Pesada where 3 ferries a day go to Zakynthos. No buses seem to
cross the island from Sami to Pesada. Are we doomed to go by
taxi? I go to the Blue Line Travel Agency for a second opinion.
Maybe a bus will take me somewhere and then another bus will
take us to Pesada. An elderly man is charming though not very
knowledgeable. There is a lot of discussion and some telephone
calls. I buy tickets from Pesada to Zakynthos. I am told a taxi
will be 38 euros, a necessary evil it would seem. Surprise is
expressed that we have no car. I admire a stunning photograph
of Ithaca on the wall. Stavros – on another desk – is apparently
the photographer. He says that if I e-mail him from England, he
will let me have (buy?) a copy. (When we get home, I do e-mail
him – but I never even get a reply, sadly.) There is much smiling
and hand-shaking. Lottie drifts off to the shops. She fingers the
bric-a-brac. When I join her, I look through the prints of yachts.

Then we sit right on the water's edge and eat yoghurt and honey and play cards until it is dusk. Yachts berth beside us. There is so much to look at.

We wander back to our hotel, getting a crepe on the way, under a crescent moon and stars in a dark blue sky. The sun has slipped behind Kefallonia. Lights dance in the water of the bay. Lottie sits on the balcony to sketch the moon. She can't do the hills because she has no black crayon. The moon slides behind the hill, lost except for a silver gleam above the back line of hill. A dog barks; there is laughter, a strand of music, the sudden sharp rev of a moped engine. Ithaca is lovely. I wish we could stay. I hope I return.

We talk, far too late into the night, across our twin beds, about love. What it means to be loved, and which matters most – to love or be loved. Lottie says it matters most to be loved, that it doesn't matter how, just knowing it is what counts. I wonder whether there's any point in being loved unless the manifestation of it is satisfying and since one cannot command how one is loved it therefore matters more to love; that is the feeling that counts. We agree that we both find it easy to love: different people, different ways. Lottie says that being loved by her family makes her feel good about who she is.

Eventually we sleep.

Friday 12th August

Something (the ferry engine at the quay?) wakes us both before the 6 am alarm call. We dress in a flash and in five minutes Lottie is striding out at a spanking pace – I can hardly keep up.

"I've got a burst," she declares. It is still dark. "Of course," she states, "it's only 4am in England." Of course.

The ferry is not very full for the hour's journey to Sami. We clean our teeth and brush our hair in the excellent ferry loos. In 20minutes it is light – fast. Mist hangs around lumps of land in the sea as we edge out of Vathy's caressing bay to circle the southern tip of Ithaca. The sun rises as an orange ball behind misty grey, turning yellow as it gains height. We travel close to Ithaca's rocky shore. Little pebbly coves hold sleeping yachts with naked masts. The only road cuts a terracotta slash through the green scrub. I can only see one house low on the promontory. Lottie and I play cards again with big cardboard mugs of hot chocolate.

When we dock at Sami there isn't a bus in sight – the only way to get to inaccessible Pesada will be taxi. Bother, what a waste of money. 40 euros later I feel carsick. I try and see the landscape of 'Captain Corelli's Mandolin' out of the car window. Kefallonia is hilly and vine strewn, but really rather dull. Maybe my carsickness is affecting my impressions. It takes us forty five minutes to reach Pesada. Already there is a queue of cars down the hill, waiting for the ferry. They must know they have to be there early to be certain of getting on. The port is tiny: a quay, huge yellow boulders below a vertical cliff, some motor boats, and a café – closed. No matter, they won't mind if we sit at their tables. I put my head on my hands and sleep off my car sickness. Lottie reads aloud from 'The Gods of Olympus' by the Stephanides brothers – I find it lulling.

Waking, the café is open and we share delicious iced coffee and a Greek honey cake. It is getting hot; crickets are scraping loudly. There is still two hours to wait until the ferry to Zakynthos. The queue of cars is even longer. I muse over what happens next. I have no idea where to go when we arrive at Skinari – Kate Sloane has not sent me a text with her address. I send her our ferry details on my mobile, and hope she will reply.

Waiting is a textured pleasure when not in a hurry. The sea stretches flat and mobile all the way to grey misty Zakynthos. It is dappled turquoise and dark blue with sheens of silver streaks. The sky is hot but misty pale blue. Lottie drinks a strawberry granite. I do my budget sums – we have spent 178 euros on accommodation, 100 euros on travel and 50 euros on food so far. Lottie insists on playing more cards. When the score is 68 points each we walk to the rocks to test out the water. Still over an hour to wait.

The rocks are sharp and volcanic. Sea-urchins lurk in the clear shallows but the water is clear, clean and refreshing. As we swim we can see the ferry coming blackly in the misty distance. When we eventually board, our bikinis drip wetly through our clothes.

Lottie reads 'Greek Gods' aloud to me on the one hour journey. Reading about the battle between Zeus and the Titans seems apt as we leave the boulder strewn shore of Kefallonia. Our wake is 'wine-dark'.

I ring the Sloanes as we dock and Hugh comes to collect us in a jeep. Later she tells me that they knew when I would ring because they heard the ferry horn as it approached. We go instantly to the Peligoni Club for lunch; other friends and children are there – a long table under awnings looking out to sea. We talk about American Universities, diseases in Western civilisation, our children. Lucy and Lottie soon disappear to swim. I go back with Hugh to the villa and swim and read and doze: peace. The villa is high in the hills with a vast panoramic view across the wide blue sea. The infinity pool disappears flatly into that blue water.

The other jeeps return. Hugh and Steve Covington go to play tennis. Lottie has slipped into 'separate' mode, disconnecting with me, in order, I suppose, to fully connect with Lucy. I shower and change – we are going to a drinks party at the Shearer's house. They have bought this sailing club, the 'Peligoni' which is beside their house. It had gone bust and what else, they said, would their children do when they were holidaying here on Zakynthos if there wasn't the club? My dress is rather crumpled from the backpack.

I feel a bit unsettled here with the Sloanes. It is so kind of them to have us and such an idyllic place but, though they did invite both of us, I feel an outsider. I think they wanted Lottie not me really. Rather like Royalty who 200 years ago 'visited' honoured friends: one was supposed to consider it a privilege that they chose you to stay with – but you wished they hadn't. I don't know how to play it – should I try to be unobtrusive, or entertaining? The former is safer. Better to be thought boring than a pain. Also I think by nature the Sloanes and Covingtons are very

English in their reserve. They are not effusive at all and it is hard to judge what they think or feel – though it is probably a mistake to interpret their reserve as anything more negative.

Packed into the jeeps, the children stand in the back holding onto the roller bars. I would embarrass Lottie and annoy Hugh by objecting but I do think it is unsafe: it wouldn't take much for them to be flung out. I am cross with myself both for being so protective and for not daring to say so.

The Shearer's house is wondrous. It has a Moroccan feel and is made of stone and old wood built into the hill beside the sea. A double bed under a Moroccan wooden gazebo sits on the edge of the decking. The long infinity pool is tiled in black so that it reflects blue and yellow light. We drink rose and there are delicious nibbles. Sam and Martin Elliot (from Gloucestershire) are there and are rewardingly pleased to see me (as I am them). Charlie Brocket's daughter is pointed out to me (not so much sins of the fathers but fame – or infamy – of the fathers being visited upon their children). She is desperately thin and beautiful with endless legs. Sarah Shearer is sweet (I used to teach her daughter). She has just acquired a stray dog that bites ankles. Teenagers flock on a separate level of decking. It is a beautiful setting; the sea and sky merge and dusk together – stretching forever and flat like a matt metal mirror.

We go to the Peligoni Club for supper. Lights entwine the trunks of olive and tamarisk trees; each level of terrace has a separate long table. Perhaps only big groups of families come here. The conversation becomes increasingly relaxed and amusing – or I do. The atmosphere is witty and laid back. Kate is sweet and chatty. Now the conversation revolves muchly around the children and their current/future activities.

When we get back to the villa we play cards, but I am so tired after the early start that I soon go to bed. My room is blue and white, pretty and cool.

Saturday 13th August

I wake at 9 am and it is lovely not to have had to move early for a ferry or a train. It is hot and I can hear voices. I lie and think. I would like to explore Zakynthos but the villa is so far off the beaten track that it would involve hassle for the Sloanes to do so – I'd either have to borrow a jeep (and am I insured?) or they'd have to drop me somewhere to hire a scooter. I don't want to be a nuisance so I decide to keep quiet for the moment.

I spend the morning by the pool in semi-shade reading up on Greek history and politics from The Rough Guide. There is a forest fire on Kefallonia across the sea in the distance – a regular problem apparently. I can see the blackened stubs of last year's fire on Zakynthos above the villa. There's a good breeze and I see little white sails far below on the sea.

Lunch is at the club and I spend the after noon by the pool up at the villa again. I read a book of Kate's – a gruesome American murder mystery.

When I change for dinner I decide to put on my pearl ear-rings which are in my money belt which I have hidden in the flip top bin in my bathroom. Hugh said to hide it in a safe place – not a drawer or under the mattress or pillow. To my horror the bin is empty. Someone has come today to do the villa and empty the bins (it never crossed my mind; I thought I would clean up when we left after our stay). I have a complete sinking panic feeling and rush to the veranda. Hugh and Steve are calm. Dustbin men won't have worked on a Saturday, even if the cleaner has. They ring Hazel, the cleaner. Apparently the black plastic sacks are taken to a skip beside a supermarket in a nearby village. Hugh drives me there – Hazel's husband is already at the task when we arrive. I open one sack full of empty Malboro packets and mortar rubble. Hugh is more able than we are to recognise villa rubbish, and he finds the right sack. It is there – safe (passports, tickets, money, credit cards and pearl ear-rings) thank goodness. I feel a sense of enormous relief and a cheer goes up from everyone sitting round the table on our return.

Supper – at a restaurant perched over a tiny hidden cove – is a cheerful, noisy time. Ursula and I discover she knows both Richard, my brother, and my sister Carey's sister in law, and learn that she lived near us in Gloucestershire as a child. I feel more part of things. It's as if the discovery that one knows people in common is a sort of code to enable quicker acceptance; not so much a substitute for getting to know you, but a reason to make it worthwhile, relevant.

The children are eating at the club; it is party night. Saintly Hugh collects them at 3 am – Lottie and Lucy come into my room to tell me what a wonderful time they have had. Lucy says,

"We danced with real boys." It takes me seconds to fall asleep again when they go.

Sunday 14th August

I wake earlier than everyone else and go outside meaning to swim, but it is windy and I read instead. Lottie sleeps until midday but I play in a tennis competition at the Peligoni club. Sheila, the referee, is sweet and keeps everything non-competitive by getting the score wrong and missing shots –

"Was that out – yes?" Hugh wins the competition. We swim afterwards and then swim to a restaurant called the Sunflower to meet up with a family called Colchester (Jonty and Zara who live at Hook Norton.) The restaurant turns out not to be called the Sunflower after all, and there is a panic about whether it is the right restaurant. Ursula is reading an autobiographical book by an American cook which warns against eating out on Saturdays and Sundays because the cooks are overworked on those popular days. This is proved by the owner of the Sunflower (or whatever the restaurant is really called) who, laying up for over 20 of us, takes on an oily sheen. The Colchesters and their friends Lou and Piers Cavendish arrive in a motor-boat. Jonty wades in like

Robinson Crusoe, Zara like Ursula Andress. We eat squid and sardines and local fish, and talk about climbing mountains. It is great fun. I envy the Colchesters leaving by boat. It is windy and white horses splatter the sea. A flotilla of five yachts motor across the bay, sails furled. The car journey feels lengthy and sick-making after all the food and wine.

Returning after 5 pm we read and doze and swim. Hugh, in spite of little sleep last night, goes off to play tennis again. We have a salad for supper at the villa. Alex Sloane is teased about a boy she danced with last night – provoked, she chucks a glass of water over her mother. Lottie is shocked (and shocked too by Lucy's lack of reaction and indeed by Kate's lack of anger; Lottie knows I'd have been livid). There are general high jinks and Alex and Lucy end up being thrown into the pool. We end the evening by playing poker (Texas Hold'em) and Hugh wins massively. I try and get Lottie to go to bed but she takes ages to get packed, and I find her sitting on my bed playing cards with Rory and Lucy.

I sleep badly and dream that the puppies are unfed and dying. It is dark and I pick one up and it feels like an unstuffed toy. I try and breathe life into damp nostrils – it breathes but won't eat because it's too weak. Only three puppies are left. I wake in darkness, sweating.

Monday 15th August

Double-saintly Hugh drives us to Zante town to catch the 8 am ferry to the mainland. Rory and Lucy come too. It rained in the night and everything smells good. An orange ball of sun swings fast into the sky. The scrub heather and dry stony hills are replaced by green plains and agriculture – little squares of bamboo or olive trees. Hugh is anxious about finding the quay in Zante town but the road leads straight to it. We hug and kiss goodbye and I buy tickets (discovering later that for some strange reason I have bought three) for Kyllini. Lottie feels sick so I buy her plain biscuits and hot chocolate.

We can't find any sort of bus to any station. We want to catch the Peloponnese train back to Athens. We have to take a taxi. It is only ten euros and we are taken to Lehenna station. It is deserted; café doors are padlocked, no-one is in sight. Cocks crow. We sit on café chairs on the platform in the shade. I read notices about train times. There should be one at 10.45 am but it is, I discover, a religious holiday, so maybe not. I see an elderly couple sitting at a table under a tree on the other side of the line. I flip flop across the stones and sleepers and ask them if the station is open. Apparently so. I go back to wait. A couple of Middle Eastern boys arrive and sit at a next door table. Lottie sleeps in her chair. Two girls arrive and play with ring tones on a mobile. Lottie still sleeps. An elderly man, quite distinguished looking in chinos and a check shirt, panama and moustache shuffles towards us tapping with a stick on the concrete. He chats and mumbles to himself. He goes to a pay phone and a shouted but entirely imaginary conversation. The two girls giggle. He comes back, sits down at a table opposite and farts. He gets up and sits on a chair beside the Middle Eastern boys. They smile warily at him.

The train arrives and I can hardly wake Lottie. She sleeps again, most of the six hour journey. The train jolts too much to read; I can't imagine how Lottie can sleep as she is chucked back and forth. The train is noisy and the journey dull until we reach the coast at Patra. I like this journey backwards; I see coves I missed before. I dream and think, my elbows leaning on the open window. I would have liked to go the other way to see the ancient Olympic site – but we would run out of time, I think. I do not know how long it will take to climb and then descend Mount Olympus. Lottie briefly wakes to eat biscuits and marmite. I buy café frappe and fanta from the buffet car on the train. The track is single line and we wait at stations for trains to come the other way and pass. The trees have grown so close to the line that the leaves brush my fingers on the window. If we went slower I could pick figs. A yacht, with the wind pulling out its spinnaker, whirls by. Eventually we cross the Corinth canal – I see it this time and gasp; it cuts endlessly deep beneath the train, a vivid strip of blue flanked by a high ravine of concrete. Amazing. The sea is on the right now as the line curves round the coast. Pireus must be near – rusty tankers cut into the sea. A ferry is tilted on its side, capsized, lifeboats lined above the water mark. The island of Salamia is close. Industrial Athens is ugly. We pass quarries and then piles of sand and gravel; maybe it's a concrete factory. There are vast gas chambers, and enormous electricity stations with vertical coils of thick wire and their marching pylon giants, and what looks like a nuclear plant, heavily guarded with wire topped walls and watch towers: it looks like a prisoner of war camp.

We reach Athens and take a bus to Larissa station to find out train times to Litochora – the springboard town for Mount Olympus. One train leaves at 11.55 pm. Return tickets are 27 euros for us both. We then plod to the Aristo hotel which kindly lets us leave our backpacks there for five hours, and we set off unencumbered into the centre of Athens. We go back to the Acropolis but go east this time to see the gigantic temple of Zeus – happily inhabited by mangy dogs. We return to the café that makes good milkshakes and wander the pedestrian streets of the Plaka district again. Lottie buys a T-shirt. It gets dark; we round a corner and there, suddenly, is the three quarter moon, hanging large above the floodlit Acropolis. The streets are full of colour and people and waiters trying to persuade us into gardens and side alleys. I suppose if your restaurant isn't on the main street, you have to have some way of attracting the random tourist to your doors. We allow ourselves to be so drawn. The garden in quiet and leafy: we stay. A fig plops from a tree and bursts beside my chair. Lottie eats spaghetti and I eat Tzatsiki and taramasalata. We linger; we have so much time to fill. But I feel slightly dizzy and not very well, so we pay and wander, listening to guitar music from the roof garden of a taverna, exploring dark alleys and bright shops, watching cats, admiring ruins and artistic graffiti on walls, finding at last a metro and heading back to the Aristo where we play cards in their downstairs café and bar for another hour.

Platform one is packed an hour before the train is due. A harrowing row breaks out between a woman and a man and a crowd gathers in appreciation. The rest of the platform is silenced. It is impossible to work out what the row is about (though it may have been a lovers' tiff which got out of hand and which has pulled in faction supporters). When Lottie and I eventually board the train and find our seats, another row breaks out, this time between a group of gypsies and a couple of men. This row is loud but mostly laced with humour. It is to do with seat numbers. Several of us, including me, have been double booked by the ticket office. A stout but spry well-wrinkled crone in a swirling skirt and dangling scarf leaps over the top of the seats to claim one. It is ages before people are remotely quiet. A kind Greek man diagonally opposite asks me if I am jealous that I don't come across these scenes in England. This leads to more conversation – he is a member of the mountain rescue team for Olympus but has been living in the UK for seven years studying architecture. He is kind, friendly and helpful but I never learn his name.

Lottie takes the towels and sleeps on the floor in the storage V behind our two chairs beside the partition. I doze deeply until 4 am and then uncomfortably until 5.30 am when the guard tells us to be ready for the next stop. Bleary eyed we stagger down the steep steps off the train. It pulls away immediately. I notice in the stark overhead lights that a khaki uniformed soldier has got off too. The tip of his cigarette glows red against the black sky. The station is otherwise deserted. Hardly a station: just strips of concrete beside the track. Apparently in the middle of no-where. What shall we do? Where is Litochoro? And how far? I can see a motorway sign away to the right. The Rough Guide says that Litochoro has its own motorway exit. Lottie puts more plasters on her rubbed toes, we hoist up our backpacks, and set off. I don't look at the soldier as we pass him leaning against a lamppost. I am a bit scared. It all feels like one of those morose films where nothing much happens but the music fills everything with a sense of foreboding. After a short while a black car, lacking its silencer, roars past, halts and roars past again – presumably having picked up the soldier. The Rough Guide says that there are army barracks at Litochoro.

After half an hour of walking in the dark we come to the motorway bridge. To the right in the grey dawn we can see the grey sea. To the left, town lights. I see a sign saying 'Litochoro 5 kms'. And at the same moment, over the bridge, a bus-stop. We wait there for nearly an hour. A man comes and flashes a gold tooth leerily at us and offers us a lift into town. We refuse, obviously.

Beside us on the bus is a priest, hatless but with his grey hair knotted neatly behind – a tiny flat button bun, By the way he rubs his nose I suspect he wants to pick it. In the main square of Litochoro is a church which he enters. (It is beautiful we later discover, with softwood carvings lightening the heavy ornateness of brasses and oil paintings).

As we leave the bus-stop, the sun rises – an orange ball rippling an orange path across the rippled grey sea leading along the road and up to the heights of Olympus, now suddenly visible, towering grey above the land and covered in pink and white reflection from the sun. It looks as if the ridges and peaks are streaked with snow.

The village is quiet when we arrive. Only one café is open; it's 7.30 am. Papanickolaus – the guest house recommended by the Rough Guide is not open. When I ring the bell a man eventually leans over the balcony in his pyjamas and whispers that he will have a room for us – 35 euros – but not until midday. I yearn to sleep but instead we go back to the café. I buy croissants from a nearby bakery when it opens and we order hot chocolate. Lottie buries her nose in her arm to block out the acrid cigarette smoke from nearby tables. Slowly the town wakes. Groups of young men come to the café for iced coffee and cigarettes. At 8 am the fountain in the square turns on. Taxis arrive at the taxi rank. Delivery vans pull up. The light changes. The town is pretty, really pretty, in a ski village sort of way – chalet houses but in white and wood with terracotta tile roofs, balconies, and every inch of patio, yard or balcony festooned with geraniums, roses, marigolds, jasmine or bougainvillea. It is a mass of colours. We explore, buying postcards, watermelon and a map of Olympus. We find the mountain centre and a sweet girl talks us through the route up the mountain using a model of Olympus in a glass case. She even rings Shelter A for us to book our accommodation for Wednesday night. She says it will take us three days to climb the mountain and even that will be pushing it. Apparently the descent will take a minimum of seven hours but there is no refuge for shelter on that route down – so tough, we have to do it in one hit.

We decide to take a 20 euro taxi as deep into the mountain as possible to conserve energy for the two steep climbs – to Shelter A, and then even more so to Mytikos summit – which sounds scary, along ridges with precipitous drops and down a climb which translates as 'Evil Stairway'. I learn that my mobile phone won't work up there – if there's a drama I just have to wait for another climber. We are told we will need raincoats because the weather on Olympus is so unpredictable and swift changing – Zeus chucks his thunderbolts randomly and storms are frequent apparently. I buy two waterproof ponchos. On the way back we decide we will walk the last part down the gorge – the part we will miss because of the taxi ride. It is a hike not a climb, but nevertheless the 12 kms will be the easier for being downhill. We start to get excited.

We go back to Papanickolaus and are shown up little white-washed stairs to an enchanting shuttered apartment with a little balcony overlooking spruce trees and a stairwell balcony overlooking Mount Olympus. I sit there a while watching the clouds shift shape and colour round the summit – Zeus's swirling cloak. Lottie and I sift through kit trying to decide what to backpack up the mountain and what to leave here – as much as possible. Lottie's sketching stuff and the marmite are going to weigh a ton. I sleep for an hour, Lottie reads. We discover a tiny kitchenette behind a cupboard door. We eat watermelon on the balcony and play Blackjack, Poker, Gin Rummy and Whist. We stop for yoghurt and honey for lunch, watch some Greek television, enjoying appalling American sitcoms with Greek subtitles (they are bad enough for me to prefer to work out the Greek words than to listen to the English ones). Later we wander into the square and eat chips and salad for 4 euros. The fountain splashes, church bells clang from the bell tower that rises separately from the church, and a canary in a cage by the café door shrills. It is clear-skied and sunny except for the thick clouds over Mount Olympus. We play cards until I owe Lottie so many cents that she can have an ice-cream – she chooses caramel, and it's delicious – or so I think from the small mouthful she lets me have.

We go back to our room. Old women greet each other across the cobbled streets; one makes lace at a table. Pots of basil grow on tiles steps. We shower, wash underwear, pack, chat, and watch Elvis Presley (or is he a look-a-like?) on Greek television. Tomorrow feels exciting for us both. This mountain is not only the highest in Greece but the second highest in the Balkans (so the Rough Guide tells me. Where exactly are the Balkans, I wonder? Or rather what countries, exactly, make up the Balkans? I must find out). Above all, it feels wonderfully mythical – we will climb to the throne of Zeus and reach the Plateau of the Muses. What an experience

Tuesday 16th August

Lottie closed the shutters and the curtains last night, so I wake in darkness at 8.30 am. Outside it is clear and sunny with only wisps of white cloud touching Zeus's throne which I can see clearly today, powering into the blue at the top of Olympus.

We dress, put on sun cream, leave our main backpacks with Maria (Papa Nickolaus's daughter who gives us a delicious big breakfast of croissant, rolls, cheeses, coffee and real milk) and set off into the square. The first taxi man shakes his saloon car head at us dolefully but makes a telephone call and tells us that a Volvo will be here in five minutes. Is the road too rough? Why didn't he want to take us? In two minutes we are off. The road winds steeply and our ears pop. Gaps in the fir trees show the flat plains of Priera a long way below us, and further still the sparkle of a dark sea. The tarmac gives way to rough grit. The throne of Zeus shimmers white –

"Snow!" cries Lottie eagerly, but I don't think so. I think it's just the colour of the rock. The gorge plunges through enormous boulders to our left (Zeus's battle strewn arena). Prionia, at the end of the gritty road, has a taverna, mountain water gushing from a pipe, and a huge sign declaring this to be The Olympus National Park, with pictorial prohibitions (Picking flowers, cutting trees, camping, litter dropping etc).

Off we go. I carry the backpack. It isn't heavy – yet.

The path is marked here by wooden railings. It is immediately steep but branches are pegged in as steps. We divert to a waterfall and natural plunge pool glimpsed through the leaves off the path. Lottie stumbles into the stream but luckily not enough to wet her socks. The water dashes in two parallel streams over a vertical mossy rock face. The pool water tastes good.

It is 10am. Slowly we become aware of the sound of a low metallic clank of neck bells – cows, we wonder, <u>here?</u> We round a corner: half a dozen saddled mules chomp at nosebags by a wooden shack. We stop to watch. Two mangy dogs bark loudly at us- guards; there is no-one in sight. We have a pang of yearning to do this first part of the climb on mule back – what a cheat (what fun!) – the Rough Guide says one can hire mules but it would probably be too expensive.

After half an hour of up hill walking, the railings stop and tree roots and rocks replace man-made steps. The path is through spruce and beech trees and is shady but steep. We stop often for Lottie to draw leaves and flowers – I sweat and puff under the weight of the backpack and am glad to rest. We eat a sesame bar by fallen uprooted trees. It is very quiet. We hear a woodpecker. A huge butterfly lands beside us – black and white.

It is 11.30am.

Two people have passed us going the same way; four people have passed us going down. There is too much in the backpack. Heaviness apart, the zip is tearing, damn it. We take stuff out. Lottie carries her sketch-book, I carry the camera and the biscuit packet. But I'm sure we need all that we have brought: 1 thin towel, clean knickers, waterproofs, a couple of warmer tops for Lottie, 1 extra T shirt, toothbrush and paste, camera, suntan cream, crayons and a pencil, Lottie's sketch-book, sun hats, Milli (Lottie's beloved soft rabbit), little sachets of honey, pistachios, chocolate, sesame bars, biscuits, water, and of course, marmite.

"It feels like England," says Lottie. That's the beech trees that give that impression. The path narrows to a couple of feet; steep and stony. It is hot and sunny – we can hear the mule bells far below us. They are on the move. We sit on rocks and wait to watch them pass. Daft of us to think of them as tourist accessories: they carry provisions for Shelter A in a string of sure footed strength. A man sits side-saddle on the first mule, kicking rhythmically with a sandaled heel. The dogs pant at the back, too tired to bark. Beside us, a mule halts, flanks heaving, and then moves on. The last mule does the same, heaving its load on tiny hooves up the rocks. How do they manage? We follow – much more slowly.

At 1 pm we have another sketch-and-shade stop. I sit on a hummock of scented lemon thyme. Tiny flowers are everywhere. Pinky purples and white mostly. A tall good-looking man comes past us, stops and chats in an American accent. He's called Simos (he is Greek) and he's already been to the summit this morning. He fills us in on detail. Apparently his mother screamed at him down the phone when he told her what he was doing as it is reputedly so dangerous.

"Mount Olympus claims lives." He was kind and gave us his (better) map. He walked up the gorge from Litochoro yesterday, but he is going to hitch down the road that we took a taxi up.

We part and climb on. There is hardly a path now and trees have given way to scrubby trunks. My knee hurts. My thighs begin to ache. I feel slightly dizzy. We find wild raspberries and I climb down shale to pick them – they are sweet and delicious. It is hot. We put on our hats.

At 2.15 pm we stop to eat biscuits and marmite. The view down the gorge, back behind us, is spectacular, right across to Litochoro, the Priera plain and the sea, with Mount Antonio looking like a volcano crater reaching up to our right. Apparently the ancient Greeks, too wary of Zeus to climb his peak, left sacrificial offerings on Mount Antonio. I eat a tiny sachet of honey. Lottie doesn't want one. I hope it will give me energy.

We climb on, suddenly seeing the roof of the refuge high on a rocky plateau well above us. Another 40 minutes maybe. We see lizards and a silent cricket. The lizard has a spotty back and dark striped sides, and is fearless in spite of his visibly pounding heart.

How can it be so hot? I read that for every 100metres up it is 1 degree cooler. People pass us in ski jackets and jerseys – it must be cool where they've come from. We hear mule bells, and there they are – grazing on scrub at the edge of the refuge. As we trudge the last slope, they get ready to leave; their keeper walks downhill leading the first mule. They are carrying empty water containers. One mule gets left behind, distracted and delayed by morsels of scrub. When he notices that the others are gone, he sets off at a trot, bell clanking, and slithers down the slope to join the path proper, the last dog at his heels.

The refuge is welcoming and shady. The last of the spruce – the tree line is about here – grows out of stone parapets. A stone water tank is filled by blue tubing from the river, but the river is dry at the moment. The refuge sleeps forty in dormitory bunks. We have to take off our boots or shoes and wear provided slippers. Our room is clean and simple - bed, pillow and blankets, shared loo and shower facilities. It is windy up here – Lottie is soon cold as the warmth of our exertions cools. We snack on nougat and Tzatzaki and listen and watch. People seem to walk up here and then go back down in a day; more people are pausing than staying the night. Germans mostly I think from listening to the accents. I look at the map puzzling over what to do tomorrow, which route to take. If we come back to this refuge tomorrow afternoon before a steep hours climb across the mountain to Refuge B, then we could unload some of the backpack and leave it here. The last third of the climb to the peak is best done with free hands (and I find the backpack unfamiliar and unbalancing too; it is Lottie's as hers was smaller). Or if we take all the pack, go to the peak, and come back halfway and then cut across the mountain, it is a longer but not nearly such a steep climb to the second refuge. The only essential is to avoid the short cut of the Louki couloir – dangerous and needing ropes.

In the end I decide on plan B, but reckon I will leave the whole backpack at the bottom of the final stretch, the hardest part of the climb, 'the Scala'.

"I'm not leaving Milli alone on the mountain," says Lottie. "What if someone steals the backpack?"

"Olympus claims lives," I laugh. "And who would want to carry your crayons and marmite all the way down Mount Olympus as well as their own stuff?!" I hope I am right – we can't lose Milli to the Gods.

By 4.30 pm the clouds are thick above and it is chilly. When the sun is out the view is lovely, and the light soft making the green slopes undulate. It takes thirty minutes or so for my knee to stop hurting. I hope it holds up tomorrow. I sit on warm steps looking up at jagged ridges. Lottie is sitting at a nearby table sketching. People bring trays of bean soup to wooden tables and it feels like a restaurant at a ski resort. Apart from Lottie there are no other children younger fifteen or sixteen. We look funny in our slippers – mine plush maroon, Lottie's leather.

On the way up the mountain Lottie has said she thinks we should have a break from travelling next year. I am sad. This is what we do together. I worry: does she say this because she no longer enjoys it, because she hasn't enjoyed this year here in Greece? Or does she just prefer the fun of villa, pool and sailing club with a friend better? Or is she just tired and fed up of the steep upward trudge? But coming on the back of the older girls telling me that they are spending Christmas with their father in Germany this year, it hurts. I always knew our travels had a limited shelf life; I just hoped it would be longer. I know that Lottie would be thrilled to go and spend time as a cowgirl on a ranch in America, or go snorkelling in the Caribbean (adventures she has suggested keenly) – but these aren't budget trips. After time to ponder I suspect that she may be right. I have found some of this trip (the night in the train for instance) tiring; the Acropolis lacked the thrill of Herculaneum. There are a few moments when I wonder why I am not at home with the puppies. Maybe I am not so fidgety: the acute reasons for escape no longer fret at me and my life is calmer now, two and a half years on from the separation. I think I want to settle contentedly and make a home again. In which case travel might become an adult-shared pleasure rather than a search. Perhaps I am losing the wanderlust urge; maybe there is no longer a point in travelling for the sake of it, only because I want to go somewhere – to see, to explore, to discover. And where do I want to go now anyway? I had thought Israel or Egypt, though the latter is too dangerous at the moment. But the road to Damascus? Maybe I have had enough of visions and revelations – they shift with time and circumstances anyway.

"How do you spell 'chimney'?" says Lottie. I tell her.

"Where's the 'L'?"

"'L', what 'L'?"

"The 'L' in 'chimley'." I laugh and tell her that her spelling problems are really hearing problems.

"I'm not deaf. It's always been 'chimley'." I try the 'r' and 'l' sounds. How do lip readers tell the difference?

We wear jerseys and drink hot chocolate. Lottie colours her sketches but seems to have no yellow and only the wrong green. I eye the tin of Carand'ache balefully. It has contributed I am sure to my sore knee, and now it doesn't even have the right colours.

"Funny word, cardigan," says Lottie. We discuss the good Lord Cardigan.

"It's a bit gay to wear them now," she states.

"Only on men," I say. She gives me a funny look.

"Not like that. I mean not cool." So now 'gay' means 'not cool'. Is this politically correct or not?

"Is my eye ok?" she asks. It is red on the lower lid. I hope she isn't getting a stye.

By 5.15 pm there are few people left at the refuge. We discover that the forecast for tomorrow is fine, possibly with rain in the afternoon, and that the generator (and therefore the lights) is switched off at 10 pm. I want us to leave at about 7 am: I hope we wake up in time. I think tomorrow's climb will take us eight hours. Apparently expert climbers/walkers do 20kms an hour (that sounds impossibly fast; I must have misheard), and people like us only 5kms an hour. I hope we will be ok. The girl at the refuge reception looks at us dubiously, and tells us that her father – a climber – always took his children up the summit on ropes. Well, we aren't doing the Louki couloir even though it would cut three hours off our climb time. It is the Louki couloir that the Rough Guide seems to indicate is the most dangerous climb, the place where there have been most deaths.

It is waiting time tonight. It is a bit chilly. We wrap ourselves in blankets and play cards. Everyone seems to be in thick jerseys and fleeces and jackets. I only have a long sleeved T shirt. I think I will be cold; I shall wear my waterproof and hope it is wind proof too. Lottie has a hoody and a jersey but only shorts. It was hard to get clothing right in terms of the variety of temperature bottom to top and taking into account the problems of space and weight in the backpacks.

We have supper at 7pm – tepid rice or spaghetti with insipid red sauce. I force us to eat for energy. Lottie is reluctant. Afterwards, Lottie sketches the view. I chat to Costas, a Greek who has been doing international business in America and so speaks good English. We sit on the balcony and watch the sunset and the colours change until the trees are black silhouettes. We drink Tsiporo made by a neighbour. Jet fuel. When Lottie tries it, it burns her mouth. Everyone laughs.

"I don't know how you could let me drink that stuff," she says, spitting.

We talk about Greek culture – apparently lacking because there was no renaissance because of the Turkish occupation; we talk about Greek archaeology and the buildings that were damaged by earthquake and civil war (there's a hole in the Acropolis made by Greek canon firing at the Turks); we talk about the British ownership of the Ionian islands after the war of independence, and their return to Greece, insisted on by their second king, the Dane, Philip 1; we talked about the creation of Olympus from a shallow sea and falling rock during earthquakes. We discuss how equipment and kit is got up to the refuges (probably by helicopter) and how therefore the refuges are quite recent buildings; and how Christoph Kackalou first climbed the summit in 1913, because no-one had ever dared to before in case they incurred the wrath of Zeus.

Costas had spent a year in the army, Special Forces, parachuting – so Lottie and he discuss fear, and falling, and bungy jumping and fall speeds and heights. He laughs a lot and is charming. He has an ace flying watch (complete with altimeter) much admired by Lottie. He agrees to wake us at 7 am as we have no alarm, and we mutually agree that we will be leaving our packs at the base of Scala and trust our fellow mountain climbers not to nick them. His pack weighs 18 kilograms and he said he had been totally wiped out by the climb up from Prionia. Lottie wants to leave Milli in Costa's pack but (probably to his relief) I point out that he might make it quicker to the summit than us and then Milli would disappear back to Athens with Costas and without her.

We say goodnight at 9pm and snuggle into our orange blankets – with toe pictures at one end to show which way up to have them – clever from a hygiene point of view when so many will be using the same blankets. Lottie is on the top bunk – no-one else is in our dormitory. I am scared about tomorrow – not for me but, in case, for Lottie. The last part of the climb from Scala to Mytikos sounds hard. But the weather should be clear – which helps, and I am sure we will be alright. I remember that we had to give in our passport numbers in case anything happens on the mountain. Lottie climbs down from her bunk and goes to clean her teeth.

"Golly the water is cold," she says when she comes back. "And there's no power, it just trickles."

"Not surprising," I say. "It comes through a little plastic pipe from outside."

In bed, lights out, we chat as usual, conversation punctuated by me saying,

"We must go to sleep. Sshh." We fall asleep, I think, before the generator – humming audibly, is turned off.

Wednesday 17th August

In the middle of the night I am woken by the door opening and a torch shining (it turns out to be the light from a mobile phone).

"Who are you?" I ask sharply, instantly awake and scared. In broken English a man replies,

"Can I sleep in here tonight?" Well, there are four spare and empty bunks in here, but I feel vulnerable.

"What for?" I ask ungraciously.

"There is a man in my room who is harrumphing and I cannot sleep," he replies. I love it; 'harrumphing' – what a lovely word for snoring.

"OK." I watch him as he makes his bed on a lower bunk by the light of his mobile. Once he is breathing deeply, I feel I can sleep too. Lottie never stirs.

The next morning after Costas has banged on our door to wake us at 7 am, I find other refugees from the 'harrumpher' sleeping on benches and the floor in the hall. At breakfast it is a subject of gritted teeth laughter – everyone is talking about the train-whistle snorer. Costas, who had pitched his tent far away amid the spruce so that he 'can be alone with nature', is unaware of the joke.

The sun rises hard in a clear sky and we are walking by 7.30 am. Lottie sets off at a spanking pace, refreshed. I plod along, panting immediately. It is cold, but we strip off our layers fast as we sweat uphill. We try a short cut to avoid the zigzag path but the stone is loose and the grass thistly – it is a mistake. We rejoin the path. Costas overtakes us with a smile.

"See you on Scala," we all cry. Costas has left his backpack at the refuge after all, and carries only a water pack.

The air tastes clean and alpine. Flowers splatter the edges of the path. After an hour or so the path forks right under the ridges and peaks to Refuge C (three hours away), and goes straight on for Scala. We carry on. There is no scrub now; the slopes are bare shale, the views high and especially good looking back, and the path is ugly and dull. Steeper and steeper it gets. After two hours or so, we are at the top of the ridge. We crawl to the edge. The gorge plunges away from the ridge rocks; it is dizzying. The clouds whirl and dance around the edges, above us, below us, around us, so fast, so unpredictable in their random swirls and whooshes. We see no-one. It is hot. There is no shade – but it is cold too: the chocolate in the pack never melts, and in a crevasse thick ice lies slicked, unthawed.

We plod on; it is so tiring. Suddenly (we have been climbing looking at our feet I think) we are at the top of Skala (2,866 metres) – and we look over the edge into forever. Later I learn that, about now, Olivia, my stepson's daughter is born. It seems coincidentally parallel. Around her, the stretching heights of her future; around us the very real heights of Mount Olympus. To our left is Scolio (2,911 metres), the second highest peak; a rounded hill veering gently up. We can see for miles because it is so clear. To the east is the sea – I can make out the dark shape of an island somewhere near the horizon. To the west is the Pindus mountain range. To the south (eventually Athens) are more mountains. To the north is Mytikas (2,918 metres) looming like a vast God's finger, thickly, starkly, into the blue sky. Clouds flurry and fuss, sweeping its sides and summit, filling the gorge below, hiding everything and then clearing windows of view. I look at Mytikos and I am really frightened. It is so vertical. I can see the Greek flag (metal) on top. One or two people – men – inch their way up its side.

"We have to do it," says Lottie. The cloud is thickening. She has unsuitable shoes – trainers with no tread. I am not sure at all.

"We don't have to reach the peak. We have climbed Olympus. We are here.................This....................... is..................................... amazing."

"But I want to sign the visitor's book at the top." We see a couple returning up the Kakascala (evil stairway). She is crying. She only took five steps before coming back. We watch a family set off boldly – Germans.

"They are experienced alpine climbers," I am told. "They climb many mountains." We eat some chocolate. I stare at Mytikos. I look over the gorges and the plains, across the ridges and other peaks. I am still scared.

"OK," I say. "We'll try the Kakascala and come back if it gets too dangerous." We leave all our stuff on Scala in a cleft of the rocks. I go first. Loose stones, lying on the huge blocks, shoot from under my feet. It is hard to stretch down to the next toe hold.

"Three body points must touch the rock," I say, repeating something I remember my father saying to me as a child. "Make sure you have two feet and a hand or two hands and a foot on the rock always."

The Kakascala cuts like a ravine through the mountain, almost perpendicular, falling away with no ledges fast and steep to somewhere out of sight. Red paint splodges mark the best route. Hah! My legs are shaking with fear. We reach the bottom of Kakascala – a tiny crumbly soil ledge, and have to turn sharp left. I see pitons (for ropes) hammered into the rock. I wish I was on a rope. I wish Lottie was.

"We could go back now," I say.

"No."

The next bit is jumbled rocks, very steep but made terrifying by the endless drop below them. If we can make it there is, eventually, a sort of narrow path below a ridge on the left which drops away hard to the right. If we can reach the other end of that, the sheer vertical climb up that last 40 metres of Mytikas begins. I look up at the route we have just climbed down. It is appalling. My heart is pounding. I have horrendous images of Lottie slipping – me slipping – and nothing would stop our fall. The rock is unstable – apparently solid stone breaks away in our hands or underfoot.

"We should go back," I say – though back is worse than on. It's just the thought of more 'back' later that I can't cope with.

"OK," says Lottie. "If you want." If she had argued, would we have gone on? Who knows? I am so scared climbing back. Stones dislodged by Lottie's feet rattle past me, but if she fell I couldn't stop her or even break her fall: we would both go. It takes us over an hour to get as far as we did and back again. It takes me half an hour to stop shaking when we are back at Scala. I ask a man who returns from the peak what it was like.

"Frightening," he says.

"Which bit was worst?" I ask.

"This bit," he says, pointing to where Lottie and I have just climbed. We talk to a Greek born in Australia, climbing with his Greek cousins. His father had been a shepherd in these mountains. They are getting up courage to attack the summit and are scared. They are eating chocolate chip cookies and offer them to us. We both share our chocolate too.

Lottie is quiet and sad that we haven't done the last leg. I am half sad, and half glad that, anyway, we are safe.

"Come back one day and do the last bit. In proper boots," I say.

"I will," she says. "I want to sign the visitor's book." We see Costas returning. He is chuffed to pieces at having made it. He says the last bit wasn't as scary as it looks and he confirms that our bit was the worst. He is pale and a bit shaky, but triumphant.

"Better safe than sorry," he says to us. We discover that we are taking the same route for the first part of the climb down: under the ridge, under the dangerous Louki Couloir, under Mytikos, into the seat of the Throne of Zeus (Stefani peak; only climbable with axes and ropes) to Refuge C on the Plateau of the Muses. Costas wants to see the highest church in the Balkans – a tiny shale sixteenth century chapel built by Dionysius to the prophet Elias which perches on a peak called Prophet Elias above the Plateau of the Muses. We agree to do the climb together.

The first part down from Scala is steep and slippy. Lottie falls a few times (I expect she is tired too), but it is, as she says, 'comforting' to have Costas with us. I wish he had been with us for Mytikos – we might have made it with him.

We cut away left under the ridges: it is utterly beautiful. The mountain plunges down to the right of the path. We can see the roof of Refuge A dark red in the trees, so far below that it is smaller than a doll's house. The thrusting jags of ridge and peak lurch up high to our left, the clouds whirling in a frenzy around them. One has to stop and hold on to a rock in order to look or you feel dizzy – and the path is only a foot or so wide before the ground plunges away. Not a good place to lurch or stumble. It is breathtaking.

We reach a summit – the path snakes left and a new gorge dives away, and in the distance we can see Refuge C. Mytikos towers above us.

"How did I do that?" wonders Costas. It is staggering.

We turn another corner and gasp as we enter The Throne of Zeus. Huge black rock thrusts darkly into the sky, shaped as the back of the throne. Dominating, imposing, commanding. We walk on the arm of the throne and then along the edge where back meets seat. We climb the other arm and look over the edge, now opposite Scala with Mytikos on the left but hidden by Zeus's rock. Suddenly a cloud whooshes up behind the rock, shaped like a head and shoulders with hole shapes for eyes and nose – it is Zeus himself. We laugh.

By 3 pm we have reached the refuge. Mules are tethered to a pole. We are hungry and I eat bean soup and salad. Lottie has, guess what, spaghetti. Costas has potatoes and some meat – goat probably. We drink coffee in the sun. It is actually windy and cold but we don't feel it yet.

An English group arrive – they've climbed for five hours from Gostia (our route back tomorrow) but want to reach the summit of Mytikas tonight.

Not possible, we reckon, as it means at least another two hours more climbing and it will be dark. They decide to try anyway.

"They're bonkers," says Lottie firmly – speaking from the experience of having climbed for seven or eight hours today herself).

"What is 'bonkers'?" asks Costas. We tell him, and he agrees, laughing. He asks them if they have a torch. They haven't, but there is no more dissuasion.

We stomp off over loose shale up Prophet Elias to the chapel. It is tiny and primitive but so peaceful. Just made of stone and wood. We all light candles and pray. Costas explains to Lottie about icons and talks about his (Greek Orthodox) religion. The view – over sea and plain and mountain – is staggering. It is so quiet too – nothing but the wind.

When we return to the refuge, we say goodbye to Costas who heads back down the steep short cut to Refuge A and his backpack. He is aiming to be at Prionia and his car by 9 pm and is then driving to a monastery in the Pindus mountains for the night.

"You are my second travel friend," says Lottie and tells Costas about Mark in Spain.

"I will e-mail you and you must come to my wedding." So we get his e-mail address. When we say goodbye Lottie says,

"I hope I see you again."

"You will," says Costas solemnly. "At your wedding." A kind, good man – we were glad of him.

Lottie says she would prefer to sleep at the Christoph Kakalous refuge, perched on the cliff edge down the sheep track: tiny, white-walled, sleeping eighteen in one big dormitory.

"Why not," I agree. It is very friendly and welcoming. The loos are in a separate block down the hill – tricky at night! It is freezing cold and windy but the sun shines, the Greek flag flutters on a cairn, the view is stunning and the back of Zeus's throne looms black and high. We are truly at the top of the world – of Greece anyway – and I no longer mind too much that I bottled out of the final forty metres of Mytikas. Lottie's here and safe. Zeus is on his throne and all's well with the world.

Far, far away, across the gorge, we see the miniscule figure of Costas heading for Refuge A. For the fun of it, we shout hello across the mountains and wave. We never expect such an echo. The rocks take up the echo and carry the sound to Costas, who hears and turns and waves back.

Michaelis, the refuge warden, is great. Lottie asks him how many times he's climbed Mytikas. He says,

"Oh a couple of hundred but last year I climbed Everest." It took him two and a half months and he bewails the tedium of waiting for commercial 'client' climbers to climb ahead, and the litter, and the general way the mountain has been spoiled.

He sees Lottie shivering, and he makes her hot chocolate and lights a woodburning stove in the single downstairs room. We play cards and chat to two Greek girls and a Frenchman who are going to climb Mytikas tomorrow. Later, we go outside and Lottie sketches and I find a sheltered spot in the sun out of the wind behind a wall to sit and look at the view. Zeus's throne towers darkly above me, casting its huge shadow over the mountain as the sun sinks behind it. Soon it is too cold and I go back in. The refuge is so small: one communal rectangular room downstairs filled by table and stove, with a little kitchen off it. Stairs at a forty

five degree angle rise by the kitchen door into the attic where bunk
beds are side by side in a row, no space between. We later discover
we are the only girls sleeping there. The two Greek girls prefer to
camp in a tent.

This is a proper climbers' shelter: as the dying sun casts long
lingering shadows over the green of the Plateau of the Muses, men
arrive – deep voices, laughter, the clatter of rope attachments.
They wear helmets, and kit and ropes hang off their belts and
bodies. They strip it off and sort it. The room is full and there
is a sense of excitement. Lottie finds a book of climbing pictures
– all axes and terror. We aren't hungry. Lottie eats some bread
and I have some potatoes with sauce. It feels as if food has been
scrounged from sparse supplies.

Lottie and I go to bed at 9 pm, but from downstairs beneath us
drifts laughter and chat. Someone plays a guitar. It is toasty warm
as the heat from the stove rises. Outside, through a little square
of window, I can see the curve of the hill, the full moon lighting
the mountain in silver. We snuggle into thick soft blankets and
sleep.

Thursday 18th August

We wake at about 7 am. Opening my eyes and turning my head
I see rows of sleeping men. Lottie is on my wall side. Some of
the men are up already. We slept in our clothes, so there is no
dressing or undressing to do. It is another clear day – but cold,
as we discover as we walk down to the loo block. Too cold for a
shower certainly – especially since I have gathered that the shower
trickles are barely tepid.

We drink hot chocolate for breakfast; the climbers chat.
When they discover that we bottled out of the last bit of the
summit, Michaelis says we must try going up the Louki couloir
as he thinks it is less scary. Maria, one of the Greek girls, offers to
take us. Lottie is reluctant but I feel we should accept. I am not
sure why she is so reluctant – does she feel unwell; is she scared

by stories of the Louki couloir; has she had enough? Michaelis says that the couloir is only dangerous if there are a lot of people (because rocks fall down from above), or if the visibility is bad – but today is clear, and because it is a weekday the couloir should be reasonably deserted. Maria is an expert; I'm sure we will be fine.

Disappointment a second time is a dull sadness. From the beginning of our climb up the Louki couloir, Maria is unhappy.

"The Louki is difficult," she says. "For Michaelis, he does Everest, it is easy." We get to the start of the red paint splashes marking the climb. It is steep, very steep, but in a sense Michaelis is right: psychologically, because it is less exposed, it is less scary. It is like climbing a near vertical chimney with one of its sides missing. Lottie goes first, then me, then Maria.

"Are you OK?" she asks often. The footholds are just large enough for the tip of a shoe, and they aren't really spaced too far apart, and the handholds seem stable. Some little stones from Lottie's climb clink down.

"We're fine," I say.

"It's easy," says Lottie.

But I make the mistake of looking down after ten minutes. And then I make a second mistake by saying to Lottie "Don't look down." Of course, she does. We climb slowly, precariously. My heart is pounding, my hands slightly sweaty. Maria asks us if we are ok with increasing anxiety in her voice. I look at her face and see that she is scared. It is contagious – now I am scared too. Her English is too bad to be able to discuss what the climb becomes like. Does it get harder?

"Do you think we should stop?" I ask Lottie.

"Well," she replies,"It's going to be hard coming down." I look back. It seems vertical; much worse from here than from the bottom.

"I think we should go back," says Maria nervously. We do. It takes us twice the time: it is indeed much harder.

We walk back to the refuge in silence.

"Sorry," says Maria. "I can do it alone, but with you I am scared."

We pack up, pay 25 euros for our supper, bed and breakfast, and leave, exchanging e-mail addresses. Michaelis says we must come again, and he will take us up with ropes. We want to.

We take the longer route back across the Plateau of Muses onto a narrow ridge called Lemnos. There we stop for Lottie to sketch and me to write. As we look back the peak of Prophet Elias is above us – we can just distinguish to outline of the stone chapel – and to the left is a clear view of the Throne of Zeus with the jagged thumb of Mytikas behind it, and then further to the left still is the ridge leading to Scala. There are pockets of snow and ice in gulleys, and the ridge we have just walked with little concern looks frighteningly narrow. To the right the world disappears below us into valleys and wooded slopes, plains, villages, to the sea and distant mountain ranges. Over my shoulder to my left is the coastline and the sea curling southwards in a hazy blue. It is silent except for the occasional buzz of a fly or bee. We feel totally alone. It is beautiful. We have been so lucky with the weather, lucky that it has been clear and warm and sunny. Even the wind today is a breeze.

But this is a long walk, and while going uphill is hard on the lungs, steep downhill is tough on the legs and feet – and my thighs ache from yesterday anyway. Lottie gets a rub on her little toe – we swap footwear. Her trainers are murder to wear for walking downhill – no grip. Experiencing what it is like in them I am so glad that I didn't let us do the last part of Mytikas. She is comfortable in my walking boots. Soon my shoulders ache from the backpack.

Eventually we come to an ancient pine forest. We hear the clang of mule bells – there they are, heading for the refuges on the Plateau of Muses. There is a grey mule that became a favourite of ours when they were tethered outside the refuge yesterday among them.

Shortly afterwards we come across a shady mountain farm of lean-to shacks amongst the boulders and herds of sheep and goats. The downwards plunge seems to go on forever. I slip and fall several times – the path is stony, uneven and rough. We stop by a cliff drop into a gorge to eat biscuits. Nearby a house is being built – maybe another refuge. Stone and wood and cement have been brought by mule – they are grazing near.

On we go and stop again by a hummock of grass. Up an extraordinary jagged mountain spur is, apparently, a cave where a famous Greek painter lived – so my Rough Guide tells me. We detour to see it.

This is an exciting mistake. What appears to be a tiny path soon peters out. We find ourselves scrambling up a needle and boulder strewn slope, pushing through scrub, clutching at spruce sapling trunks. This is an adventure. We force our way to the edge of the spur – there is a horror of a drop – but although we seem to be in the right place we can see no cave. Lottie edges closer to the drop; I snap at her to stop; she is annoyed with me.

"I'm ok," she says crossly. "It's as though you don't trust me."

"I do, I'm just protective."

We walk back and on through a glorious beech wood in silence. I know that she is thinking that I am too protective. I know that she is resentful that I didn't let us make it to the top of Mytikas.

The wood is lovely but my legs really hurt and the backpack is making my shoulders ache. Suddenly we hear that familiar clang of mule bell. There they are, nimbly plodding up the track laden with tiles and bricks. A load slips. The muleman slides off the back of the lead mule and goes back down the track, heaves the panniers straight and jumps back on again. He tells us it is still a three hour walk to the bottom.

At least Lottie and I are talking again. I later discover that anyway there was no cave where I had thought – I had missed it earlier.

Very tired we decide to stop for an hour. We find a spot of dappled shade in a flat place by a rock and get out the towel, cards, food. We take off our shoes and socks. Our socks are wet and smelly. I won't want to put them on again but I lay them on a rock in sunlight in hope that they will dry. The minutes pass too fast. We dress again, pack away the stuff and continue.

On and on.

Eventually we come to a sign – and hour and a half down. An Italian is staring at it.

"How long up?" he asks.

"To the top – five hours," I reply. He gasps.

"To a view?" he asks. Lottie and I look at each other and think of the endless trek through the woods. I think that the first proper view is from the ridge at Lemnos.

"Three hours, then," I say. He shakes his head in horror.

"My wife is waiting at the bottom," he says, and leaps off downhill.

On we go until at last we reach the road from Prionia to Litochoro – the joy of the walk rather spoiled by our aches and tiredness. We are too tired to go into the gorge for the five hour walk back, however wonderful it is supposed to be, so we decide to hitch to Litochoro. A Polish couple with a twelve year old daughter picks us up. In ten minutes we are in Prionia. What? Surely we were walking downhill when we were picked up? Yes, but we must have been going the wrong way. We get out and pretend we are grateful as the Polish family are heading up the hill for a walk we think. We have a can of fanta at the tavern and then start to walk back. A car approaches; we stick out our thumbs.

"It's the same people as before," says Lottie, and indeed it is. The car stops and the Polish father winds down the window, grins, and gestures into the back seat. Half way back along the road (they keep stopping to take photographs of the view) I realise that I never paid for the fanta. Lottie is horrified and wants us to take a taxi back to give the bar owner his two euros. I promise to find someone who is going there to do it for us. Soon she feels car sick on the bendy road. In halting English, we learn that the child's name is Marta and that the wife has a brother working in London.

It is 6.30 pm when they drop us in the square and say goodbye. We go straight to Papanickolaus and collapse on the coolness of the beds. We have texts that have come in while we were up on the mountain. Andrew, my stepson, tells us that his first baby Olivia weighed 3kg. We talk about me being a step grandmother, Lottie being an aunt. We shower, sort kit, watch Greek television, and at 8.30 pm we go to the same restaurant as before and eat salad and chips. The owner gives us free watermelon when he hears of our climb. We wander back to our room, buying caramel ice-cream on the way.

I fall asleep before Lottie.

"Shall I turn the television off?" I vaguely remember her saying. I think I grunt in reply.

Friday 19ᵗʰ August

I am so stiff. I can't walk downstairs. Lottie says,

"My butt hurts."

We have breakfast in the little room by the kitchen in the main house. We eat hardboiled eggs and cheese and rolls. Then we walk down to the mountain rescue centre and give the girl two euros and ask her to give it to the restaurant owner at Prionia. She looks surprised by our honesty over what I suppose to her is rather a small amount of money. She kindly finds out train times for us from Litochoro back to Athens. She also gives us instructions to find a climbing wall that we have heard of. Lottie thinks it would be fun to practice climbing skills using ropes. We make our way to the stadium where there is a cheerful game of striped-shirted football taking place. We hunt for the climbing wall and find it at last, vertical concrete with rounded hand or toe holds. Weeds are growing out of cracks. Undoubtedly there needs to be an instructor for this – and the place is deserted. We give up and decide not to bother about the climbing wall – I know they go from school next year anyway.

We take a short cut back to the town along a scrub lined dust track. Suddenly bright-eyed Lottie sees something under a bush, half in shadow. Perhaps it moved just as she looked. It was a tortoise. Quite large - about the size of Lottie's head. Lottie picks it up and suddenly the tortoise shoots out its head from its shell. Lottie is so surprised that she nearly drops it. She kisses its scaly dry head, it waggles its little clawed feet, rather crossly we think, and she puts it back on the ground whereupon it pulls its head back inside its shell again. We admire its beautiful mottled brown shell, so good for camouflage, push it further back into hiding, and leave it alone.

On the walk back I tell Lottie the story of Helone who was so reluctant to go to Hera'a wedding, and therefore so late, that she incurred Hera's wrath. Hera turned her into a tortoise, (the Greek for tortoise is helone) destined forever to travel slowly, dragging her tummy in the dust.

"More, tell me more," begs Lottie. So I tell her the story of Io, the cow, who, stung by a gadfly sent as a punishment by the Gods, bolted in pain and panic over the seas to the west of Greece. Where her feet touched the water, islands formed – ever since called the Ionian Islands.

We go back into the square and drink fresh orange juice before we gather our swimming things from our room and catching a bus to the beach at Plaka Litochoro. This is a day of rest. We had wondered whether we could walk to the beach – but it is five kilometres, so I am glad we didn't.

The beach is flat and fairly wide set back off the road that runs at the foot of the lowest hills rising up to Olympus. There is soft sand, straw umbrellas, sun beds and a clear, clean sea over gravel and sand. It is hot and sunny, lovely in the shade. Mount Olympus, a looming backdrop, is clouded at the peak. As we float in the sea and watch, the clouds clear, leaving the peak white and vivid, and then smoke with cloud again, and then clear, and then darken with cloud again.

We have lunch (Lottie and I share a large plate of spaghetti for five euros) in a taverna behind the beach. It has a pool beside the tables, but we are full of sea swimming and prefer to sit in the shade and just eat and chat and play cards. The pool, however, provides entertainment. How do Greek men manage to smoke and swim? Somehow cigarettes look most odd above a naked chest. And why is it always the largest, fattest boys that want to dive bomb into the pool? No doubt they make the biggest splash.

Back under our straw umbrella, Lottie sketches. We discuss how and where to hide the money belt so that we can swim together – we bury it in the sand and put Lottie's sketching things on top. I expect anyone who wanted to could watch this elaborate rigmarole! We drink café frappe, filling it up with water from our plastic bottle which makes it weaker and warmer but still rather good. We watch a family next door to us with a Down's syndrome daughter. She is affectionate and chatty and takes a particular interest in her baby niece or sister, until the baby gets attention from the adults, and then she plays up and is difficult and attention seeking. She likes to have her hair brushed and goes to each adult in turn for them to do so.

Bother, I have left my Sudoku book at the Sloane's villa. I will soon know every inch of Greece and every detail of Greek history if my only reading is The Rough Guide.

The day is wonderfully relaxing. We doze and swim and talk and read and sketch and doze and swim.

We catch the 7 pm bus back to Litochoro and drift into the bakery by the bus-stop. Lottie buys one euro's worth of sweets. I buy a piece of baklava – honey, nuts and flaky filo pastry. It is easy to make at home but never tastes quite the same – I think because the honey tastes different here, presumably because of what the bees feed on.

We fiddle about in our room, showering, reading, watching television. We don't have the energy to go out again to go and have supper. I look through the digital view-finder at the photographs we took on Mount Olympus. Wonderful, stunning place. Then I read to Lottie from 'The Gods of Olympus'; stories of battles between Zeus and Titans, stories of Aphrodite the goddess of wisdom, stories of Apollo the musician God. Lottie falls asleep, tiredness greater than hunger. Soon I do too.

Saturday 20th August

I wake to the single note of the church bell. Lottie still sleeps, her back brown above the blanket. Her hair is streaked very blonde. – eleven year old honey and caramel dishevelled on the pillow. I lean on the balcony in morning sunshine – myriad swallows dive and swoop with vicious speed into the cobbled streets, like little First World War Spitfires. I can hear the deep, almost Islamic, chanting coming from the church in the square. An old woman carefully steps her way there, smart in black dress and black stockings, bow-legged in high clumpy heels, grey, thinning hair carefully curled. Clearly church is an important occasion. Round the corner stumble, equally smart, an elderly couple; she holds his arm; he needs her support too. I want to be like that when I am old, holding and being held.

I feel tearful as I watch Lottie this morning. The days of childhood – and this sort of motherhood – are passing so fast. Soon she will be gone – like Sophie and Annabel her older sisters; not gone forever, gone, but gone differently: coming home to visit; home no longer the core of her world. Lucky Andrew with Olivia, at the beginning of this precious patch of time.

Maria makes breakfast especially for us – such good value at two euros each, which takes some time so we don't get to the beach until after 10 am. We settle ourselves on our sunbeds under a palm umbrella and order café frappe and strawberry milkshake from the itinerant waiter. The sea is flat and clam, the sky clear blue. As I swim I look back inland up at Olympus – it is shrouded in black. Lottie and I dive for pebbles, and practise life-saving (otherwise known as strangulation) on each other. The sky above Mount Olympus gets even more threatening and spreads. By midday the breeze is a brisk wind and the sea is bigger too – white horses, waves breaking hard on the shore, a big swell. It is the weirdest sort of storm: sunny overhead, visibly wet and stormy 20kms away with a knock on effect at sea.

I have put Lottie in charge of the rest of the money (though I take out enough to pay all the hotel bills between now and the 24th). She wears the money belt proudly – it holds her money too – 80 euros in total. We go back to the same restaurant to share our 5 euro plate of spaghetti – delicious. We then walk up the beach the other way to look at boats and little rows of chalets on the sand. We swim this time in big dangerous waves that knock us flying and swamp us. Lottie sketches pebbles and feet.

Lottie goes back to the restaurant to go to the loo. When she comes back she realises that she's left her sunglasses behind. When she comes back for the second time she says,

"And I left the money belt behind too but luckily some woman had found it and was going to hand it in but I saw her first and got it back." Sadly when she counts the money 20 euros is missing – we have only spent 16 euros (4 euros for the bus, 7 euros on drinks 5 euros on spaghetti) and only 45 euros is in the purse. A lesson not to take off the money belt in the loos – one so easily forgets it. Poor Lottie, she is mortified.

We head back to Litochoro, the day a little sullied.

"I'm so sad people aren't honest," says Lottie.

"At least she didn't take it all," I say.

I am sleepy. The day on the beach is almost more tiring in a way than climbing Mount Olympus.

We buy yoghurt and bread and a peach from the supermarket for supper, and watch a film (English, with Greek subtitles) about the life of the painter Gaugin.

Sunday 21st August

It is a pity that Lottie doesn't want to go to Delphi, but really we've run out of money and probably can't afford the detour. I can imagine it – now – shadowed by Mount Parnassus, but I would have liked to go there, although apparently the chasm of vapours that was the oracle no longer exists, closed by earthquakes. We decide to walk up the gorge. There is some discussion about footwear. Lottie still has rubs and blisters so wants to wear flip-flops. I am pretty certain this will make walking hard. But I keep her company.

Litochoro is crowded today – we soon see why: it is local market day. We wander the stalls. Lottie buys knickers (her passion) and I buy nectarines for lunch and cinnamon sticks to take home. There are piles of stringent smelling olives of varying sizes and colours, thick bunches of herbs, pale lime coloured peppers, glossy purple aubergines, heaps of nuts. I have a yearning for Turkish Delight which I resist. We finger baby clothes for Olivia, but we don't think they are good enough quality. It's all pretty cheap quality stuff except for the fruit and vegetables – but colourful. We tear ourselves away and head into the gorge. I don't think this is the right path, but the river-bed is dry so we walk – stumble – along it. There is a Judas tree with its heart shaped leaves, an odd type of evergreen oak with tiny leaves like a holly, plane trees, and a type of ash whose branches were used by the Furies (mythologically) for whipping sinners. We stop for Lottie to sketch trees and later a little waterfall. We watch a flock of sheep and goats cross a bridge (heard by their neck bells long before they were seen). The black and tan dogs shepherding at the back, nervous of us, cross the shallow river. There is hardly any water. This is the River Enipaeus. Enipaeus was a Greek God who only appeared as a river. The River Enipaeus starts as a spring on Olympus but travels underground until Prionia and again after Litochoro. It is more rush and gush in the spring apparently –

and it provides all the water for Litochoro which is piped off and explains the dry river bed now.

By 11.30 am Lottie has had enough – and I reckon this walk will only be more of the same – so we head back, taking a different route – higher.

Lottie spots another tortoise, larger and eating. Such fun. The path is thickly carpeted with lemon thyme, in pale purple flower.

Back in Litochoro Lottie buys sweets and we go to the waterfall in the park to have lunch. The sun shines on us but just behind us, covering Olympus, is thick black cloud. Lottie doesn't feel very well, so we head back to Papnickolaus, shouted at on the way by a shopkeeper for fingering the postcards.

"We're not going to waste 4 euros on bus fares to the beach just for the afternoon," she says. I rather wish I was still in charge of the money. "You can teach me how to play backgammon," she states.

Actually our balcony at Papanickolaus is lovely – lots to watch, sunny and comfy. We are given clean sheets, which inspires Lottie into a tidying spree. The room is perfect with its fridge and television. The only fault is the shower which soaks the whole room – floor, loo, loopaper, everything. But I begin to feel fidgety for home. Having climbed Mount Olympus, the purpose of the adventure seems finished. There is no time to island hop and have other travel plans. We both want to get back, and so look forward to doing so. Once again, however, the time has been very good value. Including airfares (not cheap this time) we have spent £1,400 in two weeks: £350 a week each which is £50 a day. Most of that has been accommodation (between £25 and £30 a day) and travel. If you take out the airfares, we have only spent £35 a day each. And as Lottie says – sitting at yet another café – this has been quite a luxurious holiday. If I was doing it again though, I think I would hire a car. Train and bus travel here in Greece are cheap but unreliable – travelling infrequently and not often where one wants to go. Crossing (or not crossing) Kephallonia is a typical example. And of course trains and buses so often only go to 'main' places, which, when one wants to discover villages off the beaten track, is annoying.

I discover that Litochoro station is not officially open yet although one train a day in each direction stops there if requested – probably to service the barracks. The bus ticket booth tells me repressively that there is no station at Litochoro and that I must go to Leptokaria. I like the idea of catching our 9.10 am train from a station that doesn't exist; I hope the train stops. We will catch the 8.15am Katerini bus, get off at the motorway round-about (where we got on it last Wednesday), walk to the concrete strips, and wave madly!

By about 3 pm Lottie decides that she feels better and maybe going to the sea is a good idea. No luck: there are no buses running. Cafes are closing, streets are empty. The Greeks, I learn, went back to work today, so the 'holiday' buses to the beach have stopped. Weird. We walk about, find a once full fountain emptied (for cleaning?), eat Tzaski and chips, buy an ice-cream, feel at a loose end.

Later we eat baklava and watch television lying on our beds in the sunshine that comes through our balcony windows.

Monday 22nd August

I wake up before the alarm and feel unsettled.

We have to wake up Maria to pay her and we are too early for breakfast. We catch our bus, which duly lets us off at the familiar bus-stop. The walk to the station feels even longer than it did before. A burdensome trudge along tarmac and concrete. Lizards are beginning to warm and energise. Mount Olympus is white and clear behind us. Litochoro is deserted except for a Canadian backpacker. He is the same sort of age as my nephew. Tall and blond and skinny. We sit on the benches in the sun and chat and wait for the sound of the train. We hear the rails rattle before we see it. We stand up and wave – the Canadian wonders whether we should stand in the middle of the track. When we get on there are seat problems since everyone else has reserved seats and we don't even have a ticket. There is a conductor on the train and we buy tickets from him, but not seat reservations. We have to move several times as more people get on at stops along the line. We buy coffee and hot chocolate too.

For some of the journey we have no seat at all. I stand by the open corridor window. I watch arching shoots of irrigation water. There is a green tractor under a fig tree, spikes of purple loosestrife, yellow star-shaped thistle flowers, soft fluffy cream thistle seed heads, lilac coloured banks of scabious, pinky blackberry flowers, bamboo, bulrushes, pea plants and apple trees. Dusty tracks meander along the single railway track. A siding disappears into a thicket of wildflowers and brambles. There is a deserted, overgrown station, dilapidated as we pass. The mountains are green-striped. We chug through mountain tunnels, dark and swift, Bright yellow broom bursts on the other side as we shoot out into sunlight. Time passes, lurching.

Have I missed the essence of Greece? (What is the essence of a country? How you measure it? Smell it? Feel it?) I want to go to the Epirus mountains which were once invaded by the Italians. I want to explore the islands.

A seed head drifts in through the window and floats around the carriage. We travel ever south. There are cypress trees now, narrow and pointed. I see English words on T shirts and in magazines. There are endless halts for other trains to pass on this single line. Why did the Candian boy get off at Leptokaria? There will be a three hour wait for the next train. I think he hasn't got the money for a ticket and is trying to avoid buying one.

"The mountains are so beautiful," I say to the man in the buffet car.

"They always are," he replies.

I wish on an eyelash that falls out that Lottie and I will always .... Always what? Just always. But the eyelash falls off my forefinger before I can finish the wish, so it won't come true. The mountains are always beautiful. Everything always changes.

We stay the night at the Aristo Hotel again before going back to the airport the next morning. We have time to wander the streets of Athens, but we have run out of money so we eat supper in our hotel room. Our flight the next morning is uneventful, though we chat to the man beside us about Athens, and a couple in front of us about Greek islands.

We are glad to get home, sad that our adventure is over. Glad that we climbed Mount Olympus, a 'proper' mountain, sad that we didn't make the summit. Glad we are alive and safe, sad that we didn't risk it.

ISRAEL – 2005

OCTOBER RUSHED towards half term. Lottie and I wanted to do something fun; it had been a busy and exhausting term. Various tentative plans fell through and Lottie and I discussed whether or not to find a bargain flight to a city somewhere for three days. We considered Istanbul, but the cheapest flights were still too expensive to make it worthwhile for a short break.

"Can't we lie on a beach?" asked Lottie. She seems not to mind about not having a friend with her. How on earth did the Dead Sea come into my mind? But suddenly there it was: a bold idea. We would go to Israel for the whole week, spending time exploring Jerusalem and the nearby countryside, and then lying by (and on) the Dead Sea.

Oh my goodness! How exciting! Oh what a thrill! So much so that the need for a 'bargain' flight went right out of the window – just as well; there's no such thing.

Actually it turned out to be very difficult to get any flights at all, probably because it was half term. Although my world atlas shows an airport near Jerusalem, international flights apparently only go to Tel Aviv. Recklessly, I didn't even find out how far Tel Aviv is from Jerusalem, assuming that given the width of Israel it wouldn't be an impossible distance, and some form of transport would exist from one city to the other.

However, all the flights to Tel Aviv were full; if not outward, then returning. There were some seats, at an appalling price, business class. It was going to cost as much as a fortnight in Greece anyway, so I rejected the 'appalling' option. It was interminably tedious trying to find flights on the internet. Ignorant of which airlines flew to Tel Aviv, I used 'Direct Flights' and then tried some bargain flight sites. Nothing seemed to be available.

The thrill of possibility became a mix of disgruntled resignation and determination not to give up.

Suddenly I remembered a little travel agent in Upton on Severn I had been told about. I rang them. In 24 hours they sorted flights (Thursday night at 1.45 am), hotels in Jerusalem and at the Dead Sea, and transfers, all for the same price as flights to Istanbul.

I got excited again, and brushed aside fearful comments from friends who thought that the political situation in the Middle East and the chance of a terrorist attack in Israel made it a mad venture. After all, given this year in London, we could as easily be on the receiving end of terrorism in England as in Israel.

WH Smith seemed to have no books about Israel; even their suppliers were out of stock of guide books. I was sad not to be clutching my Rough Guide, but a colleague lent me a good book full of photographs and brief descriptions: perfect. I spent a happy couple of hours listing the places we wanted to visit and outlining the sequence of historical dates and events which I précised for Lottie as follows:

"At the beginning Jerusalem was Jewish; built by David, improved by Solomon."

"David, as in 'Once in Royal David's City'?"

"Yes. After Solomon, the country was divided into Judah (with Jerusalem) and Israel. The Babylonians forced the Israelites into exile and then the Romans conquered it and by 150 AD

Hadrian called it Palestina and banned the Jews from Jerusalem which he named Aelia Capitolina."

"Hadrian, as in Hadrian's wall?"

"Umm. I suppose so. Christianity was legalised in 300 AD and it became The Holy Land."

"We learned about the crusades at school."

"Round about 600 AD the Persians and then the Muslims conquered it, called Jerusalem 'El Quds' (The Holy) and Islam ruled. During the 1000's the Christians took it back again, 200 years later the Muslims grabbed it back again, and from the 1800's the Jews began to trickle back."

"How confusing."

In 1917 the Turks surrendered the city to the British …"

"At the end of the First World War?"

"That's right….but in 1947 at the end of the Second World War the United Nations split Jerusalem with a wall between the Jews who had the new West Jerusalem in Israel and the Arabs who had Jerusalem Old City in Jordan."

"Is that what it is now?"

"No. 19 years later, in 1967 the Jews tore down the wall and reunited Jews and Arabs in Jerusalem."

What a struggle over a city in arid land – just because

a. Jesus was crucified there and

b. Mohammed ascended into heaven (his night journey) from there.

I can't wait to smell it, breathe it, feel it.

Two days before we left I managed to buy a Berlitz pocket guide to Israel, with Hebrew phrases and maps. Good. I have bought, commission free from the Post Office, £300 worth of brightly coloured shekels. A shekel is worth 13 pence (7.6 shekels to the £1). How wonderfully biblical 'shekels' sounded. I poured over the photographs in the Bonechi guide. The Dead Sea looked extraordinary.

I tried to think. No visas were needed. Our passports were in date. Our insurance was valid. The weather, apparently, would be in the 80's. I hoped the travel documents would arrive in time. Only two days for the first class post to prove its efficiency.

At school mine and Lottie's excitement rubbed off; suddenly Jerusalem, the bible, Jesus, was cool and interesting.

Not much in life is ever plain sailing. On Wednesday my travel documents arrived. I put them safely in my luggage pile only glancing through them cursorily to check the existence of hotel vouchers and tickets. On Thursday Tim from Poundsavers, the travel agency, rang. Panic. Kindly ringing to confirm our flight for us, he discovered that the tour operator had messed up and issued us with tickets for 24 hours earlier. We should have already left in the middle of Wednesday night at 1.45 am.

When I tell Lottie she says,

"But we are still going aren't we? <u>Aren't</u> we?"

Amazingly Tim sorted out seats for Friday morning at 9.40 am, and he added an extra day on to the end of our journey to make up for losing eight hours. Whew!

We were getting swift at packing. We shared a suitcase and dug out the electrical adaptor, cards, books, towels and swimming things, suitable clothes shoes, and, of course, the marmite. We went home after school on Friday, bathed, changed and headed off at about 5 pm to stay with a friend who, living a bit closer than us to Stanstead airport, had offered to drive us there early on Friday morning.

Friday 21st October

Security for El Al is fierce: separate baggage checks from other travellers; endless checks at every point. Replacement tickets are at the ServisAir desk – everything goes smoothly – and as usual I am there ages in advance. The security is reassuring. At the departure gate our names are called over the tannoy. Security guards take us and two others downstairs, through pass-locked doors. It's slightly scary – I think we are about to be body searched. A door is opened onto the tarmac and out suitcase is pulled from outside, wet from the rain.

"There has been an incident. Please open your case and check that everything in it is yours." It looks alright but .....

"How big might anything else be?" I ask. The guard shrugs and tells me to open sponge bags. So: any size. Eventually I am sure that there is nothing odd in the case and we close it up again. I slightly wonder, as we head upstairs again, whether the case will end up on the plane or not.

We board and are given free newspapers: The Jerusalem Post and something colourful in Hebrew (right to left pages and words). Our seats have pillows and blankets on them. It is a five and a half hour flight. There is good food, and Lottie watches a film.

"What is it called?" I ask. She doesn't know. Her view is blocked by a vociferous Jewish woman.

We fly, I note, over Greece: almost over Mount Olympus. I do Sudoku puzzles – the time goes fast. We land at about 3.30 pm Israel time. They are only an hour ahead because they changed their clocks last weekend and we don't change ours until next weekend. There is a wonderful stand-up, screaming, Jewish row about the behaviour of some small, rather uncontrollable, boys. As we wait for the cabin doors to open after we have landed, Lottie feels a bit claustrophobic. I think she is tired too.

After passport control – and a pentagonal green stamp – we see a white sign with our name on it. Such fame pleases Lottie. Jacob – our driver – waits while we collect our suitcase (it is safely on the carousel) and takes us to his car.

"Welcome to Manhattan," says Jacob gesturing to the high rise skyscrapers of Tel Aviv. Palm trees line the motorway and orange groves are sheltered by lines of cypress. It takes 40 minutes to reach Jerusalem. Jacob gives a running commentary in heavily accented English, pointing out olive groves, cemeteries, kibbutzes, settlements of different nationalities on the outskirts of Jerusalem.

Buildings are white, flat-topped cuboids – lots of them; Jerusalem has clearly spread widely beyond its old city walls.

It is dusk when we reach the 12 floors of the Jerusalem Tower Hotel. It looks glamorous in the reception lobby – gold and mirrors and palms. An armed guard sits in the doorway. Our room is small, dark, and comfortable. We are so tired that we picnic in our room. Lottie watches television while I go for a short exploratory walk, but it feels uncomfortable alone in the dark. I find a Macdonald's and buy Lottie a strawberry milkshake and head back to her.

Back in the hotel room my mobile rings. It costs me to answer but this is a good friend, Tim Spicer.

"I can hear that you are abroad. Where are you?" he asks.

"Jerusalem."

"Are you mad?" he asks. It sounds like a statement. And he knows about such things – not madness, but about political situations in foreign countries.

Lying in bed later, we hear shots.

"Maybe it's just a car backfiring," I say to Lottie. But there are shouts, and then more shots. I look out of the window but I can see nothing untoward. The roads and pavements are mostly empty. Isn't that unusual at 7.30 pm on a warm Friday evening? Or is it normal here?

We are both asleep by 8 pm.

Saturday 22nd October

I wake first at 6 am but Lottie is still immobile with the turquoise blanket pulled up under her chin, so it is 8 am when I wake again. The sky is bright blue through the window. We get up and go to breakfast which is odd: mostly pickled fish, salad and yoghurt. Lottie has bread (and marmite), I have fish and yoghurt which turns out to be delicious (though I can taste pickled fish for hours afterwards) – and I avoid the salads and olives and eggs.

We set off towards the Jaffa gate of The Old City. At a drinking fountain on the way, a scruffy man is washing his willie. It is both shocking and funny. We avert our eyes and hurry past.

The walls are pale yellow and made of huge uneven blocks, too clean to be very old, with a castellated top. I read that we can walk around the ramparts, and we intend to, but they are closed for another half hour. As we stare at the signs on the wall by the stone steps leading up to the ramparts, the man we come to know as Zaki greets us. He offers his services as a guide round the Old City. He is middle-aged, bearded, wears glasses, Palestinian, tidily dressed, surprisingly unpushy.

"How much?" I ask.

"200 shekels," he says. "But if you do not enjoy, you do not have to pay."

"I just want to discuss it with my daughter," I say.

"I will move away a little so you can talk in private," he says.

"What do you think?" I ask Lottie. "It might be useful because my historical knowledge isn't that good. We might learn more with him than on our own. Can you understand his accent easily?"

She shrugs, and then nods and agrees, so we take on Zaki – and are glad.

He strides ahead, forging a pathway through the crowds. He makes us feel safe. He takes us first to the Church of the Holy Sepulchre –

"To avoid the long queues which will come soon."

The alleys are crowded, lined with market stall: a mass of people, goods and colours. I smell spices, rich and scented. A woman sits among thick bunches of mint and basil stiff with freshness.

"She is Palestine woman," says Zaki, "because Palestine men not allowed in Old City so women have to come to sell the things."

It is the Jewish Sabbath so all the Jewish shops are shut, only Arabs are working. But it is Ramadan so the streets are even more crowded than normal with streams of Muslim women. I cover my head with a sarong that I have brought – and feel more comfortable. Lottie says it suits me. I ask Zaki if he is a Muslim, and he replies,

"International." Tactful. Later when he refuses to eat because he is fasting I suspect that actually – and unsurprisingly – he is a Muslim.

The Church of the Holy Sepulchre is an extraordinary building, home to not one church but a roof over many – Coptic (Egyptian) chapels, and Catholic, Franciscan, Armenian, Greek Orthodox – Christian denominations. One of the key holders, however, is Muslim.

"Why?" I ask.

"Because Muslims are closer to Christian than Jews."

"How?"

"Because Jesus is special to them too, special like Mohammed. And they pray to the Virgin Mary." (Do they? I didn't know that).

Inside the door is the stone slab that Jesus was laid on to be anointed after he died on the cross. There is a beautiful (modernish) mosaic of the event on the wall behind. We go round the corner (Zaki's tour is not at all in chronological sequence) to Jesus' tomb. There is a guardian priest at the entrance making sure there are not too many people inside. The outer room contains a case holding a piece of the rock from the stone rolled in front of the tomb. The silence is broken by the two men on a stepladder refilling the lamps with oil and replacing and relighting wicks. A hymn we sing at Kitebrook 'Give me oil in my lamp keep me burning' comes to mind. I think their presence spoils the moment, and then I think that perhaps it is symbolic that oil and light and men should be part of this place, not separate. We go into the inner room and kneel by the marble topped tomb. My bad knee shoots with pain. A woman beside us sobs quietly. The cave ceiling is low over the tomb which suffers from over decoration but in spite of myself as I touch the tomb I feel a sense of tearfulness. Does that mean there is something to this room? Or is it a ricochet of the emotion of millions of believers? When we emerge Zaki tells us that everyone believes that this is where Jesus is buried except for the Protestants who believe his burial place to be in a garden outside the Damascus Gate in east Jerusalem. He tells us how the original city wall surrounded only the temple – this tomb and Golgotha were outside the city, as was all the Via Dolorosa that Jesus walked carrying his cross, but that when Constantine built a church over the sacred sites he rebuilt the wall to include it. Zaki shows us the tomb of the architect who was executed for forgetting to include the tomb of King David inside the walls.

Zaki takes us next upstairs to Golgotha, where Jesus was crucified. A life size Jesus hangs from a wooden cross. We kneel under the altar and thrust our hands through a hole in the floor to feel the rock of the hill underneath. The chapel to the right shows a mosaic of Jesus being nailed to the cross before it is hauled upright. The room along the side wall is built over the place where Jesus was stripped of his clothes, whipped, and crowned with thorns.

With this church built over the land, it is so hard to imagine the actual event. Zaki leads us up more steps to the roof of the church, where the Africans have built a community, and out through an archway. He takes us to the rest of the Stations of the Cross – places where Jesus fell, or was offered water of help during his walk with the cross. Imprinted in one stone, apparently, is his handprint. A chanting pilgrimage passes us, led by a man carrying a cross. Some more of these wooden crosses are leaning against a wall. Lottie and I try to pick one up. It is heavy, too heavy for her. This is salutary, since it isn't even full size or weight.

We ask Zaki if we can find somewhere that sells baklava (Lottie yearns for this since Greece) and he finds us a shop owned by a 'friend' who gives Lottie two small pieces for free. Encouraged by this, he takes us to another 'friend' who owns a shop. Politely, we look round, but do not wish to buy anything. The 'friend' becomes desperate and blocks our exit talking in broken English of starving children and of us being his first customers of the day. I appeal to Zaki, explaining that we do not wish to buy anything – Zaki speaks harshly in Arabic and we leave. He buys Lottie a leaflet about the Stations of the Cross and takes us to a café owned by another 'friend' who apparently makes the best hummus in Israel. It is a tiny little basic room through unprepossessing corrugated metal doors. Locals sit squashed together at the three plastic tables. A pale-skinned, balding, Palestinian fills two soft pita-bread semi-circles with a nutty brown goo. It is a gift. And delicious – spicy and crunchy and not like any hummus I've ever eaten (later I discover it is falafel – like hummus, in that it is made from chickpeas, but with spices) – but I feel it is impolite to eat in the streets especially during Ramadan so I wrap them up in their paper and put them in my bag for later.

Zaki takes us to the Temple on the Mount – which is closed today – so we can see the Wailing Wall. Here he leaves us – as a Muslim he says he is not allowed there. (What about the mosque, I wonder?). He points out that women go one side, men the other.

Lottie and I walk through a metal detector doorway rather like airport security, down steps to a huge courtyard and to the right hand side of this huge wall, the only standing remains of the original temple. It is all very Jewish. Little boys with short, short hair and long, really long, bits hanging from their temples emulate the adult men. The 'uniform' is a skull cap or wide brimmed black hat, black suit or dress with white tights and black shoes, a belt with long wispy bits, and a black and white striped cloak. A group of male Jews walk past.

"Come up and we will have koshid and then a scotch," I head one say. Apparently 'koshid' is a type of blessing. Koshid and scotch seems a sort of contradiction.

The area by the wall has bookshelves – filled with copies of the Torah in Hebrew – and plastic chairs. Jewish women, young and old, read verses aloud from the books they clutch (I see that the writing is very big) with eyes half closed and sorrowful yearning expressions. They rock back and forth. I wonder to myself: shouldn't religion be a joy, a celebration, and a thanksgiving?

Lottie and I find some paper and write wishes (prayers?). We find a space between the women to approach the wall and a space, somehow, between the huge stones to push in our folded wishes, along with everyone else's. The stones, I feel, are cold.

"Somebody else's nearly fell out," says Lottie. What is this power of the written word? Why not a silent prayer offered to the wall, to heaven? And does it count if your piece of paper falls out? And are they 'cleared' sometimes? I am reminded of the wall below Juliet's balcony in Verona, covered in love messages.

Afterwards I see square holes cut in the canvas that separates the men from the women and Lottie and I go to peer through. It is much noisier that side. Chanting is full on. It is a sea of black and white, like magpies. And more bookshelves and white clothed tables and white plastic chairs and white awning to protect from the sun

Lottie and I leave towards the Damascus gate. It is so crowded. A gaggle of school children in stripy dresses over tracksuit bottoms giggle and poke at Lottie in her knee length skirt and T-shirt. The alley heads steeply uphill. The stalls spill into the alley making it even narrower: spices, fruit, vegetables, tacky toys, even tackier clothes, a basket of live chickens, souvenirs. We burst out of the Damascus Gate into the width beyond. It is a relief.

We catch a bus to Bethlehem. It is air-conditioned and cool and it is good to sit down. A man who gets onto the bus behind us finds himself mistaken as being with us and paying for our tickets. He joins us to explain the error and we talk. He is Swiss and has been at Gaza researching the current political situation for an NGO (non-government organisation) He says he finds more tension in Jerusalem than at Gaza.

As we drive to Bethlehem I think about this, remembering the looks on people's faces. Yes, perhaps the Jews look more cautious, wary even. Their faces are more guarded, closed. The Arabs seem pushy but friendly. I haven't really felt any tension, I don't think. Just a strong feeling of difference in character.

But the possibility, proximity, of violence is clear at the check point. I am horrified. It is like old Berlin (I lived there for two years in the late 1970's) – check point Charlie. A heavily armed (Machine gun I think) Israeli boards our bus to check passports. And then we have to get out; our bus driver is allowed no further. Bethlehem is inside Palestinian territory. There are guards, watch towers, sandbags, wire and barriers. Lottie and I and the Swiss man share a taxi for 10 shekels to the Church of the Nativity. The driver tries to take 15 shekels when we get there. The Swiss man is firm and sharp. We are glad of his protection.

The Church of the Nativity is plain and straight lined, almost fortress-like. The door is tiny, only four foot high or less. Inside there are huge plain columns holding up a raftered roof. There is space and peace here. Down steep, steep steps is a cave where apparently Jesus was born – the original stable – and a wide niche in the rock which is supposedly the manger. Who knows? In a parallel street is a church with the 'milk grotto' – a series of low roofed connecting caves where Mary apparently hid and lived with Jesus and Joseph while she was breast feeding him. The grey walls of the cave have milky white deposits mythically from feeding Jesus. The chapels are lovely and peaceful, if rather too tackily ornate. We are the only people there.

Nearby is an olive wood factory. Drawn by the buzz of saws and the smell of resin and sawdust, we go in. We watch the olive branches turn from twisted tubes into short planks into shapes. Eventually we buy several pieces as presents for Lottie's teachers. The shopkeeper offers to take us to the roof above his shop to see the views of Bethlehem. The little simple flat-roofed building feels authentic. Isn't this the sort of building Joseph would have lived in as a carpenter; the home Jesus would have lived in as a child? The view shows Bethlehem white but built up, the surrounding hills dusty and barren. Bethany is in the distance one way, the Herodian hills another.

We wander round the streets and alleys. There are camels in the square and old Palestinian men wearing what, just as in nativity plays at school, look like drying up cloths on their heads. They are sitting around, squatting on their haunches, chatting, smoking. They smile a lot. But Bethlehem is a far cry from the mental image I have created from the Christmas carol. Shops, of course, don't help. I rather wish I hadn't seen the real town. It spoils the fantasy.

We stop in a coffee shop owned by Franciscan monks for a rest as well as a drink. We have just ordered when our Swiss acquaintance appears. He joins us and his friend arrives – a Palestinian who owns a French school in Bethlehem. Lottie has a fanta; my iced coffee is delicious. Lottie has pita bread (and marmite from my bag) and I eat one of the hummus parcels. The courtyard is shaded and full of geraniums. What a relief.

We take a taxi to the Shepherds' Fields. Oh dear. I had in mind a stony dusty hillside. Well, there probably is one somewhere that looks the way I imagine it to – but not here. A concrete path goes through a sort of stony field fenced with metal and barbed wire. It leads to two shepherds' chapels; cave structures with dusty model sheep scenes. Horrid.

In the taxi again on the way back to the check point the driver tells us his brother was shot by the Israeli's here in Bethlehem. I remember what Zaki said to us when we were looking at the Wailing Wall with the Temple on the Mount behind it:

"We are all human bees and life is beautiful and we should be brothers. It is all the same God and he is God of love. If people say they fight because of God, they are wrong because God not like his people to fight. He want them to love each other because we are all human bees."

The driver asks me if I am a Muslim because my head is covered. I say no, and he says he is glad I am so polite. He is less happy when I refuse to pay him more than the agreed price when we get out.

"You are friend," he claims, waving my 20 shekel note. "This not enough." But it is what we agreed so I am firm. I hope it doesn't make him hate the English because I don't give in to him.

We walk up the road, away from and out of Bethlehem to the check point, leaving the vast wall behind us.

"Salaam," I say to the border guard. He is darkly handsome, but he looks at me with cool disdain.

"It is 'Shalom'. I am Israeli," he snaps. How am I supposed to tell or know? He's not wearing a skull cap, (soldiers presumably can't); he's working on the Saturday Sabbath. I sigh inwardly and smile outwardly, apologising and saying "Shalom." I am only slowly beginning to get the hang of the difference between Israeli Jews who, olive skinned and dark, look far more like Arabs or Palestinians than like the Orthodox Jews we have seen who are very pale skinned, and a different sort of shape. I also don't quite understand why the Israeli (Jewish) soldiers should guard Jerusalem against people leaving the city as well as people coming in.

Anyway, the soldiers wave us on past piled sandbags, metal barriers, watch towers shrouded in netting ("Perhaps to stop birds from flying in," says Lottie) and coils of barbed wire. We wait for the bus on the Jerusalem side, sharing a corrugated iron shelter with one male and one female Israeli soldier and a mess of litter. We talk, or try to, in half sentences of simple English.

"Isn't it your Sabbath today?" I ask the girl.

"Yes, but army work more important than that," she answers. Lottie is rather quiet – the visible closeness to potential war is shocking. We watch an aggressive stop and search routine. The man is spread-eagled against his car. The boot is emptied.

The bus takes us back to the Damascus Gate - or nearly: the stationary traffic of rush hour suggests the wisdom of getting off early. We dodge people and cars to cross the road and walk to the Garden Tomb, the alternative site of Jesus' burial and crucifixion. It is very pretty (kept by an English association) and flowery. The rough cliff top (Golgotha and Calvary meaning 'skull') still has rock formations on the side that look like the hollowed facial features of a skull. Meandering through the gardens past an ancient wine press and water cisterns, we go down steps well below road level to the tomb supposed to be that of Joseph of Arimathea that he leant for Jesus' body. On a wooden (hardly original!) door is carved: 'He is not here for he has risen'. Where the stone opening has crumbled and collapsed, new blocks of stone have been used for repair; apparently, even so, the opening would have been much smaller. Inside, the tomb has a first section – for people to cry in – and a second with stone pillows where up to three or four people could be laid. It is interesting but it doesn't have the emotional feel to it that the tomb in The Church of the Holy Sepulchre had. Nearby is a round tomb entrance stone of the sort that would have blocked Jesus' tomb. It is large and heavy but I feel a strong man could roll it away. Not surprising since someone must have rolled it there in the first place.

Lottie and I sit on a bench overlooking the tomb and eat tangerines that we have bought from a market stall on the way there. At least here, unlike the Church of the Holy Sepulchre, the imagination is not stretched so far. But I do not feel much here; it is rather antiseptic.

It is getting late in the afternoon, and cooler, and we have had enough. Our feet ache and we are weary. We head back to the hotel, plunging back into the Old City through the Damascus Gate into the crowds. We begin to feel as if we know the way – I only have to confirm the direction twice: over the cobbles through the narrow alleys of the souk, past the olive wood carvings, rugs, mosaic boxes, spices, hubble bubble pipes, swathes of material, silver, leather, nuts and sweets, past the Church of the Holy Sepulchre (with huge crowds gathered outside). We pause to haggle for an olive wood nativity scene that I want to buy for Lottie to give Kitebrook as a leaving present (though later she insists that she cannot wait that long; it must be given this year). The shop is closing and I get it for what I think is a reasonable price.

I begin to notice where and how the hill slopes as we walk. We leave by the Jaffa Gate and plod to the hotel. The relief when we get there of not walking! We eat pita bread and marmite (the bread was saved from Bethlehem), talk, watch television, write diaries, and go to sleep at about 9 pm. An hour later we are woken up by explosions.

"Is it bombs?" asks Lottie as we wake up with a start. But I recognise the sound, run to the window and open the curtains. Fireworks! Beautiful, Glorious gold and silver stars over the Old City. We watch for fifteen minutes until they finish.

"Do you think they happen every night?" asks Lottie. Who knows, but it was a wonderful sight – what a view we had. Sleep comes again easily.

Sunday 23rd October

We have displayed the nativity scene on a table and when I wake the light is shining on it. It is pretty, the olive wood soft and pale, streaked with dark lines.

Half an hour later Lottie wakes. The routine is the same as yesterday – pickled fish and dill yoghurt for breakfast for me, and bread (and marmite) and yoghurt for Lottie. I take an extra bread roll for Lottie for lunch (though in the end she eats it for supper).

We set off to walk the ramparts. It is nearly 10 am. We have the wall more or less to ourselves. The battlements are on our left as we go clockwise from the Jaffa Gate. The Old City is more or less an irregular quadrilateral with the Jaffa Gate in the centre of the side apposite the Temple Mount. In the centre of the next side clockwise – on the east, the Arab, side – is the Damascus Gate. This first part of the rampart walk takes us past the Christian sector. The top of the wall is quite narrow, the railings (where there are any) rather wobbly.

"I don't think they've heard of 'health and safety'," says Lottie. It's very untouristy – the downside of that is the litter and the general state of disrepair. We don't like the large cylindrical gas containers and batteries on the roofs (not to mention the satellite dishes). But there are vine covered trellises over gardens, bougainvillea and geraniums. We see a little school playground and stop to watch a Muslim woman dressed in a tobacco coloured robe and head-dress pull small boys onto a bench. She holds two netballs, but when a whistle blows the small boys run around and cartwheel on a hankie sized square of tarmac. Another Muslim woman walks gracefully through a door holding A4 sized exercise books, The whistle blows again and the small boys are lined up to go back inside.

We walk past a prison, a monastery, little houses, roof gardens, and all the time have a view over the Old City roofs to the golden dome of the mosque – the Temple of the Mount.

I stop to take photographs and we are caught up by the only other people on the ramparts; an Arab family with a small tearful girl dragged along by her mother. In any language – "Let Granny carry you," is clear, as was the petulant childish rejection. Lottie and I think that the little girl is frightened of the height – the drop, the steep stairs, the wide arrow slits – and we overtake them again.

The walk is shaded now by drooping fig tree branches; over ripe squishy figs have rotted between the stones. As we pass New Gate (half way between the Jaffa and Damascus Gates) a couple come the other way and tell us in broken English that the gate is closed further on and we have to go back and exit through New Gate. I ignore them (I think they mean Damascus Gate is closed, and I know that and want to go to Lion Gate beside the Temple which I read was open on a notice beside Jaffa Gate).

On we go. Beyond Damascus Gate, the Muslim quarter now, there is more dirt, more bustle, more crowded houses. We pause to stare at an archaeological dig, probably untouched for a couple of years given the size of sumac trees growing in crumbly walls. The tiles on the watch towers are broken after Herod's Gate; at one point the wall is almost the same height as the ground outside. I can see the Jewish cemetery, row after white row, on the opposite hillside, from which the Messiah (when he comes) is supposed to raise the dead and lead them in triumph through the Golden Gate (closed) set in the main Temple wall, and into Jerusalem.

I cannot find Lion Gate. A sign saying 'Danger' ropes off the ramparts and I think it leads to steps down so I duck under. Lottie refuses to come too – and she is right; the steps crumble into nothing. We retrace our path and find other stairs and a rusty metal turnstile to the pavement below.

We are so close to the Temple on the Mount. There are eight entrances: the first is surrounded by armed soldiers, and the next. At the third I decide this is just typical Jerusalem protectionism, and we go down an alley towards a smaller entry and only a couple of soldiers. A beggar woman chants what I later realise is words that mean 'closed, closed'. The soldiers shake their heads,

"Muslims only," they say. Segregated entrances? We go down the next dark alley, stone roofed, to the fourth entrance.

"No, closed," states the soldier.

"When will it be open?" I ask.

"No, only Muslims," he uninformatively replies. I don't understand at all. This is a Temple area sacred to Jews and Christians because of Abraham, who tried to kill Isaac on the rock there, and Muslims because of Mohammed (who stopped here on his flying horse on his night journey to heaven and hell). How come any of them are prohibited from entering? The soldiers are unaggressive but adamant. Through the arch I can see bareheaded Muslim boys running, and head-dressed women walking. Maybe entry is by the Wailing Wall. We walk on through the souk, up alleys, down alleys, and there is the metal detector gate to the Wall. We walk through (at least we are allowed there), our bag is checked, and I ask the guard when, if ever, and how, we can get to the Temple area. She shakes her head.

"It is Ramadan. Muslims only. No Jews or Gentiles. Maybe 7.30 for one hour with a policeman for tourists." Or maybe not. Was that 7.30 am or 7.30 pm? It is so frustrating. Above the Wall

– the old original Wall of the biblical, Solomon temple – gleams the golden dome, soars the minaret. The Islamic faithful are called to prayer while the Jews pray by the Wall and the bells of the Church of the Holy Sepulchre ring out.

We cross the square to the Dung Gate set in the western wall. This is the Jewish quarter and it is the feast of Succa. (I had discovered this in the hotel after breakfast. A sign on the lift door said, '1st Floor – Succa'. I asked a Jewish man in the lift and he explained that it is the celebration of Abraham coming from the desert and the Jews represent this by living in little wooden shacks shaded with reeds: a succa. There is one out of the fire escape on the flat roof of the hotel above the lobby. I went and peered at it: it looked plasticy, rather like a pony club picnic tent. I wish they'd made it look more biblical. I don't think they do more than eat in it either). The square is awash with Jews in the traditional dress code – from velvet skull caps to black fedoras to wide brimmed fur hats – all carrying long plastic wrappers of reeds. I think they are hurrying to the synagogue on the east of the Wall at the foot of the Temple Mount wall. There are more succas at the edge of the square, slightly less plasticy than the one at the hotel. They seem to be a sort of meeting place/café: inside at plastic tables there are small gatherings of people talking and snacking.

At the Dung Gate we ask the woman selling tours for the big archaeological dig by the gate for directions to King David's tomb. She sends us up the hill to the next Gate – Zion Gate – on the top of Mount Zion. Up we trudge, a bit hot, a bit tired, a bit hungry. Almost crossly, we come out to a view, to the left, of the Mount of Olives. We are clearly looking puzzled so the custodian of Mary's Church takes us under his wing and lets us in (he was about to close it).

Here Mary, or rather a statue of her, lies in prayer, or sleeping. Our friend tells us that this is probably not her tomb; it is more likely that she is buried with her parents in a church at the foot of the Mount of Olives.

"Though some say she buried at Ephesus in Turkey. When Jesus die he say to John to look after her and he go to Turkey to preach and maybe she go with him. So maybe she die in Turkey," he says. It is a modern church, but the mosaics around Mary's tomb are lovely: biblical women - Rachel, Judith, Sarah, for instance.

Our friend takes us next to The Room of the Last Supper. Blissfully simple, it is just a plain stone room with a beamed roof and lovely arched columns. Though I am not sure it can really be the original building, it is easy to imagine a long wooden table and chairs for twelve in here, just outside the city walls and, appropriately for Jesus, near the tomb of his ancestor David.

Now there was disappointment. King David is, in fact, buried deep in a cave leading under Mount Zion and is inaccessible – to visitors anyway. All that can be seen is the upper mouth of the cave entrance in front of which is an altar. The room around it, tiny though it is, is a synagogue. Some women are seated, reading and praying. We do not stay for long. We say goodbye to the custodian.

"What do you want to do now?" he asks.

"We wanted to go to the Temple Mount, but we weren't allowed in," I reply.

"It is a difficulty," he says. "I am Jew but I am Messianic Jew."

"What does that mean?" I query.

"I believe in Jesus."

"As the Son of God?"

"Of course. We are all God's children," he states simply. "We were allowed to Temple until year 2000. But then, no."

He leaves us in the church coffee shop where we have a drink, more to sit and rest our feet than for the drink. I am not sure what we will do next – I feel somehow that Lottie will not be up for a trek to the Garden of Gethsemane. We chat – and then suddenly our Israeli custodian reappears.

"You want go to the Temple Mount? You want see the Mosque? This man my friend. He will help you. He is Muslim." The man beside him looks kind and smiley.

"Well, thank you, yes," I say, "but.." – and I know how the 'let me help you' mentality works now – "how much will it be?"

"No, no, nothing. Only what you feel like giving to say thank you." I know Lottie is tired, so I don't even look at her for her agreement – just in case she looks reluctant.

We set off, the man, in a red 'Israel' baseball cap, setting a fast pace. Lottie has a flip flop rub on her foot but races along without any fuss.

"Sorry," I say, "but this may be our only chance."

We are back in the souk when the man stops.

"This will be difficult. How much do you care?"

"I care," I reply. "I want Lottie to see the Dome of the Rock; I want to see it for myself."

"It is Ramadan. Only Muslims, Arabs, allowed. You do not look like a Muslim." He looks hard at me. "But if you really care, maybe we can do something. But it will be difficult. Do you understand what I am saying?" I nod – but do I? I wasn't sure what hidden messages – if any – I was supposed to be understanding. He tells us his name. Lottie and I call him Moo from now on which is the only part of his name we remember, and he sets off again through the crowds – so fast we nearly lose him. It makes me think of a James Bond film. We stop, suddenly, at a cheap clothes stall at the junction of two alleys. Moo talks fast to a toothless gypsy-looking woman who takes us into the back of the alley behind her stall which is lined with clothes in plastic bags on a rail. Moo rips one open and sniffs the beige material.

"It is new. Clean, anyway." He thrusts a bundle at me. "Put them on." There is a shapeless tube of a skirt with an elasticated waist. I pull it on over my dress. It is too long; I have to wear the elastic under my armpits. Moo helps me on with the top – a sort of poncho with a hood. The hood is too large. Moo takes me outside and the gypsy woman unpins a little gold pin from another item of clothing on her stall, pulls the hood tight under my chin, and gives me the pin to fix.

"Hide your hair," orders Moo. "It too blonde. It must not show." When I am ready, he nods. "Good. Now you a Muslim woman. If they ask, you my wife. She (gesturing at Lottie) your daughter, not mine. Your first husband he dead. Do not speak English. Stay behind me. Look down. Do not look at soldiers. Remember my name (and he repeats it)." I nod. Moo takes Lottie's hand and sets off again.

I feel different – apart from just feeling rather scared and rather hot in the all-covering clothing – sort of demure and anonymous. I am worried too – is this right? Perhaps Lottie and I entering such a sacred place in disguise may be religiously offensive? I don't want to upset the Muslims – and yet since we are being taken into this sacred place by one, perhaps it isn't unacceptable? Or is it even a common tourist trick to earn money? Or is it, in fact, a very dangerous and incredibly stupid thing to be doing?

At the first alley to the Temple Mount entrance Moo pauses.

"Did you try here?"

"I don't think so." He goes on anyway to the next alley.

"OK. Remember all I tell you," he says. I follow Moo and Lottie closely, a strange trio to my mind. My eyes are lowered. Don't my shoes look western? I have to hold my elasticated skirt up high under the poncho thing. It would be a worry to trip over it. At least I'm not wearing any make-up. I see the soldiers' black boots, but nothing else of them. Moo strides on. I can feel sweat on my face – and then we burst out of the darkness of the alley into enormous space and brightness – the Temple Mount. I gasp. It is truly phenomenal. We are high above Jerusalem but can see none of it. The minaret leaps into the sky to the right, ancient arches curve at each edge of the square; in front of us, blue and gold and so <u>there</u>, is the mosque. There are orange trees growing – but most of all so much space. It is frighteningly different – every man, woman or child is an Arab or a Muslim: flowing Arab head-dresses (lots of teacloths and rope), shrouded women.

"Well done," says Moo. "You are good Muslim woman." He smiles.

We go to the Mosque. Moo tells me historical facts, some of which I know already, some of which I don't really hear or listen to because I am too busy trying to see everything, take it all in, check that Lottie (who is utterly silent) is alright, hold up my skirt, take surreptitious photographs (Moo says it is okay to do so but I am sure that he is wrong, that it makes me a tourist), and still look like a Muslim woman.

At the entrance of the Mosque, the Dome of the Rock, Moo tells us to take off our shoes.

"I have brought socks in my bag," I say. "So we don't have bare feet."

"It is okay," he says, "but men are not allowed in here today. It is women only. So you go in. Do not speak English. I will wait here." Moo speaks in a hushed whisper. It is both exciting and frightening. The women are seated everywhere inside the Mosque, some clutching open copies of the Koran, some in a group listening to a sort of priest figure (a man). No-one looks at me, but Lottie attracts glances – jeans (lucky that; yesterday's skirt showing her legs would have made this adventure impossible), and such long blonde hair even if it is in a ponytail. We hold hands. The carpet is incredibly soft underfoot. Suddenly Moo appears and whispers,

"They say I can come in."

He leads us round the Mosque, listing Lottie so she can see the Rock behind the wooden trellis. He tells us about the pillars, windows and arches representing months and days and weeks. The inside of the Dome is phenomenal. Unutterably beautiful – a rose of gold and blue mosaic. Moo leads us to a grotto under the Rock where women are praying, rocking, murmuring. The cave ceiling is low and there is a hole in the middle where Moo tells us is where the blood from the sacrifices made on the Rock fell through to the floor below. The atmosphere in this domed Mosque is electric. In contrast, it is quite dark – the only lighting from oil lamps.

We melt, unnoticeably I hope, outside again, put on our shoes, and walk down wide steps across the Mount to the Aksa Mosque.

"You cannot come in her, it is men only today," says Moo. But he takes us to the doorway and the interior reminds us of a beiger version of the Mesquita at Cordoba – pillars, striped arches, empty spaces. Lovely. The men were quieter inside, leaning against pillars, seated, lying down even.

"I can take you to the original temple," says Moo. We take off our shoes again.

"Do not speak. Only Muslims ever allowed in here," he says. The carpet, pale green, is soft. Men (only men) line the walls, reading, sleeping, praying. We go deep under the Mount. The repairs are modern but the columns (huge and thick) and the roofs (arched) are original. This is all that is left of Solomon's temple and we are on the far side, the hidden side, of the Wailing Wall – parts of it are visible through the shoring up and the restoration. The Muslims have turned the far end into an Islamic library – bookshelves line the walls. It is peaceful. I feel as if I am incredibly privileged to be in this place. A trio of Arab children are playing tag around a pillar. Old men sleep against the walls.

An elderly Arab, who is seated by the door into the library like a guardian with a copy of the Koran on a lectern before him, speaks sharply and angrily to Moo, gesturing to Lottie as he does so.

"It is your hair," says Moo urgently. "You must cover it." Lottie has a jersey knotted around her waist. We take it off and use it to shroud her head. The old man nods without approval.

Slowly we potter out again. Moo takes us to the place where legend has it Mohammed stabled his winged horse when he ascended from the Rock to heaven. With reluctance and yet a sense of liberation from fear, we walk past the soldiers again, a different entrance gate this time, Moo holding Lottie's hand, me politely behind – and we are safe. We round the corner, out of sight, back in the souk, and stop. Moo grins.

"We did it. Thank God. God has smiled on us. He has willed it so!" I wipe the sweat from my face and thank him (Moo, not God).

Inevitably there is some haggling over the size of Moo's fiscal thank you. He asks for 400 shekels. I give him 50 shekels. He points out the risk he was taking and I give him another 50 shekels. He says that it is not enough because he has to pay for the clothes I wore. I give him another 50 shekels. He says, again, that he should have 400 shekels, that less is an insult to his kindness. I tell him, as I give him another 50 shekels that there is no more, that we will have no supper tonight by giving him this 50 shekels.

"You must come to my house to eat," he says hospitably, pocketing the 50 shekel note nevertheless. "You must eat with me and my family. My mother is Armenian but my father is Arab. I have six children." What an adventure, I think, and accept. He arranges to meet us at 4 pm at the Zion Gate – "beside where I show you the bullet holes in the wall from the Six Day War." They eat, he says, at 5.30 pm after the sun has set because of Ramadan.

"What will I do about the food?" asks Lottie anxiously as we sidle our way back through the souk, ignoring the calls of "Please, Lady."

"Say you have a tummy ache," I suggest. "They probably won't be insulted by your not eating anything if they think you are feeling unwell."

We have an hour or so to kill. We find ourselves back at the Church of the Holy Sepulchre and it doesn't look so crowded. A minaret points skywards beside it. We go in – Lottie reluctantly – to potter in the coolness. Away from the religious pull of Golgotha and sacred tomb the church is dark and cavernous. I realise that there is no electricity, only candle and oil lamplight. We found a dusty little cave with a broken altar to Mary with a tiny grotto cave, like a tomb, off it. At the other end of the church rough hewn stairs led down and down – again seemingly right under Golgotha. The cliff edges jut out and are shored against crumbling in places. An altar, of sorts, is in the corner. A mass of little crosses are carved into the stone.

Making our way well in time to the Zion Gate, the streets are packed with Jewish families – this is the Jewish quarter – and I realise that I hardly ever see them in the souk and over in the Arab/Muslim quarter; there were none by the Damascus Gate. They keep themselves very separate. Or are they, tacitly, not allowed?

Moo is sitting by a wall outside the Zion Gate beside a wide barrow where an Arab boy is trading peanut brittle slabs. Moo looks surprised to see us.

"I think maybe you not come, you get lost," he says. But it is only a quarter to four. We are far from late. We sit on a low wall overlooking the high city wall and the Mount of Olives and wait for Moo to be ready.

"I have to take motor bike round outside of Old City," says Moo coming over to us. He looks discomfited.

"If it is a problem, don't worry," I say, getting off the wall.

"No problem, no problem," says Moo looking around. "Okay, you know Lion's Gate?" I nod. "I meet you there in fifteen minutes."

"Okay," I say. "You will find it? You not get lost?" asks Moo – but there is something in his voice that makes me think he hopes we will. We shake hands goodbye and Lottie and I go back through Zion's Gate.

"Are we going?" asks Lottie.

"No, it's far more than a fifteen minute walk anyway. And I don't think he wants us to come. Not really." Lottie looks relieved.

"He didn't think we would turn up at all," she says. "And if we bump into him again, we can always say we got lost like he expects us to."

Back by the Jaffa Gate we write postcards at a rickety table in a back alley by a shop that sells stamps, and post them at the post-box (red, like in England). We are sidetracked into buying a little knickknack – ("Please come to my shop, it is not in a favourable position"), and some baklava on a paper plate covered in clingfilm. On the plate too is another sort of pastry which looks like green beads wrapped in rope. A sort of nut and shredded wheat thing.

Although it is earlyish it is beginning to darken and chill and we head back to the hotel.

We know we have to get up early tomorrow for our journey to the Dead Sea, but we cannot sleep. Lottie, who has eaten rather a lot of chocolate, gets the giggles. Outside, the noise of revelry keeps us awake.

"I can't believe we were really smuggled into the Mosque," says Lottie. "Being burnt by a volcano was my biggest adventure. But now this is."

Monday 24th October

"What's the time?" shouts Lottie, leaping up in bed in a rush. The alarm has not yet gone off, the early morning call has not yet rung through. I look at my watch – 6 am.

"I suppose you thought it was later because of the sunshine?"

"Yes," she says, and goes straight back to sleep.

The reception calls, at the time I asked to be woken, to say that the taxi is waiting. No matter, the taxi's early, he can wait. We are already packed so take five minutes to wash and dress. We even have breakfast first: more pickled fish and yoghurt (not such a good idea actually, before a drive) – and Lottie braves the toast making machine.

We get 50 metres down the road when I feel an uncomfortable lump in my pocket: the room keys. Our driver turns round. As I leap out I see him drive off and have a momentary panic: white child slave trade for Lottie? – but he's only turning round again. He turns out to understand much more and better English than he speaks, so we stop making whispered comments even when he goes the wrong way out of Jerusalem, gets lost, asks the way from other taxi drivers, and stops at a garage to ask the way.

"I am from Tel Aviv," he says in explanation. No matter – he's kind and gives us peppermints. They are so strong we have to secretly take them out of our mouths and rewrap and hide them. I slide down in my seat so that he can't see me doing this in his mirror.

It is an exciting drive. The yellow hills of Jerusalem, stony and scrubby, scattered with shack shepherd huts, flocks of goats, the occasional donkey, give way to the red hills of Judea, harsh and barren. The road is a tarmac scar, imposed not belonging. Our first glimpse of the Dead Sea is a shiny blur some time after passing the sea level line – which is marked by a large sign-board. So now we are below sea level, but above ground. Odd. The road runs all the way south alongside the sea. At the northern end there is Jericho but that belongs to the Palestinians. We drive through two armed check points – Israeli soldiers – just to remind us that we are at the southern end of the Palestinian held 'West Bank'. The Dead Sea here has reedy banks and looks dark. Later, the shores are flatter, streaked white from the salt and the water becomes a milky turquoise. We pass a sign for Qumran where the Dead Sea Scrolls were discovered in 1947 in caves. I'd like to go there but apparently there is nothing much to look at – and looking up at the red cliffs I can see just the sort of inaccessible caves – shadowy and dark holed – that they are. There are danger signs on the shore – land mines – and then more danger signs - pit holes. The road is empty of other traffic and of verge-side signs of life.

It is further than our driver thought: not to the Dead Sea (only half and hour) but to its southerly tip where there is a cluster of hotels, the Crown Plaza amongst them – and the best, because from it one can see none of the others and it is the nearest to – right on – the Dead Sea. We are at the foot of Masada – the ruins of the fortress besieged by the Romans where all 960 of the besieged (Jewish rebels) killed themselves rather than be captured and taken into slavery.

There is a breeze in the palm trees, and our room is, of course, not ready (it is only 8.30 am). Reception gestures to us to leave our suitcase in the Ladies; we unpack bikinis and head outside. The hotel is huge and light. Outside the glass doors are palm trees and a glorious pool, and half a step away is a strip of sandy beach and the milky turquoise of the Dead Sea.

We are so excited – we are in the water in a trice. Under foot it is soft, soft like sand but it is white; it is pure salt crystals. We wade in up to our waists. The water feels oily and quite warm.

"Look!" I say. "If I relax my leg, it bobs up!"

"So does mine!" It is fascinating; like no gravity. We plunge forwards meaning to swim but our bums pop up above the water and above our feet: it's impossible to do other than doggy paddle. It is easier to roll over onto our backs. One can sort of sit float with ones body in a sort of V. Very comfy. We practise different positions, rather yoga like. Lovely. Moving is hard though. We discover we can bicycle with our feet while breast-stroking with our arms – that works. And so does lying on ones back sculling in either direction.

"Lucy said that if you put a book on the Dead Sea it wouldn't get wet," says Lottie. (The Lucy that is her best friend whom we stayed with in Greece).

"I think she must have thought it was solid salt and no water," I reply.

"That's what I thought too," says Lottie. "This is much better. It's wonderful."

And so it is until we splash some of the water into our eyes. Stinging agony. We rush to the beach to the showers. Back in the water again, we discover this time that it tastes repulsive. And no-one would want to wee in it, we also discover, because doing so makes ones bottom sting so painfully. But if you keep your head out of the water the whole experience is utterly blissful. The hills of Jordan, visible on the other side of the water, are misty. On our side, the red Judean hills chunk out of the land beside us.

The day passes slowly, contentedly. We swim in the pool, we sunbathe, we read, we swim in the Dead Sea.

"I'm popping," we giggle, which means our centre of balance has gone and either our bums or our feet have shot up and popped out of the water.

There is a fashion (if one can call it that) show around the pool which Lottie loves (it is fun watching prettyish girls sashay in inappropriately high heels past us: one can see at close quarters the safety pins holding folds of material). Afterwards Lottie goes to the hotel lobby to look through all the clothes on sale, and finds things she likes. They aren't expensive so I buy her an embroidered spider's web shawl and a flimsy green and gold top.

There is, on a patch of grass nearby, a bouncy castle giraffe which Lottie doesn't go on much although she likes it – is it boring on ones own, is she too old now, does her bikini fall down when she bounces? There are hammocks under palm trees, comfortable sun chairs, bubble massage machines in the pool. I collect some pieces of crystallised salt from the sea to take back.

The sea is flat milky glass – an infinity sea. As we swim in the evening a Hebrew boy pushes out on a flat surf board to collect chairs floating in the sea (People sit on them in the shallows). It is not crowded at all, but everyone is friendly. I talk to an elderly couple about how good the waters are for bones: he was in the Israeli navy and spent five years in Liverpool and Portsmouth. A kind fat woman rescues Lottie when she splashes her eyes again. A young man with a broken wrist holds his cast comfortably out of the water above his head while he floats. A group of women bob contentedly chatting in a triangle. It is impossible to sink. The temperature is in the 80's I am sure, but the breeze is lovely.

Time is weird. It feels like late evening by 3.30 pm because of the angle of the sun. By 5.30 pm it is dark.

When eventually we get around to it, we discover our luggage has disappeared from the Ladies. There has been a misunderstanding about where we should have left it and 'security' have removed it, searched it, and locked it in a vault.

"This is Israel," says the girl at reception. "We are always suspicious about everything."

Our room looks out over the pool, across the Dead Sea to Jordan. The milky turquoise dulls to grey in the dusk, and then turns to black. The misty hills of Jordan come alive with twinkly lights as they darken. It is warm on the balcony – we are glad of the air-conditioning. We watch trashy television on something called BBC Prime and eat fruit (a big bowlful has been left in our room) and bread and marmite. Lottie tries to find the cold water machine which we have been told is somewhere either on this floor or the one above. The door shuts locked behind her. She fails, repeatedly, to find the machine. At the nth knock on the door I say,

"Oh for God's sake!" – but outside is a girl from the hotel with little chocolate bars saying 'Sleep Well'. I am embarrassed. I go and find the cold water machine – it is through a door marked 'Laundry'. Not that obvious.

We turn out the lights by 9 pm and lie and chat until we fall asleep. We talk about school and Lottie's school friends. One of the advantages of teaching at the same school Lottie goes to is that we know the same people, and we know them almost as well as each other. It makes for good 'tapestry'. We talk about this. Other advantages include being able to see most of the plays or concerts or sports or whatever that she is involved in without having to take time off from my job. It is also useful that arriving and leaving (my job, her school day) coincide. The downside is to do with teaching her. I always feel I have to be careful to make sure that I give her less time and attention than other children in the class, regardless of her need – I can, of course, always make it up to her at home, but I never do, partly because it's good to separate home and school, and partly because it somehow feels unfair. I often think other children get more help with difficulties or homework from their parents than she does. This may of course be an advantage long term for her because she has to learn to work things out for herself. Worse, though, is my tendency to be less kind and loving to her in the classroom than I am to the others, partly in order not to show favouritism (which I obviously feel), and partly because, through familiarity, I am less patient with her and feel I can be more forthright and blunt than I would ever be with other people's children. This, however, makes her far more popular with her peers than she would be if it was the other way round. Luckily, for her and me, she is pretty hard-working, reasonably well-behaved (not good enough to be labelled a goody-goody by her peers, not naughty enough to get into too much trouble or be a pain to my colleagues), and a pretty decent average at most subjects so that she neither struggles at the bottom or causes envy at the top.

Tuesday 25th October

It is remarkably relaxing here. We wake up very late. There is nothing to do but read and chat, bob in the Dead Sea, swim in the pool. The sun is warm but not burning. We sit by the swimming pool. Lottie dives and swims lengths. The pool, initially, is quite crowded, but it empties and Lottie is the only one in there. A pool attendant kneels by the poolside and tests the water and the temperature. Lottie, however, comes out in a painful rash all over her body. She first realises it because her skin burns and stings when we wade into the cloudy turquoise water of the sea after lunch.

"It really hurts Mummy. It's agony."

"It must be the salt or the other minerals in the Dead Sea," I say anxiously. "But it is odd. The water is supposed to be good for your skin. People come here for the healing properties of lying in the Dead Sea. I can't understand why you should have such a nasty reaction. Poor you."

We go back to sit by the pool and Lottie is about to dive in to get off the oily salty feeling of Dead Sea minerals and stinging sensation, when we see a sign by the pool forbidding swimming for a couple of hours because chlorine has just been added. We realise that it had probably been added before Lottie swam earlier – and it is the chlorine that has caused her allergic reaction – or the combination of chlorine with Dead Sea water. It is a sad waste of the swimming day – although I float around for a while on my own. I can see Jordan on the other side of the sea, blurred and bluey. Behind the hotel and the palm trees the cliffs are red. I would really like to go to Masada. Apparently part of the oath taken when joining the Israeli Army includes the words "And never shall Masada fall again." I can see, I am sure, the rearing red hill of the site. I know it is a 3 kilometre taxi ride away. Then one has to walk 3 kilometres up a 'snake path' before taking a cable car to the top. Lottie says she is happy enough to tag along but would prefer just to chill. I am keen however, and go to hotel reception to find out about the cost of the taxi and other fees.

But we are short of money and I discover the cost to be prohibitive. Later I regret not spending regardless. I am sure I will never return to Israel and will never again have the chance to see Masada.

Wednesday 26th October

It's lovely here – rather surreal, but lovely. The landscape is alien; the colours so unusual. The contrast of pale blue water over salt against red cliffs and misty distances makes it feel as if buildings are ugly intruders. Even palm trees seem out of place. (Perhaps they are; imported for hotel adornment). I would like to bring my parents – my mother would love it, and it would be good for her arthritis.

"She's probably been here already," comments Lottie. "Granny's been everywhere."

Our taxi back to Jerusalem is booked for mid-afternoon, so the day feels disjointed as waiting days often do. Lottie still doesn't dare swim, and I like floating around in the sea better with her for company – the silliness of a cumbersome body is less fun alone. I spend some time in the water though, people watching, day-dreaming, landscape gazing. We are packed already and ready to go when the taxi arrives.

It is odd that this taxi driver doesn't know his way around the city either. Perhaps the hotel we are in, though not far from the first one, is rather insignificant and unknown, but he certainly has trouble finding it. Becoming bad-tempered at retracing his wheels over the same roads he swings in a u-turn into oncoming traffic, and there is a crash. Luckily we are not travelling fast. My first gladness is that the crash is on my side and not Lottie's. I cannot open my door to get out, but have to slide along the seat and get out on Lottie's side. Nobody is hurt, but the car and its driver have to stay put and exchange voluble aggression with the other car, and wait for the police. For some reason our driver is keen that we should not be there and hurries us away, accompanied by a 'friend' who shows us where the hotel is, though not helping us with our luggage.

The hotel is rather soulless – a huge entry hall of marble and armed guard, belies small rooms with dull furnishings.

We plan our last day for tomorrow, and rather wish we had been able to stay at The Dead Sea.

Thursday 27th October

I am beginning to get used to fish and yoghurt for breakfast – it is delicious and healthy.

We have decided to explore Jerusalem outside the old city walls, and we head for the new Jewish quarter. It is quite a long walk. The sun is warm and the streets are full of orthodox Jews in their 'uniform' of black suit and skull cap and ringlets. I read that the wearing of these clothes is to set them apart from non-Jews, so that they can be seen to be Jews and can be treated as Jews. I like better the idea that they look as they do in order to be 'Torah true'. Apparently in the 3rd book of Moses it says that they 'should not round the corner of your head' – and so that is why they do not cut their hair at their temples – thus the long ringlets. They wear black as a symbol of 'fearing heaven', to show their avoidance of frivolity. They wear the prayer belt, the kippa, to separate the superior upper body from the functional lower body. In the same way the skull cap separates them from God.

There is a particular street which is undoubtedly solely Jewish territory. We are the only non Jews we see, and although we are appropriately dressed, we are stared at and feel uncomfortable. Not threatened at all, just uncomfortable. There are little treasure trove silver shops which we dip in and out of. I buy a little silver boat for a new friend at home who used to be in the Navy, called Nicholas. It has delicately carved sails and ropes. The haggling is a different sort of exchange. Our shopkeeper – tall and bearded with piercing eyes – is cold and uncommunicative. There seems to be no pleasure in the haggle. I do pay less than has been asked, but I do not feel he has enjoyed the process and I certainly have not.

The street feels shadowed and dark, although I know the sun is shining and the buildings are not so tall as to block sunshine. We shiver in the shade, and walk on the sunnier side.

We walk on quite a long way to the Israel museum to see the Dead Sea Scrolls. Having driven past the Qumran caves on the way to and from The Dead Sea, and not been able to explore them, it seems important to go and look at their contents.

The Israel Museum is an extraordinary white dome of a building, reflected in a surrounding pool of water, with black basalt walls. Two thirds of it is below ground. Our tickets do not allow us to enter for a while, so we wander around outside.

Inside, eventually, we walk down wheel-spoke tunnels to a central circular room, peer at reconstructed parchment fragments on the walls, and learn about the lives of the people who lived in these caves. We learn how all their possessions are shared.

"I wouldn't share Milli with anyone," says Lottie. I can think of quite a few things I wouldn't want to share either. Strange how the more belongings people have the more possessive and unsharing they become.

These cave dwellers appear to have been mainly men who lived strictly religious lives, to whom the desert was a symbol of purity, who could only utter prayers or psalms from sunset to sunrise, who immersed themselves in water before communal eating. We read the Temple Scroll – the longest - which is a plan for a perfect imaginary temple, but find it dull and move onto the Biblical scrolls. Fragments in a darkened room; treasured, revered. I overhear someone saying that they are copies; that the real fragments are held more secretly in vaults below us. Surely not? Surely they wouldn't have needed to go to all this trouble with glass fronting and dim lighting and underground rooms, for replicas. It is hard, however, to understand the ceilingless value that is put upon these scraps of 2000 year old writing. I feel an irrational sense of awe. Lottie is marginally bored.

We leave cool darkness for hot brightness.

Friday 28th October

It is even harder to get out of Israel than to get in. We are interviewed at length, and our luggage is emptied, thanks to something suspicious showing up on the scanner. The 'something suspicious' turns out to be The Dead Sea mud packs I have bought as presents.

We feel a little sad leaving Jerusalem. It is dawn and the white walls are pinky gold on the hill behind us.

"It's not the sort of place that would be easy to come back to," said Lottie. "Perhaps I never will."

"How not easy?" I ask.

"Well, because of all the problems they have. There don't seem to be any answers and so the violence probably won't stop. And anyway I suppose any answers would mean either the Arabs or the Jews or the Christians not owning their bit of Jerusalem and then it wouldn't be the same anyway. Part of the reason it feels the way it does is because of all the mix. You know, the mix of the Jesus bit, with the Mohammed bit, with the Wailing Wall bit. And some of the bits – like Abraham's stone – belong to the bible and to the Koran and to the Torah. And, like Zaki said, some of the people – like Jesus – belong to all of them, just in different ways. And it doesn't look as if they'll ever all be friends, so the fighting won't stop, so it'll always be a bit dangerous to go there – and if it wasn't dangerous, it would be because it had changed into a place that wasn't so interesting to go to anyway."

It feels as if we are the only non Jews on the flight. We try to work out which of the Jewish women are wearing wigs – Lottie is transfixed by this ingenious alternative to covering your head. We reckon they all are. During the flight, while they sleep, many of their wigs slip drunkenly to one side. Lottie says it reminds her of the witches in Roald Dahl's book.

Once again England curves greenly into sight below us. The slightly sicky smell of the aeroplane and the airport is replaced by autumn air. We are laden with Christmas presents (though none of the things look quite as special two months later when I take them out to wrap) and dirty laundry in our luggage. When we unpack, everything smells of Dead Sea saltiness.

CROATIA - 2006

AIRPORTS HAVE been on red alert (the highest possible security rating) since Friday, with flights cancelled and hand luggage banned. By today really only Heathrow and flights to the USA are badly affected (23 terrorists have been caught: the fear is of a liquid bomb). I confirmed my flight on Monday afternoon before leaving to stay the night with Nicholas in Suffolk (nearer to Stanstead airport) – and all seemed normal according to the internet.

I am excited about this trip and Lottie has been excited for ages. I was slow this year to book, although when people asked what adventure we were about to launch on, I had said 'Croatia'. Because I hadn't booked it Lottie wasn't sure I really meant it. Nor was I. Partly I had a new man in my life – Nicholas, Partly I wasn't sure of what dates other things were happening. Partly I had really wanted to go to Turkey but the increasingly tense political situation regarding Iraq, Hezbollah, Islam, etc made it seem a potentially stupid place to be travelling. (This was borne out by the bomb attacks made on holidaying tourists during exactly that fortnight.)

I am not sure whether it was the late decision that meant direct flights to Zagreb or Split were so expensive – but they were. I had had it in mind to fly to one and from the other, hiring a car and exploring mainland Croatia between them. I was on the point of giving up when a chance comment to my brother Richard triggered the information that that there are ferries to Croatia from Italy. He and his wife had taken a boat from Venice – but on the net I discovered firstly that the cheapest ferries go from Ancona – further south – and secondly that Ryanair flies to Ancona. Brilliant! £25 each outwards and £52 each back again. I book. Then I look at a map. (Is this the right way round?) Perhaps we will go island hopping instead of mainlanding. I hear that the waters around Croatia are wonderfully clear and clean. We will backpack and snorkel our way around the islands. No need for car hire; we will hop on and off ferries and/or buses. I buy The Rough Guide for Croatia.

So there we are: flights booked, flights not cancelled, no specific destinations after our arrival in Ancona – other than Split by ferry – heading for Croatia and her islands via Italy – and a civilised 9.50 am flight.

We are old hands now, and Lottie is twelve – the packing is easy and we know what to leave out and what not to leave out. So, we take a towel each. We travel light: exercise books for writing diaries – plus biro, pencil, pritstick glue and a pair of scissors, - toothbrush and toothpaste, swimming things, nightwear, a sweat shirt in case it's cool at all, two T-shirts, a pair of shorts, a skirt, knickers, a pair of flip flops. Most of the space in the back packs is taken up with masks, snorkels and fins. We have bought our snorkelling equipment from a diving shop deliciously called 'Aquaholics' in Port Steward in Northern Ireland at the beginning of the summer holidays. We had our masks and fins professionally fitted and feel well kitted out. It wasn't cheap – about £60 each – but probably worth it to have stuff that works properly.

Tuesday 15th August

We stay the night with Nicholas and he drives us to the airport, but, oh bother! How could I be so stupid? I have forgotten to bring any marmite. Luckily the newsagent's in Great Finborough is open as we leave at 6.30 am, and joy of joys it sells marmite – a rather bigger jar than usual, but never mind.

Stanstead is crowded at 7.30 am, but pleasantly so, everyone in cheerful humour, even the heavily armed police presence. (After I get home in a fortnight's time, I read articles in the papers extolling this very British attitude). I change sterling for Croatian kuna – 10 to the pound – taking £700 with me having budgeted for £50 a day. We check in – passport and money in clear plastic bags, no other hand luggage – and join the long queue through security at the departure gate, waving goodbye to Nicholas. There isn't much to put through the x-ray machines, but we have to take our shoes off and put them through too, and we have to have nothing in our pockets. Inside we are allowed to buy water or food for the plane. I get some eye drops from Boots: Lottie has an eye infection (and a sore throat; I do hope she won't be ill). We take a shuttle train to gate 30, try on a few scents at the tax free booth beside it (Lancombe's 'Tropicana' is much loved by Lottie; it leaves her smelling of mangoes), listen to a cracking marital row in the queue, and eventually cross the tarmac and board.

It is a great flight. It passes in a trice – I mug up on Croatia from The Rough Guide, and Lottie reads Bliss magazine, full of quizzes – 'How independent are you?' and so on. Starvation forces me to buy an in flight sandwich (egg and bacon, really good). Lottie has a fruit salad and a cinnamon bun that we bought at the airport.

Oh bother! How can I have been so stupid again? I realise I have left the jar of marmite in Nicholas's car. So, here we are without marmite for the first travel ever.

"Don't worry Mummy," says Lottie. "I can make do with honey. They are bound to sell that in Croatia."

We arrive at Ancona - warm and sunny with clouds. Lottie goes to the loo in baggage reclaim so we miss the first bus to the ferry port and have to wait an hour. The baggage reclaim machine eats the straps of a fellow traveller's case, totally preventing its reclaim: – increasing numbers of Italians come and scratch their heads and tug uselessly at the straps. It is rather funny.

We sit on a bench and wait for the bus. Ancona airport seems to be in the middle of nowhere. It is very quiet, almost deserted. I think our aeroplane is the only one on the tarmac – and that not for long with its 25 minute turnaround. Lottie changes out of her tracksuit bottoms (warm for early morning travelling) and into a skirt. She sits on the pavement and plays clock patience. Our bench is in the shade.

Waiting is part of travelling. Minutes are slow but don't matter too much. Lottie loses her game by one card. She takes photos of herself with my camera and makes one of them my screen saver. My backpack is leaning against the bus stop post. A policeman strolls past and gestures at me to move it almost at the same moment that I gesture to him that it is mine, at the same moment that he sees it, half pauses, half looks about. Tiny, slow motion actions that take place in the same moment but in sequence.

At 2.45 pm the bus rolls in. You know it is coming by the Italian woman who stands in the middle of the road watching for it. When she walks back everyone gets up from the benches. The tickets are 2 euros each. According to a car rental man at the airport, the bus only goes to the railway station where we have to change to get to the port.

The journey seems long, but of course airports often are at least 30 minutes from the town centre. We strike up acquaintance with two English girls who are also going to the port. They have booked passenger tickets on an overnight ferry to Split. I find out the line name from them – Jadrolinja. An Italian standing near (they like to stand even if there are seats empty it seems) tells me that, today, the bus goes all the way to the port. We drive through modern suburbia and follow the railway line along the coast where blue and yellow umbrellas flutter on shingle by shallow turquoise water. A large man wades waist deep with arms aloft. Odd not to want to get your arms wet if your legs are. At each stop the bus gets standing-deep fuller – girls with strappy tops and dark armpits, girls with nose rings and tattoos and henna red hair. The shoes speak differences: trainers, sandals, heels, flip-flops. Toes even more so: dirt, plum varnish, peeling varnish, clean.

The port is overloomed by a golden dome, a stone cathedral, and russet cranes. We head for the ticket office. Lottie sits on a bench to wait for me. Twice I queue in the wrong aisle. Moving into the third and correct aisle my backpack snags on the barrier tape. The ticket man (tired? Italian?) blows up in a fury and walks away. I think I hear him say, roughly translated,

"Probably bloody Americans". He flings his arms about and mutters darkly to his colleagues. Abashed, and anxious that he'll refuse me tickets, I am contrite and apologetic. He returns, demands passports, demands information, refuses us a cabin, charges me 129 euros return and pushes immigration forms at me. Did I want a return? I have in mind that we would return from Zadar, further north than Split, - or....? Never mind. Having explored the possibilities in The Rough Guide I reckon the Split to Dubrovnik coast holds more possibilities than Zadar to Split – and anyway it is only 3 to 4 hours by bus from Zadar to Split from the sound of it.

We fill in our forms, and we queue at immigration control to have our passports stamped. Our ferry leaves at 21:00; we may board at 19:00. We go to the loo (clean and 3 sheets of loo paper given to us in return for 20 cents.) Then we go to the tourist office in search of leaflets for Lottie's Eye Spy Diary – and she finds a brown paper book – a Diario – and buys it – "For my own private diary". We discover it is a feast day – no wonder it is so quiet. Apparently cafes will be closed, but we find one only a few steps away – cream coloured umbrellas by a huge old wooden door with a long rusty bolt. The café itself is almost a shack but we share a pizza (I have to have the thick cheesy excess from the top) and a café frappe (Lottie has most of the froth and ice cream bits, though they give me extra milk so it is 'soft' enough for Lottie to drink too). She feels less tired now,

"My eyelids aren't heavy any more and the eye drops have worked too".

It is only 4pm so we sit there for a couple of hours writing, playing cards (rather dog eared – they are the ones we bought in Greece with pictures of Greek gods and heroes on them), eating, watching the world.

It is good to be in Italy again – Italian voices, Italian cigarette smoke. Sunshine and timelessness. Waiting becomes a pleasure.

Eventually we wander through high iron gates into the port, past an enormous ferry (where is Durres?): the fenders are vast black rubber loo rolls and the anchor is clamped brown and rusted on its side. We sit on the harbour edge in the sun, our feet on a sleeper, and watch little fish swim beneath us. The sun is full on our faces; an empty crisp packet floats fat air-bellied like a little mattress on the ripples. A warship, gun pointing high (A 5364) is docked beneath the cathedral. (Later, looking at photographs, Nicholas tells me that he thinks it is a coast guard boat – golly). Europalinks Finnlines has scaffolding up her sides. Tugs are moored in single file; cranes hang chain limp. The harbour wall curves embracingly; the little shoals dart and scurry. Lottie sketches. (I mistake her 'pool of water with droplets' for a candle burning – "blame my sunglasses," I apologise).

When I look up from writing, the crisp packet mattress has gone, the sun is lower. We board at 7pm in order to bag decent chairs.

They are navy blue plush and don't recline much – or even at all - but no-one seems to be interested in this darkened room (do they all have cabins?) so we take two chairs each side by side so that we can sleep curled up. I am so tired, but we go up on deck to admire the view, look at boats, watch the sun set and our ferry cast off. We like seeing the fat ropes unhitched and the water churn. Lottie is hungry so we go to the pretty basic self service café on board and Lottie has chips and I have a plate of prestad which is a local smoked ham – salty but good.

The night is long and disturbed and cold. A light above our heads has no means of being turned off – I wrap Lottie's tracksuit bottoms over my eyes. Lottie uses most of the clothes in her backpack as a pillow.

Wednesday 16th August

By 6 am we give up trying to sleep and stumble blearily on deck to watch our approach to the Croatian shore at Split. The sky is clear and blue and the air is warm. Lottie looks as tired as I feel, but actually I think we slept adequately if fitfully.

In Split we have our passports stamped (much to Lottie's pleasure – "All this travelling and because it's Europe, there's nothing to show for it in my passport", she grumbles. "Sam's got loads of pages with stamps on them") and go to a café for breakfast of hot chocolate while we decide where we go next. I think we should head straight for the nearest island; Lottie agrees; we buy tickets for the ferry to Brac (so cheap at the equivalent of £2.00 each); we only have an hour to wait. We play cards and Lottie takes some kuna and goes off to explore food possibilities. There are a range of little cafes and ice cream shops opposite. She comes back with a huge slice of baclava (remembered with passion from Greece and Jerusalem) – but made with walnuts so it tastes different. She eats the honey soaked pastry, I eat the nuts. We order more hot chocolate. Our waitress wears strange trainers – white, but open toed and heeled – with short white socks and short black skirt. Come to think of it they are all dressed like that.

I'd like to explore Split later. It looks attractive. But we board our ferry and sit on a bench at the prow; the journey takes less than an hour. The sea has ferries dotted all over it – white wakes foaming in angles lines, and it's hard to tell in the purple light where one island starts and another ends. Split fades behind us, red roofed and palm treed, and Supetar on Brac looms ahead, red roofed and palm treed.

The Rough Guide tells us that there is a dive centre to the West of the town, attached to the Kactus Hotel. Sometime during our journey we have talked our way from snorkelling to diving. Lottie is dead keen to do a PADA Open Water Diving course.

"Sam has got one", she pronounces. Sam is a friend from home, the son of Tim Spicer who rang us in Jerusalem. It would be exciting. If we could do the course, pass the exam, and get our licences, then we could dive our way around the islands. Underwater exploring.

But first, somewhere to stay. I am nervous. The Rough Guide states, and my brother Richard assures me, that ferries are met by touts offering rooms, and that this is the cheapest way of getting a simple cheap place for the night. But I worry in case our ferry isn't met, that all the rooms are full, that we'll end up sleeping on the beach (not what Lottie wants to do at all – I get a very old fashioned look when I mention it as a possibility). Why DO I worry? It's always been alright and today is no exception. We hardly have time to admire the clear water and the darting fish in the marina – "Which is amazing", says Lottie, "since there must be pollution with all these ferries coming in and out" – before a smiling brown bespectacled face greets us. Stephano (we learn his name later) is clutching a pad and pen (for writing prices), a card saying OOMS, and a map of Supetar. He speaks no English but he makes himself very clear. The room is 5 minutes walk away (he shows us on his map). The price is 300 kuna – we haggles it down to 250 kuna which seems reasonable. Pretty good actually, the equivalent of £25 a night for the two of us. Stephano is a grandparental figure; cheery, chatty, brisk. We set off at a cracking pace along the harbour, with no concessions for the weight of our backpacks.

"Good restaurant", says Stephano. "More good restaurant. Supermarket. Good sun. Good, all good. Super. Supetar!"

We go up a steep cobbled alley behind a souvenir shop (marked by a no entry sign for old people!), wiggle into a broken cobbled lane and stop by a fig tree.

"Maria, Maria!" shouts Stephano, and a child in lime green sticks her head out of a window and there is a Croatian chat. Actually, I later discover, she isn't Maria but Maria's granddaughter. Maria is old and grey haired and large and smiley and welcoming. We go through metal gates into a small irregular courtyard and climb stone steps to an apartment of bathroom, kitchen, sitting room and two bedrooms. Ours is whitewashed and shuttered with a fan on a chair beside the bed. Maria makes up a large double bed for us and brings coffee and orange squash to a table in the sun at the top of the steps. The view is over tiled red roofs and vines and fig trees. Old stone roofs with slipping tiles cover ancient wooden stable doors. The coffee is black strong and very sweet, just how I really hate it – I sip gingerly: it is utterly delicious; Lottie tries it and likes it too.

We change into bikinis – Maria interrupts with towels; I hold up a shirt in front of myself for modesty. "Ah, no, no," laughs Maria, unbuttoning her dress to show huge white naked bosoms. Far from putting me at ease, I am more embarrassed, but laugh and smile and mutter about the heat. Lottie unpacks her whole backpack, neatly, into the drawers and cupboard. It seems a bit pointless for only one night, but I do the same to be companionable.

Lottie has only one goal – to find the dive centre. She is distracted on the way by shops, but only for a while. We head, Rough Guidebooked, west towards the long shingle beach and package style hotels (hard to recognise because all single storey – clever planning that; it keeps the skyline pretty). The concrete path turns into gravel and dust. It takes a while to find the dive centre – the hotels don't seem to have names on them – but in the end there was a huge orange plastic sign: 'DIVING CENTRE' and an arrow pointing.

The girl in the office (shelves of neat diving equipment behind her) has wonderful blonde braids ("it took two girls eight hours" she says) and is Polish. We talk diving. They don't do PADI but something else. I wonder if it matters. They say not, but they would, wouldn't they.

She offers us a 'discovery dive' in an hour's time. Lottie's gleaming eyes are pleading. In spite of the 300 kuna each cost, I agree. We go to the café beside the dive centre to wait and play cards.

"No thanks, no food," says Lottie. "I can't eat before we dive." Privately thinking I might be sick during the dive (a friend Debbie Liggins told me she had been sick when she had tried diving), I concur.

There is an oldish man – Marcek – as our instructor and a ten year old German girl who joins us. A quad bike is loaded with tanks and jackets and weights and driven to the shingle bay close by. Before we dress we go through some theory – not much; just the signs one gives for okay, up, down, something's wrong.

We put on fins and flip flap backwards into the water. Lottie has a sleek black and yellow fluorescent wetsuit. We have already had our weights belted round our waists – golly, they're heavy; I feel so cumbersome and keep falling over. Once waist deep, Marcek puts on our jackets which are floating in the water behind us with air tanks attached. I am first – which is just as well because it gives me time to practise breathing with my head under water. Yes, I need to practise. I am in such a panic my breathing is just gasps and is so loud. I clench my teeth and lips round the mouthpiece, terrified that water will come into my mouth as I breathe in (later my jaw is so stiff). By the time the other two are sorted, I feel a bit better and my breathing is slower and quieter. But what does one do with ones spit? I daren't swallow. If I relax my lips will it dribble out or will sea water leak in? Marcek makes us hold hands in a circle under water. He deals with the valves on our jackets that inflate or deflate (for up or down) – down we go. How lovely the fish are, especially the silver ones with black bands at their tail base. I am sure there are more than I notice but I am concentrating on breathing and things. Marcek takes underwater photos of us. We go deeper, huge bubbles coming from us. My ears hurt. Marcek has told us how to 'equalise' so I hold my nose (quite difficult through the plastic of the mask) and blow. It seems to work. We swim a little and then go deeper still. My ears hurt again. Everyone else is making okay signs. I try to equalise. Nothing happens. I try again. I think I must have opened my mouth – suddenly it is full of water. Salty, stinging my throat, going into my nose. I turn to Marcek making 'something wrong' signs. I can't breathe. I shoot myself up to the surface (I think Marcek must have helped by inflating my jacket too) and cough and retch above the surface. Horrid. Someone says "Are you ok?" and I'm not at all sure I am. Ah well. I recover and sort myself out with Marceks's help and, mouthpiece back in, down I go again. It's not very peaceful because of the noise of my breathing and I still feel heavy and cumbersome. Lottie, however, is clearly at home.

Surprisingly quickly an hour passes and it is all over. My ears hurt, I feel dizzy and headachy and seasick. Lottie, who regards me with uncomprehending pity, is in raptures.

"And I'm starving," she says. We rinse out our equipment in fresh water, agree to collect our CD with the photos of us at 7pm and head for a seafront café. Lottie orders spaghetti Bolognese. I still feel sick. Then she eats a sugar and lemon crepe. I nibble a piece of bread and begin to recover.

We spend the afternoon by the diving bay, our towels spread on the quay. We snorkel – brilliant fun; I really notice the fishes now! I love swimming through the shoals or following a big fat one. Lottie dives to the bottom and collects little twirly shells which she puts on the quay. They promptly walk away! I don't quite have the courage to dive properly in spite of Lottie's encouragement. I like just looking at the coral (and the sewage pipe!) and the sea urchins and sea slugs from above.

We meander back to our room, greeting Maria. On the way we buy bananas, bread and honey and what Lottie thinks is yoghurt but turns out to be cream cheese. I slip in the doorway of our room and the bag falls with a sharp crack onto the tiles floor. I know the honey jar has broken. Yes. I rescue the other food, cut my thumb on glass and bleed everywhere. Eventually food is in the fridge, honey in the bin and my thumb wrapped in loo roll.

On the way back to collect the CD we visit a white stone cemetery – very grand and marble slabbed with an enchanting cupola of a chapel. What a view of the sea across to the mainland! We stop again a few minutes further on to watch a game of volley ball in the sand. In the dive office is Marjej – with piercingly blue eyes and a powerful smile. His son (about 3 years old) has propped up oars across the doorway and is kicking a ball with them as some sort of goal.

The next Open Water course starts on the 19th. It would be a drag to come back in 3 days time. We decide to do the course somewhere else. There's always the option of returning if we can't find anywhere else – but The Rough Guide mentions dive centres on other islands.

We buy little sachets of honeycomb on the way back and sit outside at the top of the steps in the evening sunshine to eat supper. Swallows swoop and dive all around us. Maria laughs and chatters somewhere below. It is lovely.

Thursday 17th August

Although Lottie nicks the sheet and wraps herself in it like a mummy all night, we both sleep well, lulled by the baby roar of the fan. We wake at 8.30 am and eat the bananas at our table outside for breakfast. Maria kisses us goodbye "Good luck," she says. She is wearing lipstick today – or is it just the morning and it hasn't worn off yet?

"The camera doesn't work," says Lottie. "It didn't like being put in that bag underwater." When I had bought the snorkelling kit I had tried to find a totally waterproof bag to put passports and money in so that Lottie and I could snorkel together. Eventually I had found one in a chandler's shop in St Tropez. I had thought I could put the camera into the bag and then take underwater photos yesterday, but the lens had refused to go in and out once it was airtight. Now it doesn't work at all. The letters ERR appear in the window. Irksome. I splash out on a disposable camera using my credit card – and we buy a disposable underwater camera too.

We have decided we want to go by bus to Bol on the other side of Brac. Luckily we get to the bus stop early – I say luckily because firstly the bus is already full - we are only just allowed on – and secondly (being full) it leaves 15 minutes earlier than timetabled. It is a good way of seeing the island – green tamarisk and larch, fig, vine and olive, hills. Piles of stones are heaped everywhere. The Rough Guide says they are caused by years of land clearance by peasants scrabbling a living from the soil. We stop in little sun soaked villages. There is a wonderful 'marital' between an elderly couple, because he gets off first without carrying any of the bags. She, overladen and screeching abuse at him, chucks one of the bags off the bus at his feet. Things half spill onto the road. Teenagers clutching towels climb on.

Having woven our way up the mountain ridge we now descend towards the sea on the other side. I can see the island of Hvar (I think) across the water, little while sails dotted.

I am disappointed that the bus isn't met by room touts - but of course, it's a local bus, not a tourist transfer. The agency is less romantic – but we are offered a room just up the hill above the harbour. On the way past the harbour – extraordinary – Lottie suddenly says –"That's Matilda!" – and there is the Jacobs family, acquaintances from Gloucestershire, Matilda is at Kitebrook with Lottie but a couple of years younger. Poor Matilda, she looks so embarrassed to see us – you don't expect to see your teacher on holiday, let alone weighed down with a backpack and looking scruffy. I find myself apologising for being there. They say they have bumped into other friends in Dubrovnik a few days earlier. It's a small world.

Neno Petrick is even older than Maria, waiting in the road to show us the way, a pink flowered dress instead of Maria's blue check one. Her legs are hard skinned, well veined and solid as they stomp up the hill ahead of us. She shares the bathroom with us. I see her single room later (ours is a double room off the gloomy hall) – everything is in there: a single bed, kitchen table and a chair (she is playing patience there) a cooker and a sink and a door to a veranda. We dump our backpacks, not bothering to unpack and head straight out again to Zlatni Rat (the Golden Cape) – a promontory extolled by the Rough Guide for its swimming. The paragraph omits to mention the crowds. Lottie sees watermelon ice cream – unmissable given her passion for watermelon. We happily sit and watch boats in the marina. There is a gorgeous wooden yacht. My iced coffee is delicious and covered in sticky chocolate sauce most of which Lottie eats with a spoon – best for my figure that she does. I'm half a stone or so overweight at the moment and my clothes are beginning not to fit. I'd like to lose it if I can during this fortnight. Lots of fresh air and exercise.

Having said which, because I can't work out how long a walk it is, we catch a little train from the harbour to Zlatni Rat – how lazy is that! (It looks quite a long way on the map; in fact we later discover that it's only about a twenty minute walk).

"Where are the nudists?" asks Lottie – The Rough Guide tells us the far side of the Zlatni Rat is a naturist beach. She is disappointed not to see entertaining naked flesh on this – Hvar – side. She decides that The Rough Guide is fibbing. But we do see a dive school. This one, on the beach front, does SSI courses (whatever that is). We look at all the photos of underwater creatures that are pinned to the walls, read the details of dive excursions – I think for experienced divers – and glance at the equipment store. We say we will come back later, and find shade under pine trees to lay our towels. We watch several groups come out for lessons. But it still isn't PADI so we decide against it.

We snorkel most of the afternoon. Now I dare to dive to the bottom. Lottie says I don't do it properly. Apparently I don't go straight down. I photograph Lottie but it's really hard to see things through the view finder with a mask on. We snorkel above the dive school students, watching their huge pale bubbles and black seal shapes. It's fun.

We sunbathe to warm up between snorkelling sessions. The water is cool, not at all cold, to get into and then delicious until ones body starts to chill after about twenty minutes. We play cards and Lottie wins more often than I do. I wonder why the sea water doesn't seem to dry as salty and sticky as in Cornwall. The beach is crowded. A Belgian woman asks where I got my waterproof bag (it is brilliant – I put all the money in it and hang it round my neck and arm like a handbag). "St Tropez" is clearly not a useful answer for her.

We walk back along a paved promenade between pine trees and flanked by the sea on one side and little market stalls on the other. Suddenly we see a dive school sign – The Big Blue - the one the Rough Guide recommends.

We have to wait for Igor – the boss – to return so we eat chips (Lottie) and fish soup (me) nearby. Igor is great and speaks fluent English. They do a six day PADI course, he tells us, and it all sounds reassuringly safe and professional and difficult with lots of theory and an exam at the end.

"It's just like pony club," says Lottie ruefully. "I'm going to have to know what everything's called, how to put it together – just like tack – and how to look after it and clean it – just like tack."

I book us both in – Lottie is so excited.

"Are you sure you want me to do it too?" I ask her.

"Yes, of course. You heard what he said. I have to have a qualified adult to dive with me – so you have to, so I can do it again, more, later." Oh the sacrifices one makes as a mother. I hope I stop feeling sick. I wonder whether a Joyride (travel sickness tablet) would help? It's quite expensive too - £200 each – so I wouldn't mind it only being Lottie who does it - but it is actually cheaper than pony club camp.

Lottie is thrilled. Is this really only our second day? It feels as if we've been here for ages. I'm sad that our travelling and exploring has been curtailed – and we won't have that long after the course. I want to go to the islands of Hvar and Lastovo (they sound so romantic, these names) and I want to go to the town of Dubrovnik. I want to go to the islands of Vis and Mijet too but I know there won't be time.

"We'll have to come back to Croatia and go to the islands we've missed," I say.

"And then we can go on excursion dives since we'll be qualified," says Lottie keenly. "You know, to the wrecks and the caves and things." She's read the blurb in the dive schools that's for sure. Oh dear, I hope I get to like it better. She's hooked.

We spend the evening in our room – once I've torn her away from the shops. We eat bread and honey and yoghurt. Lottie goes for a shower (the towels are the size of postcards) and realises she's left the shampoo and conditioner in Maria's bathroom back in Supetar. She goes down to the supermarket on her own to buy more. She chooses mango scented stuff.

As I write I can hear Neno's television – Croatian music and voices. Lottie locks herself in the bathroom but Neno, laughing, rescues her, and then cleans the bath for ages with Cif and scrubbing noises. Perhaps she thinks English children are particularly grubby – or maybe we looked it. It fits with the soulful picture of a saint above our bed –

"Freaky," says Lottie. I offer to take it down and hide it in the wardrobe – but in the end we leave her there. Jesus is quietly being crucified in the bottom corner.

Friday 18th August

Hyped up on an iced coffee drink from the supermarket with supper, Lottie takes ages to get to sleep. Lottie pretends she is a mosquito – funny to start with and then irritating – and is giggly. She lies heavily on my legs – I push her off. She giggles more. Eventually I get ratty. Nevertheless we sleep well eventually and wake at about 8.30 am.

We breakfast at what has quickly become our favourite café on the harbour. Baclava and scoops of kiwi and pineapple ice-cream for Lottie, coffee for me, total bill the equivalent of £2.20. We play cards and watch the boats.

Clutching fins and snorkels we head east away from Zlatni Rat to the other end of the town. Nicholas has asked me to find out berthing costs and the harbour master's office nestles under the church there.

"300 kuna a day in the high season," I am told – and I am given telephone numbers for marine offices here and in Milna – a port and little town round the coast to the west. There is a different feel this end of Bol – more sophisticated and quieter. We walk round into another bay and the water is so clear. We can't resist – we are in in a trice. Brilliant. We can see so far underwater. Lottie and I dive for dead sea-urchin shells; she finds this enchanting little crescent shaped shell of burnished mother of pearl too. We snorkel and dive until we are cold and then spread towels on a wall to warm and dry ourselves – but only briefly, and then we are in again.

We have lunch nearby – extravagantly: 100 kuna for an omelette and delicious taggliatelli and freshly squeezed orange juice. We are right on the very edge of the sea which is just six inches below us, sitting under a cream umbrella on wrought iron chairs. We are obviously early by Croatian standards; we are the only ones here. As we eat, a black VW pulls up on the sea wall and unloads dripping boxes of shellfish. It's rather a grownup restaurant I think. Inside it is high ceilinged and elegant and cool.

It is a good half hour walk back along the marble promenade to Big Blue, our dive school, but we get there early. That's ok; it's nice sitting in the shade at trestle tables looking at the sea and half listening to the instructors and other divers.

Our PADI course starts by feeling like being back at school – a lesson in a classroom with a whiteboard. Six of us: Lottie and I, a Polish couple and two Croatian girls. The lesson is in English and is about bars (pressures) and depths. Lottie understands. Then we go through the equipment thoroughly, learning how to put it together, what bits are called, and how to use it. After an hour we are on the beach sorting out tanks and jackets and putting everything together ourselves. Our instructor is a great bear of a man, dark and swarthy. A good teacher – he has a calm manner combined with lots of big smiles and he explains things clearly. I wonder what his name is – everyone else seems to know already.

The dive is slow and careful. Soon we are kneeling on the seabed, on sand, at about 4m deep. We have to take the regulator (the bit you breathe through) out of our mouths and put it in again. I am a bit worried about this – surely everything would be full of sea water; the mouthpiece, my mouth, everything. And it is, but amazingly when you give a little blow into the regulator all the water goes out and you can breathe just fine. Then we have to fill our masks with water and blow the water out again through our noses. Everyone else can do this easily. Lottie finds it a doddle. It takes me about six blows. But I don't panic, I don't feel sick, I equalise, my ears don't hurt. I can regulate my buoyancy myself. (Quite fun that – you press a button on the end of a tube attached to your tank and to your jacket. It puts air into your jacket and up you rise. Another button lets the air out and down you sink.)

Lottie is like a fish. She mooches along the sea bed turning over stones, poking in the sand. I see a translucent fish doing the same on a miniature level but using its nose to poke with. Lottie has got her balance perfected and is so full of confidence. If she thinks I'm not low enough she grabs my hand and yanks me down. This happens quite often. Once she presses my deflator bossily. She is my buddy (we are all in buddy pairs) and this means we have to check on each other and look out for each other. But

Lottie gets cold. We are alone, kneeling on the sandy sea bed, for some time while the others are shown what to do before it is our turn. We invent new signs. Crossed forefingers and a point to the other person means a kiss. Holding your crutch means you want to pee. Wiggly downward fingers means go on then, pee!

I look up at the surface, sunshine shiny above. My air bubbles cascade upwards. But something restricts the air flow when I tip my head back; there is somehow less air to breathe.

The other four are down. We follow our instructor and swim slowly about. All too soon we are on shore; our first lesson over. We carry tanks and weights back; go up the hill to the big Blue centre to wash equipment. We get medical forms and a PADI manual and arrange our video learning session and our lesson tomorrow. I am so thirsty and drink a lot of water. Lottie drags me down to yesterday's café for iced chocolate.

The sea is misty mauve. It must be about 6.30 pm. It is quiet and flat; most people have gone.

"Let's snorkel," says Lottie. Mermaid child. I wouldn't have chosen to get wet again, but why not. And it's fun. We wear masks and fins only – too idle to fit on the snorkels – and dive and play until we are puffed.

Walking home in twilight we have wet patches on our clothes. A wasp comes too. Lottie dances away from him. I blame sticky patches of honey on her towel from supper last night. She makes me carry the towel. The wasp stings my leg. Perhaps it wasn't a wasp – the swollen red lump itches not hurts.

We are starving so we stop at a restaurant by the sea wall and eat spaghetti Bolognese (Lottie) and a tuna fish salad (me). 100 kuna well spent. I count our money later – we are not being sensible. We have spent half our money and we haven't been here a week yet. I know I am being more relaxed about food and drink – it is so nice to sit in a café by the sea. Everything is so reasonable – even cheap – it is tempting to be less restrained – and why not maybe? There is a bank in Bol; I could exchange some euros for kuna.

We walk back to our room at 9 pm and are diverted by little stalls that have sprung up all along the harbour wall. We chat to a student from the Zagreb Academy of Art who is selling oils on canvas. I buy one – a fishing boat on sand – because it is so peaceful. It is only 30 kuna. Nicholas will like it I think. I have no money left so leave Lottie chatting and admiring a particularly orange wave. It isn't far to our room – Neno Petrich is still playing Patience at her table; I can see through the open door – and back again. Lottie returns not long after me. I wash fins and masks in the bath before I shower.

"Test me on Chapter 1 in the PADI manual," says Lottie. My eyes droop. I turn out the light.

"If there is 2 litres of air in my lungs at 20m and I hold my breath, what will it expand to above the surface?" I murmur.

"6 litres."

"How many bars of pressure are there at 10 metres?"

"2." There is a long silence.

"Are you asleep?"

"Mmm."

"I'll test you."

There is another long silence. I think we are asleep.

Saturday 19th August

I wake up before Lottie and step outside to the table in the garden. It is shaded, beside rose bushes, lavender and geranium pots – and so quiet. It looks backwards to the green and white hills and higgledy-piggledy houses – low, cream stoned, red roofed; a mass of stairways and balconies. Swallows sit on telephone wires. Church bells clang. The sky is milky blue.

It is lovely here. Not so hot as the Greek islands, and cleaner, and in a funny way (because I never felt unsafe in Greece) it feels safer. The water is so brilliantly clear too. Everyone is so friendly and feels so honest.

I wonder if this is the last travelling adventure with Lottie? Four years we have had – Italy, Spain, Greece (and Jerusalem) and now Croatia. She, of course, has changed and grown. All long brown legs and long blonde hair. She wants to eat in restaurants and drink iced coffee. She wants to shop! Luckily she has her own, limited, amount of money so it's really up to her what she buys, but she is a more expensive companion now, if still an excellent one – great to talk to, always up for adventure.

We go to our usual café for breakfast – coffee and baklava, and Lottie has a banana milkshake. Why do I fuss when the bill is 40 kuna? It's only £4 – but one gets a mind set. Anyway, it seems to go fast, all the 25 kuna drinks. And it's illogical – better to enjoy the drinks and eat from supermarkets instead of restaurants.

We get to the Big Blue in time to watch our theory DVD PADI Chapter 2. People from another dive group join us. The little room is hot and smells of neoprene. It reminds me slightly of the gas I used to have at the dentist's when I was a child. The DVD follows the chapters in the PADI dive manual but it is good repeat learning.

With only a couple of hours before we have to be back for our dive we go down to the beach, put our towels in shade on the shingle, and snorkel. That makes us hungry. We eat chips (Lottie) and tomato and anchovy salad – two large chopped tomatoes and one lonely anchovy – (me) at the restaurant nearby. We snorkel a little more and sunbathe.

Back at Big Blue I notice we are beginning to bond as a group. Martin and Martha are the couple from Poland – they are physiotherapists. She is dark and pretty with pale skin and big eyes. He is crew-cut, designer stubbled, hairy, attractively gnome like – but he speaks good English and therefore speaks for both of them. The blonde Croatian girl whose parents live in Sweden has tiny ruptures in her ears from not equalising in time and so isn't diving until the ruptures repair. Her place is taken by Artem, a Russian boy with a dour father who hovers and bosses. Inis is the tall dark haired Croatian girl. She is freckly, smiles a lot, is always late or on her mobile (she works in Bol as a sort of travel agent I think). Her English is quite good but she mostly chats in Croatian to the instructors. Jurica (pronounced Uritsa, George in English) is our instructor. Dark, swarthy and stocky, he is jokey and full of banter. Under water, however, and in our debriefs, he is strict and critical. A good mix.

Our lessons start the same way. We gather round the wooden table outside the Big Blue centre. Jurica has a big sheet of paper on which he writes down everything he teaches us with diagrams. He tells us what we are going to learn and explains how we do it and why. Most of the exercises we are doing underwater seem to be to do with how to cope in emergencies. We learn how to take our masks on and off under water – and clear them (I am still useless at this. It takes 7 or 8 snorts while everyone else does it in one. I must be doing something wrong but neither Jurica nor I can work out what. Perhaps I just can't snort!). We learn buoyancy skills. We learn how to breathe (basically all the time regardless. That sounds normal, but it is a surprising, or perhaps not so surprising, instinct to hold your breath underwater). We learn how to undress underwater, on the surface, and dress again. We learn how to take off and put on our weights underwater. We learn how to use our buddy's emergency regulator; we learn how to share a regulator (I am really bad at this because I start to panic, and never quite trust that I will be able to breathe because every time I do the regulator always seems still to be full of water). We learn how to check our tanks for air, and learn what to do if we run out.

The surface of the sea is lovely from underneath. The fish are not afraid and swim all around us. There is a pair of large silver ones today who stay close.

The time passes so fast underwater. It is hard getting in and out of the water from the shore because the equipment is heavy and cumbersome. Getting out is worst. Jurica says that most diving accidents happen on the surface: I can imagine that – drowned by the weight in a foot of waves.

After our lesson we decide to walk around Zlatni Rat – to look for the nudists. Lottie still doesn't believe the Rough Guide and wants to prove them wrong. We set off, after iced chocolate on the beach, taking the beach walk. The rocks tumble down to the water edge, sometimes topped by little pine trees, their roots straggling over the edges. Little coves curve; people are packing up to go. Zlatni Rat – this peninsula finger – is heavy unshaded shingle. At its point is a strong current. A man tried to swim against it, gave up, and was 5 metres away (sideways) in a second. Now I understand the no swimming signs.

We see no nudists, just a couple of topless girls.

We walk back through pine trees to the marble promenade and drift back to the town. It is about a half hour walk between the pine trees and, soon, little stalls.

The sea is purpley green, the colour of sea-urchin shells, on our right. The evening drifts upon the day, warm and soft.

Walking along the harbour I see dark fish. Lottie sees a glinting light –

"Look! Look! A mother of pearl!"

"OK," I say, "Let's go and get it."

"Oh do, yes do!" says Lottie. My bikini is under my clothes, my mask and fins are in the bag I'm carrying. I strip off the former and put on the latter in a few seconds. I slip into the sea off the harbour wall. The water is cool and it's just light enough to see. Lottie stays, clothed, on the wall – encouraging put not participating! The glint she saw turns out to be silver paper. But something a little further away…… I dive; it's a coin. I slip it into my fingers, turn to surface, and there, between two stones, is, yes, a mother of pearl. I have enough breath, I dive deeper, grab it and surface. Lottie is impressed. I am wet but amused.

Later we come back to the harbour for supper having showered and changed. We eat a (shared) spaghetti Bolognese and a tuna fish salad in a new restaurant – but I am beginning to realise that they all have the same menus at roughly the same prices anyway. What is lovely is that they all seem to cook on open fires – the wood is cut and stacked at the sides, crisscrossed logs. Once I see a boy bringing a wheelbarrow full down from the hills behind the town.

Having hummed and ahhed for ages, Lottie buys the picture she likes so much – the oil on canvas of a very orange sunset on the sea. She and her Zagreb artist are warm friends by now.

Sunday 20th August

We must, surely, economise. We have breakfast on the harbour wall, not in our usual café. I wonder if our waiter misses us. We eat bread and honey (we have bought another jar) and drink packets of iced chocolate. There is more of it at half the café price. We watch life in the boats that moored for the night – sluicing down, breakfast, slow paced starts. Croatian flags flutter – red white and blue with a central red and white check that makes them look like football shirts. It is early because our first dive is at 9 am. I had to set the alarm and Lottie is tired.

There are warm greetings when we arrive at Big Blue, conspirators in sleepiness, even Jurica. We are briefed, we lug equipment to the sea, we dive, we debrief. I am ticked off. During the dive I practised a skill that I didn't think I was good enough at, while the others were having their one to one teaching.

"You will not do what you want. You will stay still and watch me and be patient." Says Jurica severely. I am contrite. Interesting though – being a pupil. Salutary. How stung one feels when ticked off, but how easy it is to do one's own thing when one isn't on the direct receiving end of teaching attention.

We finish late and we have to be back to go on the boat at 2.30 pm. We go back to our restaurant on the beach and eat chips (Lottie) and tomato soup (me). I'm hungry but otherwise it wouldn't have been anything special.

The boat dive is exciting and there is a busy sense of activity at Big Blue. We are going with another group and their instructor Caesar who drives the boat. We are briefed with a dive map: we

are going to Pigeon Cave to explore. Equipment is sorted. Lottie
and I now know how to connect up on our own and can tell DIN
connections from INT ones – she prefers the latter because DIN
is sometimes stiffer. We slip the tanks into the holding straps on
the jacket and attach the octopus (regulator hoses) to the tank,
and the inflator hose gets attached to the jacket. We open the
valve and test the pressure gauge and the regulator. On the boat
you then turn off the valve to save accidental loss of air due to
pressure on the regulator from someone's foot or someone else's
tank. The kit is lined up on the dock, weights (heavier to offset
the greater buoyancy of long wet suits) fins and masks beside the
jackets. The kit is put aboard by Jurica and Caesar (luckily; it is
so heavy) and then we climb on. There is quite a swell and Lottie
goes pale immediately.

"Look at the horizon," I say. It takes 10 minutes to get round
the coast to our dive point. We pass the nudists in the coves on
the far side of Zlatni Rat. Mostly male. Lottie is amazed that The
Rough Guide is right, and at their lack of modesty.

"You don't have to look," I say. Sadly it doesn't distract her
from her seasickness which gets worse.

The other group is first to kit up and go – it takes some time,
so we six jump off the boat into the water to cool off (or in Lottie's
case to get out of the swaying boat); it's hot in the wet suits out
of water. We are so buoyant; it's like being in the Dead Sea. We
float about laughing until Jurica calls us in to kit up.

We get off the boat by being flipped backwards off the edge.
I am scared. I hate this.

"Shit. Shit. Shit." I mutter as I perch on the boat rim.

"I wish you wouldn't swear, Mummy."

"Shit." I say.

"One, two, three," says Jurica and flips me. I don't hold onto
my mask and salt water washes up my nose. I bob to the surface
and signal ok. It isn't too bad really. I look down into the water.
Pretty.

I rather wish I could just swim and look. As we set off there
is so much to think about: breathing (nearly instinctive now),
buoyancy (awful – I'm either scraping the bottom with my tummy
or I'm a metre above everyone else. If I tip my head down to look
at fish I go down and if I lift my head to see where everyone is I
go up – I don't seem to have this wonderful thing we have learned
about called neutral buoyancy), equalising, my mask (the strap
came off my head this morning – water pressure kept the mask
on my face so I never noticed, but I did wonder why the mask
was leaking and swilling a quarter full of water). Where is Lottie?
Ah. Exploring the shells under me. She passes me a mother of
pearl that she finds half covered by sand, which I stuff inside the
top of my wet suit. We swim deeper, following Jurica religiously.
We pause to look at an octopus that he points out and then at a
scorpion fish (apparently; I never see it, only a large stone: that
was it; they disguise themselves). I see a cowry under Martin's
feet and grab it (it gets lost) but begin to feel we should let the
sea keep its own.

"It feels like a privilege to be here," says Lottie later.

We dive even deeper and enter the cave, dark and beckoning
with watery treasures. A kick up, and I look up – heavens the
surface is now close – and down again and there is a ragged
hole towards brilliant blue which we swim through out of the
cave. Lottie has had problems with her ears. Earlier she couldn't
equalise properly and Jurica took her up slowly and brought her
down again. Waiting without her felt horrid. Partly I worried
about her, but I think I have relied on her to look after me – she
is such a better diver; confident and competent. She seems odd
during the rest of this dive; sort of spaced out. Her eyes look
woozy through her mask but she signals ok.

Back in the boat (so hard to climb in up the ladder with all
the weight) she is green.

"I feel sick," she says, "and dizzy and odd. My ears hurt and I
couldn't equalise." I think she has been waiting until her ears hurt

before she equalises and you have to do it right away, the moment you start to go down, and keep on doing it every minute or so.

In the boat we swig brandy mixed with Croatian herbs from a bottle Caser produces and passes round – even Lottie – to celebrate.

We are tired. We buy bread and nectarines and watermelon and eat supper in the little garden by the rose bushes and the lavender and geranium pots. The evening melts away into darkness. The sky is thick with stars. It is warm. Lottie and I talk about her sickness and decide that it all stemmed from the seasickness on the boat. We have some Joyrides. She can have one of those in future.

From the balcony above us there is a guitarist and singing – Croatian folk songs. They are so good I feel they must be a group or band practising for later performances. It is so romantic. They are still playing when Lottie and I go to bed. We hardly talk tonight. We are glad we have all begged for, and got, a later start tomorrow – 10 am – even though we have two dives in the day to accomplish. We fall asleep listening to the songs and the guitar strumming.

Monday 21st August

There are great storms in the night: thunder, lightening, wind and rain. All Neno Petrich's geranium pots are tumbled over this morning. The sky is grey and the sea choppy. Waves break with white foam on the shingle.

We are late this morning and have to rush our café breakfast. Martin and Martha pass us as we are sitting there, and tell us to hurry.

There is a drama during the morning dive when Martin runs out of air. All learning (go to your buddy, use their emergency regulator, go up slowly together) goes out of the window and, making a cutting motion across his windpipe, he shoots to the surface. He seems to use a lot more air, faster, than the rest of us.

Luckily we were not very deep and not very far from the shore. We have also done all our skills exercises, so Martin only really misses the slow fin back at the end when we fish watch.

I leave Lottie on the beach on her own between dives and walk back to the bank to get out cash to pay for our dive course – the £200 each. The machine only lets me have £300, although I try and encourage it to give me more by requesting smaller amounts. I'll have to get the rest out tomorrow.

We are now a close group. This last dive – off the boat – this afternoon is not a training dive as such, but what Jurica calls a 'proper dive'. We laugh and joke. We know all the drill now – and Lottie takes a seasickness pill for the longer sea journey. We chug across to an island by Hvar (though I think I work out later that it is actually part of the mainland) and chuck the anchor onto the rocks. Flipping backwards off the boat is fine this time. Lottie doesn't feel sick.

We mooch along underwater by the reef in buddy pairs (though I still find it hard to stay at the right level, either too low or higher than the others.) We see red starfish. Lottie picks one up but I refuse to touch it – poor thing, I think. The anemones are huge fronded. We slide over the reef and there is – gasp! – nothing. We are on the far side of the reef wall. The sea bed is apparently 65 invisible metres below us and the surface is 20 invisible metres above us. I can understand how one could get disoriented as to where is up and where is down. Actually, at this depth the sea is a brighter blue above us than below. And I suppose our bubbles go up. We swim beside the wall. Jurica points out sea life. It feels like a dream. We are all sort of suspended in watery space. One could panic about drifting down and not being able to get up again but somehow it doesn't feel as if it matters. Time is nothing. All I can hear is my breathing bubbles. I swim behind Lottie – she is fine today. (God bless Joyrides).

We slip over the top of the wall back onto the reef. Jurica takes underwater photographs of us. We surface.

In fact it has been quite a brief dive – 40 minutes or so – because Martin is nearly out of air.

The spray pours over the prow on the way back to Bol. The red roofs nestle at the base of green hills and I scan landmarks to try and find Neno Petrich's house. The sea is awash with white horses and sails – dinghies, windsurfers and big yachts. Suddenly it is a sad moment – the last dive of our open water diving course.

Back at Big Blue we debrief. Tomorrow is our last theory lesson, the last training DVD and our exam. The Russian boy has watched none of the DVD and won't pass the exam unless he does. They insist he watches it on the premises and he arranges with his father to spend the whole of tomorrow morning in the classroom here. Lottie and I talk about him. She hasn't liked him much; he has been pushy, always wanting to swim beside Jurica instead of keeping with his buddy.

"Probably he feels a bit scared," I say. "He really doesn't speak much English and he hasn't got someone he knows to do the course with so he must feel a bit lonely too." I suspect that if I hadn't done the course with Lottie, she and Artem would have been buddied up and they might have had quite a good time together, managing the language gap perfectly well.

We sit on the beach and drink iced chocolate. The woman who runs the drinks shack now knows us so well I don't have to ask for iced chocolate – she just pours it for us when I arrive at the counter. The sun sinks behind the pine trees and we are in shade. We wander home – Lottie buys a Big Blue Diving T-shirt on the way. We go out to supper – chicken kebabs – on the harbour (a new restaurant, same menu!) to celebrate. The boats are touchably close, the water clear dark. The breeze gutters out the candle on our table.

We see Jurica walk past with friends, wearing a blue striped T-shirt. We remember that he said he would be singing tonight. We follow him to outside the Big Blue shop where they render Croatian songs with gusto. We sit and listen. They are selling a

CD of their songs, but we don't buy one, although we quite like their singing.

Our room is getting messy – our towels are damp and dirty and so are some of our clothes. I pack sea urchin shells in tissue inside large water bottles with their tops cut off so we can get them inside the protective plastic. Lottie spreads them all out on the bed and exclaims over the colours and stripes and size of them. When I have finished all the wrapping there are still crumbs of sand and dry sea-urchin innards on the sheets.

We sleep more quickly but my ears feel rather odd. Perhaps it will be a good thing to have some days rest from diving.

Tuesday 22nd August

Have we been here a week or a day or a life time? I wake up earlier than Lottie. She is sprawled, mouth slightly open, on her back. I go and sit outside by the roses and lavender and geranium pots (now set upright again and tidied). It is a peerless day – the brightest blue sky and a breeze.

We breakfast at our usual café. I leave Lottie writing her diary – the table covered with bits she has cut out from tourist office leaflets ready to stick in – and go to the bank to get the rest of the money out that I owe Igor. Panic – it refuses my request for kuna. I go to the Post Office where, with a passport, I can withdraw money – the card is invalid there. I only have my credit card; I left my debit card safely back in England, so I can't use that instead. I do have cash but if I use that for the diving course I will be 1000 kuna short – and since we have been extravagant that will leave us very tight indeed. Bother. Perhaps it will work later – maybe it only allows me to withdraw £300 in a 24 hour period rather than each day. I am fidgety though – this I had not foreseen. It's not funny to be short of money and have no way of getting more. I do have some euros and some sterling I can change though – but not as much as 1000 kuna. I wish I hadn't let Lottie have a banana milkshake for breakfast today, or had two cups of coffee – or indeed had breakfast at the café instead of out of the supermarket until the money problem was solved. And I hope it is or we won't be able to do any dive excursions for the last week from other islands as we'd hoped.

We go and sit on a jetty beneath the harbour wall in the opposite direction from Zlatni Rat. We snorkel and find sand dollars. Or are they? They aren't flat but spherical with a small hole at the bottom like a sea-urchin shell has. The dotted black pinprick pattern at the top is like a sand dollar pattern though. Apparently snorkelling is called 'skin diving' – it is quieter, freer, easier than diving with air tanks and equipment, but you still have to look out for boats above. I love it. Shoals of black and silver fish flutter beside us, unafraid. I see a tiger striped fish near the black spikes of a sea urchin – I am sad to see tin cans and bits of metal pipe. Perhaps metal is better than plastic though.

I have rubs on my feet – sore. Luckily we packed Elastoplasts. I take photos of Lottie snorkel diving with the fish with the underwater camera. As the bay curves the seabed drops sharply, deeply, away. I look up for Lottie and notice that the tide has come in fast and waves are breaking over the jetty where our things are. Calling for Lottie I head back fast. The tides never seem to go out or come in very far, but they seem to do it faster.

The pleasure of the day is spoiled by worry about money. We go back to our room, buying nectarines for lunch on the way. It is 1.30 pm – 24 hours since I last drew money out with my card – so I go to the bank and try again in the ATM machine. The card is still blocked. I know what has happened – because I tried to take out more than my daily limit of £300 yesterday that has put a block on the card altogether. To prevent fraud I suppose. Back in our room we count money. I have about £200 in euros and sterling to add to the pot – but it does leave us without emergency funds.

"You can have all my money, Mummy," says Lottie. "I have 10 euros left."

To be on the safe side I have to sort out the card problem. I make telephone calls. My mobile bill is going to be unpleasantly high.

In spite of our financial situation, we buy Jurica a box of chocolates as a thank you. (He is pleased but everyone else at Big Blue eats them while he is out on the dive boat in the afternoon. He doesn't even get one.) We have a two hour theory lesson about dive tables and decompression limits, a ten minute break, and then our Open Water Diver exam.

During the ten minute break I find out that my card has been unblocked. Igor lends me a bicycle and I pedal furiously down the marble promenade (luckily not too crowded) and take out the last kuna that I owe Igor. It works. Whew. Such a relief. I pedal back, weaving through people, dogs and other bicycles, and get back just in time.

Lottie and I finish the 50 question multiple choice question paper first. We sit apart and treat it very seriously. I don't help her at all, but Martin has to translate all the questions into Polish for Martha so we don't know if they help each other. When the papers are marked Lottie gets 82% and I get 90%. Jurica is impressed because we get none of the same questions wrong. Perhaps he thought I would help her – he didn't bargain for her strong sense of independence.

We get certificates (with an award ceremony in the dimming light under the pine trees) and say fond goodbyes. It is well after 7 pm as we walk back feeling proud. The sky is soft pinks and purples.

We book our ferry to Hvar Town – one way on a 'fish picnic' excursion boat; the same price as the evening ferry but with the advantage of being in the morning. We buy bread and wafer biscuits from the supermarket and picnic on our beds while we pack. Pictures are rolled up and slide inside a large coke bottle with its narrow top cut off. Shells, in their bottle, are placed in the middle of the clothes inside the backpacks. We are tired and our intention to wander to the harbour for our last night in Bol is cast aside. We read the Rough Guide to find out about Hvar ready for tomorrow, and make plans for dives and island visits and trips. Neno Petrich lets us (after a lot of sign language) put a load in her washing machine.

"The water coming out of the hose into the bath is black," says Lottie.

"It's the towels," I reply. There is honey on our sheets and an irritating fly buzzes. We finish packing and chat.

I have liked staying so long in one place. It has become home, this tatty, simple room, this pretty harbour town. Lottie has loved it too. One gets used to things, to the way to go, to the places one prefers. Things become a habit quite easily. But it is time to move on. We love Bol but we have done what we wanted to do here. There is not going to be time to go everywhere we wanted anyway. Jurica says we must go to Dubrovnik but I'm not sure we'll have time unless we rush – and we don't feel in a rushy mood.

Wednesday 23rd August

Neno Petrich is still in her night clothes and her bed rumpled when we collect our things off her line. They are stiff and hard – particularly the towels - and I slightly wonder if there had even been any washing powder in the wash, let alone fabric conditioner. Perhaps they don't 'do' fabric conditioner in Croatia.

The 'Veli' is a wonderful wooden boat. We buy iced coffee and milk buns for breakfast on board. A basset hound comes too. We sit on the top in 9 am sunshine and breeze and chug gently and smoothly to Hvar Town. Lottie doesn't feel seasick. We see speedboats and yachts and gin palaces as we near – Hvar Island is very green with steep rocky edges. We dock in a busy, full harbour – our backpacks, which had been stowed away – are handed to us, and we head for the town centre. No room touts greet us, sadly. I suppose because it is an excursion boat. They wouldn't expect travellers to want to stay, maybe. We scan the shops along the harbour for agencies to find a room.

The first one we get to, Peregrine Tours – says they may have a room though they are all very full at the moment – and they make a call. There is one. It is double the price of Bol but this little wizened, smiley old woman that comes to fetch us, shows us up a narrow alley and steep cobbled steps lined thickly with green plants right beside the marina, to an enchanting light filled room at the top of her house that is worth every kuna. The windowsill is low enough and wide enough to sit on, and leaning out you can see the marina and the sea to the right and red tiled roofs and green hills to the left.

Our landlady leans against our bedroom wall and puffs a bit. She smiles a lot and nods and bobs. We exclaim in appreciation, dump our stuff and go. We eat spaghetti and salad on the harbour front beside palm trees. It is very Cannes, very St Tropez. The harbour is full – gin palaces, yachts, catamarans, ribs, water taxis.

After lunch we walk all the way round the harbour to find the dive centre. Round in the next cove is package holiday hotel land – not so alluring.

The dive centre consists of a table on a jetty by a dive boat (a grander vessel than in Bol). I suppose they have an office and equipment stores somewhere else. We book a dive for tomorrow at 1 pm

"Her too?" they ask gesturing to Lottie. We show our temporary licences. They are surprised at how young Lottie is to have got hers. We knew that from Bol and had discussed it with Igor. Twelve is the youngest PADI allow diving and Lottie has to upgrade her licence when she is sixteen with a half day check up course. Until then she can dive anywhere and as deep as I can, and like me can only dive if accompanied by a Dive Master or Dive Instructor.

It feels a bit scary to be planning to dive away from the comfort and safety of Jurica. At least I think so. It doesn't bother Lottie a bit. We buy freshly squeezed orange juice from a stall on the way back. It is good, but rather watery.

We go back to our room to put on bikinis and collect masks and fins, and we head in the opposite direction to find some rocks to lie on – success. We snorkel amid buoy ropes and we photograph starfish underwater. The water is clear and even more full of fish than Bol. I hear later that the water this side of Hvar is particularly wonderful because all the sewage is pumped to the other side of the island.

Lottie makes a friend – Emma – and they snorkel together. Emma is the same age, dark, pretty, fun, from Dorset. Her parents are friendly.

Research has indicated that the only ferry to Vis goes tomorrow when we are diving. I decide we should take a boat trip to Bisevo and Vis the next day, Friday, so that we can swim in the Blue Cave (extolled as more beautiful than the one at Capri) and explore Vis. I invite Emma to come too to make it more fun for Lottie – she and her family are pleased. They take Lottie back to the house they have rented. I spend the free hour sorting out ferry times to Lastovo on Saturday. Lastovo is said to be tiny and sparsely populated – there may be nothing much to do there except that apparently the diving there is the best – but a little peace and quiet will make a change from the glitz of Hvar.

I meet Emma and Lottie at Mama Leona – the pizza place by the steps up to our room where we had lunch. They have been given free bunches of lavender tied with ribbon. I take them to a café that I've found that sells baklava and buy one for us all to share. They are like locusts with it. It is new to Emma and she loves it. We wander back to Atlas Travel (via the little stalls selling lavender oil and jewellery that both the girls rifle through) to book our trip to Bisevo and Vis. We arrange for Lottie to have chicken instead of the fish that is provided for lunch.

Emma takes us back to their rented house above but in front of the harbour – at right angles to our room. They found it through 'owners abroad' on the net. Through double green doors is a courtyard filled with bougainvillea. The house is on several different levels and another courtyard shaded by a thick trunked vine tree is at the top. Bob and Nicola (and her mother Jane) give me a glass of beer and we chat. They are friendly easy people. Jane and Emma have been parascending (Lottie's eyes gleam) and Chris, their son, is going white water rafting tomorrow (Lottie's eyes gleam again). Lottie and Emma disappear to play and get a ball – and the broom they use to try to retrieve it – stuck in a tree.

Lottie and I go back via the supermarket of the town square, spending almost as much as if we'd gone to a restaurant because we buy half a cooked chicken. Mind you, 67 kuna is hardly extravagant once you translate it into sterling (£6.70). We eat up on the roof terrace where there is also an Australian girl (travelling Eastern Europe) with a heavy cold. There is a strong smell of salsa which she is eating. The swallows swoop low over the medley of red tiles. Beside us is the upper half of an old ornate bell tower. Weeds grow from its tiled roof. Below, in the marina. masts sway. Up on the hill to the right the old castle walls are floodlit. The sun sets pink behind the little 'resin' islands in the bay to the left.

I read to Lottie tonight, two chapters from 'Harry and the Wrinklies'. It makes us laugh. Lottie belongs to the Kitebrook Book Club and since her reading is reluctant I have agreed to read chunks of the books to her. We read 'Ingo' earlier in the summer, which we loved. It was about the sea and mermaids, which seemed appropriate preparation for our diving. We talk afterwards about our diving trip tomorrow – sort of mutually reassuring each other. She is asleep quickly. I run through in my mind all the things that can go wrong at 20m and how to sort them out, until I sleep too.

Thursday 24th August

What a noisy night! Muted music, less muted voices. Church bells. Clattering plates. Giggles.

Leaving Lottie to sleep I come out onto the terrace to write and read. There is still a strong smell of salsa, and muesli crumbs are scattered over the table cloth. There are little white clouds in the blue sky but not much of a breeze today, and not much boat movement on the sea. Behind the glitzy façade the town is crumbly and poor. The little yards below me are tatty. Wooden shutters have string and pegs between them for washing. Weeds grow in stone gutters, a dormer window is half built, bricks and sand lie, weed covered, on a terrace, chimney pots are broken or rough repaired. On the far side of the marina, a hotel is being built. Pity. Creamy old church spire rises above red roofs nearby.

Our landlady puffs her way up the narrow stairs. Conversation is stilted but I think she wants to know when we are going and I think she understands more or less my reply. Perhaps 'Saturday' sounds similar in Croatian. I must look it up.

The sun is hot on my shoulders. It is 10 am. When Lottie wakes up, we eat bread and honey and peaches for breakfast up there. Emma joins us. I leave them and head for the rocks to read – I only manage a few pages before they get there too. We snorkel and collect more mother of pearl shells and sea urchin shells. I find a perfect pale purple one. At about noon we pack up and leave Emma and head for the dive centre round the bay, stopping for banana milkshake and baklava on the way. We have butterflies of excitement and fear.

It is all very different. The dive boat is more luxurious than the Big Blue dive boat – not just a rowing boat shape with an engine but a proper big motor boat. All the equipment is stored on board – it feels strange not to be collecting stuff and sorting it ourselves. An Australian couple join us – Maria and Adam. Our licences are checked again, and off we go. I give Lottie a seasickness pill, but she is a bit green all the same. We anchor. Merlin – our Dive Master – passes round wet suits and connects up regulators, tanks and jackets for us – I feel uncomfortable not doing it for myself.

"That's resort diving for you," says Adam. He tells us about diving in Australia where it all appears to be more laid back – in other words they ignore the rules. We are all only Open Water divers and therefore shouldn't dive without at least a dive master with us, but he dived with mates near Sydney who were no better qualified or more experienced than him. I am full of the potential dangers and don't approve.

We step off the back of the boat and immediately I have problems. My jacket is far too big, or loose, and my tank swivels round and tips me to one side. Merlin tries to sort it out in the water, and it is a bit better. Then I can't sink. I have far too much positive buoyancy – not enough weights, a very thick long wetsuit. My jacket is completely deflated and I can't get under water at all. Merlin swims back to the boat and fetches another weight and puts it in a pocket of my jacket – nothing much happens, so he gets another, submerges himself and tugs me down. It is a bad start and I have to make a big effort to breathe calmly. Once I am deep enough down, the water pressure keeps me there better.

We swim along a reef to a wall drop – very like the one off Bol but not as high. It is very clear and the 'wall' in covered with wonderful stuff – fan coral, sponges and anemones. We see so many fish – I particularly like an orange striped one. We swim at about 20m deep – endless blue above and below – Merlin in front, me behind, Lottie below, Maria and Adam to one side. I skim the wall face – I could probably see more clearly if my mask wasn't full of water up to the bottom of my eyelids. Mask clearing as taught by Jurica has no effect. All the same, it is beautiful. We swim I into a dark cave which goes 20m back into darkness. A white starfish (maybe it is pale yellow) rests on a rock.

We dive for about forty five minutes and I am down to 40 bars on my tank gauge – I suppose I have used more air than normal, probably from all that thrashing about trying to submerge.

We shed kit, dive back into the sea to have fun, and eventually chug back.

There is a rather elegant hotel near the water sports quay with colonnades on the sea and terraces with long sofas and cushions and low tables under pine trees. Lottie and stop there for a milkshake (small and expensive) and lazily watch boats and swimmers and wonder whether to go parascending – cost the only inhibiting factor. There are shouts and a commotion – two men have dived into the sea off the terrace parapet and are admonished by the waiters.

We snorkel from rocks where wild thyme pushes through cracks. Lottie finds a beautiful shell and some more mother of pearl shells.

"I could see the edge peeking out of the sand," she says. Bright eyes.

We have agreed to meet Adam and Maria at Gromits the cocktail café on the harbour: Adam has burnt photos that he took today underwater on the dive onto a CD for us. They are fun and chatty. She's a remedial masseuse; he's an industrial engineer who has taken service leave. He's also recently qualified as a teacher and is thinking of changing careers except that it's paid less well.

Lottie goes back to our room to write her diary while I go to the supermarket to buy supper. Afterwards I get back to our room by cutting across the jumbled maze of alleys. It's easy to get lost – steps meander up and down and across, sometimes coming to a dead end. Balconies are white wrought iron, or stone 'Juliet' balconies – very Verona. It's pretty – open doors show tiny courtyards or stairs winding up inside houses. Bougainvillea spills over walls.

We eat our bread and chicken up on our terrace. I notice a weather vane of a little blue yacht. We go to bed early and I read more of 'Harry and the Wrinklies' to Lottie. Harry has to go back to school after long and idyllic summer holidays – it makes us think of having to go back to school in ten days time. It feels a planet away.

Friday 25th August

We are up promptly for our journey to the Blue Cave at Bisevo. The 'Vagabond' is ready on the jetty – but the crossing is cancelled due to bad weather over on Vis. It's sad but very honest of them – they could have taken our money and us, shrugged when they got there, and brought us back again. Here in Hvar it clouds over. Emma and Lottie go off to snorkel from the wild thyme rocks – Lottie likes it there. I go to the travel agent to reclaim the money for the Bisevo trip.

What shall we do today? Maybe this is the moment to rent a boat? I find Lottie and Emma in a children's playground.

"I've hurt my head," moans Lottie.

"On the rocks?"

"No, on the swings."

For heaven's sake – we do dangerous sports like diving and she hurts herself on swings! I suggest the boat renting idea and Lottie is thrilled – and Emma is too, but I can see Lottie has reservations and when Emma runs off ahead to get her towel and bag from the rocks, she says,

"I want it to be just us; it's our holiday." Bless her. But I don't want to hurt Emma's feelings and so I change the plan - we'll go parascending.

"I don't think they'll do it today; it's too windy," says Emma. "I suppose I could come and watch but then I'd be on my own. I'll go home." There is certainly a stiff breeze blowing. But they are happy to take us parascending straight away. They don't have any other clients on this grey cool blustery morning. They peer at the sky and nod and help us into a bright yellow speed boat. We motor out of the bay; they help us into life jackets and a harness.

"I'm scared and excited," says Lottie.

"Me too." Actually my tummy is twisting. I've never wanted to parachute; I'm not great on heights. Still, at least all I have to do is be there – I don't have to jump or anything. They pull out armfuls of red and white and blue silk from a trapdoor and fit it to a sort of pulley and let the parachute billow behind the boat, steadying the speed of the motor just enough to keep it mushroomed. Then they attach us by our harnesses to the bar on the parachute. My tummy twists again. We sit side by side, backs to the sea on the yellow plastic. We are told to hold the straps (all in mime – neither of the men speak any English). I clutch the straps tight.

Oh my goodness. We are lifted so gently up into the air. I suppose they let out the rope because we steadily get higher and higher – oh lordy, so high; the sea is so, so far below, blue and ridged and shiny (the sun seems to be out now); and above and behind us, huge and arched, the wide canopy of blue and red and white; and there is Hvar Town and the coast and a lighthouse and the 'resin' islands; and I'm so glad Lottie is there beside me (she waves at something to show me. "Hold on," I command fearfully); and we are so high and it is so gentle and quiet too, just the flip-flap-flutter of silk above, so peaceful, like flying – surely this is what it is like to be a bird, so beautiful, so soft.

It ends too soon. The pulley winds in the rope and slowly we are winched in. I only realise it because nothing is so high anymore. We land, gently, on our feet, on the yellow plastic back of the boat. I want to do it again. Lovely. I like it best of everything scary I've ever done. Just lovely.

Elated I suggest we rent a boat for the rest of the day. While we wait for a boy to motor out and collect one from the mooring on a buoy, Lottie sits on the quay and watches little brown jelly fish clench and unclench themselves along.

We have a little motor boat complete with sun canopy, oars, anchor, life jackets and engine – backwards, neutral, forwards off, and a lawnmower pull starter. We have a little lesson on how to operate the boat before we set off, and I am glad to see that there is a telephone number painted on the boat for us to ring in an emergency. It's good to know we can be rescued if necessary. We head for the Pakleni Otoci – the string of resin islands off Hvar, some them so tiny they only have names on nautical maps. We anchor off a blob of rock and pine beside some mewing gulls, and Lottie snorkels. I stay on board uncertain as to how effective the anchor is – I would hate the boat to drift away while we were both snorkelling; it's a long swim back to Hvar; too long. Lottie finds a broken saucer which she uses to carry a seahorse to the surface.

"I think he's dead." I slide my fingers under him. He curls a hard tail at my tough.

"No, he's alive!" And we let him drift down to the sea bed.

"I wish we had photographed him. A real live seahorse. The only one I've ever seen out of an aquarium," says Lottie. She flops into the boat (it's much harder to get in than out); we raise anchor and chug off.

Elevenses, we agree. We head for another chunk of rock and pine opposite a glimpse of bamboo café in pine trees. We are useless at docking. After endless attempts to get the boat near enough the rocks for Lottie to jump out onto them with the rope, a kind blond man (German, I think) comes to our rescue and sorts rope, anchor, all. There are shallows from this island across to the other (Marinkovaz). As we stumble across the uneven rocks (it is quite hard walking in water with flip-flops; the water sucks them off your feet at every stride), the sky behind, towards Vis, is black sheeted with violent, vertical lines – extraordinary. It is suddenly chilly. At the café we order hot chocolate and sit at a wooden table under bamboo roofing by the shore. Pine trees grow twisted through the shingle. We try to play cards, but they are whipped away off the table by currents of wind.

Suddenly thunder booms. Lightening shimmers. The sky is black. Suddenly from the blackness pour ice-cubes. People hide under tables; we go into the kitchen behind the counter which has a solid ceiling. It's a bit crowded in there. A huge ice-cube bounces from the ground and hits my ankle. It is painful. The sea spouts as the hail hits it. No-one can believe it – the hail is truly huge. It crashes through the bamboo roofing and breaks cups and saucers on the tables. It covers the shore in white baubles – and still the lightening cracks in the black sky and the thunder booms. We peer through a gap in the metal screening at the spouting sea. Everyone is exclaiming and talking and gasping with amazement and some people are taking photographs and we are all looking at them through the digital viewfinder. And then there is only rain. And then the sky clears. Slowly we emerge from shelter. The waitresses upend tables to drain and dry. Slowly the ice-cubes melt until they are small and insignificant. The sun comes out.

We make our way back to the boat exclaiming. Our helpful German friend is wringing out sodden towels. We wonder where he took shelter.

"It is a tragedy for the olives and wine," the girl at the café had said. Did she mean bottles have been smashed or that the harvest would have been ruined? Lottie thinks the former.

Our little boat is fine – rather full of ice-cubes and water, but fine. We motor round rocky outcrops, watching the black in the sky move away south. Lottie drives. She is rather a zigzag pilot. We see masts round a corner and head that way for lunch. It turns out to be the island of Palmizana. We dock almost as incompetently as before – but this time without help. The anchor just doesn't seem to hold. We tie up to bits of projecting rock.

The Captain's Bar gives me the best scampi soup I've ever had – utterly delicious. We wage a lunchtime battle with a wasp who falls into Lottie's bottle of fanta. The Croatian waiter speaks good English with an Australian accent. Everything is wet but the sun is out so the wet gleams. A shop has a nautical map which I look at to see where we are, have been, want to go.

We untie our rope and chug off to find flat rocks for sunbathing and snorkelling. It takes a while for us to realise that we have forgotten to lift the anchor. It seems to have made no difference to our progress – as I said, it doesn't seem to hold.

We find a perfect bay. Again we dock incompetently – but we are improving. Still the anchor is irrelevant. When we snorkel, I dive down to the sea bed and look at it. It sits on the sea bed with its spikes tilted up – merely a little heavy in the shingle. How does one get the spikes to catch? Or is it just supposed to be heavy enough that the boat doesn't catch?

It feels as if we are on a desert island – no-one is in sight though sails and boats are jaunty on the sea. The rocks are flat and warm and rise up into pine trees. The sea bed is full of fish, dull ones, and also, sadly, some rubbish: a shoe, a tyre, a tin can.

We find more mother of pearl shells (known locally, I have learnt, as 'St Peter's Ear'). Or rather Lottie finds them; I don't seem to see them as easily.

When the sky goes grey, we leave. The sea is rough and our boat plunges in the swell. Lottie, lying on the prow, flies into the air and slams back onto the hard surface.

"Get back into the boat now," I yell above the wind and engine noise. Spray pours over us. We wiggle round islands trying to keep to calmer waters until we reach a jetty on what we think is a new island (It turns out to be the far side of Marinkovaz), and moor – better this time. We buy a drink at a café perched on big shingle above the sea which bursts hugely on the rocks. There is a rather gloomy atmosphere. Lottie makes friends with a little white and ginger kitten. It sleeps on her lap while we try (in the wind) to play cards. She inspects its ears for fleas and pronounces them clean. Neither of us feels like snorkelling; anyway the sea is too rough.

Back in Hvar we have an early night with supper again on the terrace. The weather vane yacht has swung from East-West to North-South.

"When the wind is from the south (did he mean north?) we always have rain," Jurica had said. And we do. At first it is just drizzle. We venture out during the late evening; the sea is high, almost over the harbour walls. Yacht masts swing crazily. There is a feeling of excitement. Everyone is deeper inside restaurants; the pavements shine wetly. We have a photo of us together taken by a man with a camera and a laptop, who puts it on a postcard of Hvar for 10 kuna. We get two copies and send one to Granny and Grandpa ("Look who's on the front!"), and keep one.

In bed, the rain sluices down, and the thunder and lightening keep up a steady tirade. I read to Lottie – she falls asleep after two pages.

Saturday 26ᵗʰ August

Thunder wakes us. The sky is black – it is quite dark inside our room, so much so that we have to turn on the lights. Outside our window the cobbled steps of the alley are a pouring torrent, a river. We stay in bed. There doesn't seem anything else to do. Lightening flashes and the electricity flickers. I read last night's chapter to Lottie again. We giggle at the ludicrous antics of 'Gestapo Lil'. Lottie likes a character called 'Huggy'. I have given her a German accent which Lottie copies exaggeratedly. Lottie goes downstairs in rolled up pyjamas to photograph the river alley (the photographs don't actually come out very effectively, sadly), and comes back damp and grinning, with our landlady hot on her heels asking us to leave.

"More tourists, more tourists," she says, wringing her hands in apology. We dress, pack, leave our backpacks in her sitting room (bless her), and as we venture into the alley, the rain stops. There is even a patch of blue sky in the north. Two little boys are paddling in the water at the bottom of the steps, but it is draining away quite quickly. We pay our bill at Pelegrini and buy tickets for the Catamaran to Lastovo this afternoon – 20 kuna each – from the Jadrolinja offices next door. I read about Lastavo in The Rough Guide and worry that we land at Ubli and catch a bus to Lastavo town – which may not work so well at 4 am on Monday morning which is when the ferry leaves to get back to Split. I read that the dive centre is in the opposite direction from Lastavo town. There is one hotel on the island. I use my mobile to ring it and a book a double room for two nights. The Hotel Solitudo, 3kms from Ubli, right beside the dive centre. They will send someone to collect us off the ferry and also take us back to the ferry at 4 am on Monday morning. Bed and Breakfast is only 50 kuna more expensive than our room at Hvar was anyway.

We go to Hotel Dalmacia above our snorkelling jetty (Lottie hopes that she'll meet Emma) and drink coffee and hot chocolate and play cards indoors until the sun comes out, which it does in half and hour. The sea is still, the air is clean and warm. We go to the jetty. I watch a diver undress in the water, decanting his gear into his boat. He's hooded and jacketed and wet suited – I think he's been fishing too for he has a rod. Undressing down to trunks, he's rather good looking. It is gloriously sunny now. Perhaps the towels will dry. Emma's parents turn up and tell their stories of the ice-cube storm. Lottie goes snorkelling.

"I bet the storm has washed up more mother-of-pearl shells." Or broken them, I think. I go snorkelling too and find a big one under a boat; the sun just catches it and it glints. I swim back up, short of breath, through a triangle of soft ropes tying boats to buoys. I see another and dive again through the looming darkness of hulls. There is another jammed on black sea urchin spines, and, yes, another. I put two in each bikini side, but when I climb onto the jetty, my bikini top has come undone; one side has fallen down. I am more upset about the loss of my two mothers-of-pearl than the indecency.

The Jadrolinja Catamaran for Lastavo via Korchula leaves at 4 pm – it is late. I sit on the quay waiting, the sea and the 'resin' islands to my left, Hvar Town with its campanile, ruined fortress, red roofs, palm trees and yachts to my right. My brother Richard came here in the spring. He says they climbed the hill behind the fort and found a hidden path leading to an old shrine surrounded by olives. I meant to walk in his footsteps but there has been no time. I scan the slopes. There is a glimpse of stone in the green to the left of the fort. Maybe that is it.

I can see the catamaran, huge compared with the yachts, gliding across the sea towards the quay.

Lottie has the last seasickness pill. Unthinking, we sit on the sunny side of the catamaran – at least it is the sunny side once it has turned round to head for Lastavo. It is hot and crowded, and Lottie feels sick anyway although it is a smooth fast run. I read some more of 'Harry and the Wrinklies' to Lottie to try and distract her. Suddenly a woman pushes in to sit beside us, disregarding my bag on the seat. I protest, trying to pull my bag out from underneath her. A man appears behind our seat.

"Don't be frightened. She is not well. She only wants to stroke you," he says in strongly accented English. Looking at the woman I understand and am ashamed and sorry that I have been so antagonistic. I move our things gently, smiling at her, and she nods and smiles and strokes us. I wish I had realised from the beginning. The man, who smells strongly of beer, gently admonishes us for our lack of charity.

We stop on Korchula and I go out on deck briefly. The Rough Guide talks about the medieval attractions of Korchula Town, but this port, on the opposite end of the island, looks more industrial. Below, on the quay, the mentally handicapped woman is greeting an older woman with child-like hugs and guttural cries of pleasure and a big goofy grin. I am touched, moved. Tears sting the back of my eyes. They walk off holding hands – like me and Lottie do sometimes. I am blessed. She too, to have someone who loves her.

Then we are upon a mass of little islands - an archipelago - of which Lastavo is the largest. We dock at Ubli – 10 km from Lastavo Town according to the sign – a wedge of concrete jetty and a strip of buildings. I am glad we have allowed ourselves the luxury of a hotel; their minibus is waiting for us.

Hotel Solitudo sits 3 km round the coast on the curved arms of a wooded bay. It is a low white building with only a narrow road between it and the sea. Tall masted yachts sway at a harbour wall in front. It is quiet. The reception is cream and blue and cool. Our room is cream and blue and cool, with a balcony with steps leading down to the sea. Lottie immediately drops her clothes and heads off with her mask and fins. Sorting things out inside the room, I hear shouts.

"What's happened?" I ask as she returns.

"I don't know. I saw this pink machine thing in the water. I thought this diver in the water too had dropped it, so I took it to him and he shouted at me." We wonder what it could have been

– some sort of fishing device maybe – and watch the black suited snorkeler fin his way back and forth across the inlet.

We have dinner – pork kebabs (Lottie) and char grilled scampi (me) – on the hotel terrace looking at the sea and watching the sun set behind the island hills. It is utterly peaceful.

Sunday 27th August

Proper breakfast! Lottie feasts. In spite of her eating more or less what she wants when she wants, her skirt falls off her now. I hope the fortnight has had the same effect on me but I don't think so. It is irritating because I don't eat much and I take a fair bit of exercise, and I don't seem to be able to stay as slim as I used to. It must be an age thing. Perhaps I shouldn't mind – all that really matters is health and energy – but I'm still vain enough to care. I know all the things people say about your face looking younger as you get older if you are a bit plump – well great; a little compensation.

We ponder on our day. We discover that there is no bus to Lastavo Town (pity, I'd like to see it: seventeenth century and, oddly, facing away from the sea, according to The Rough Guide) because it is Sunday. We could hire a scooter. Lottie is keen. I am dubious. The last time I drove a scooter was 30 years ago on my honeymoon with Tom, my first husband, and it and I fell over on gravel and I was hurt. Lottie, however, is still keen even though I tell her she is too young to drive it herself. We go to the hire place and knock on the house door up steps – the workshops is deserted. An elegant older woman makes a telephone call and a younger woman with a baby in a pushchair turns up to deal with us. She goes into the workshop and discovers that electric cables have ignited a fire on some fuel soaked rags beside them. There is a quick drama. The older woman hurries in; the pushchair is given to Lottie; a hose is turned on; the rags are flicked off the table and stamped on; the fire is put out. (I am sure the health and safety training to do with fire at school tells us not to use water on electrical fires – perhaps there isn't too much health and safety in Croatia – thank goodness). The younger woman gestures to the plastic barrels of petrol in the store to explain her panic. We discuss scooters, and she indicates a smallish one and suggests that I have a try before we hire it. I wobble up the road and have to get off to turn round. I feel like a child learning to ride a bicycle. We are all of one mind. I should not hire a scooter!

Lottie goes back to our room to go to the loo. I decide to walk down the path by the sea away from the hotel – and almost immediately see air tanks and diving jackets on a jetty. Paradise Diving Centre. I meet 'Kicks'.

"You went to school at Big Blue? I work with Igor there for five seasons!" There are warm greetings and I book a dive for 3pm. Lottie is thrilled, though we have no way of getting more seasickness pills since it's Sunday. (I wish we'd brought more in the first place. Actually when we unpack after we get home, Lottie finds four more at the bottom of her backpack). There is a paved terrace area by the sea with umbrellas and white plastic sun loungers, presumably owned by the hotel, though locals seem to use it too. Lottie and I settle ourselves there and go snorkelling.

I find myself in a throng of shiny little brown fish with tail fins like swallows' tail feathers. Enchanting. I am right in the middle of them – they swim under my chin, through my legs, under my arms. Glorious. Lottie and I discover what looks like a sea urchin cemetery. We dive and dive until we are breathless – they are huge, pale purple, pale pink and pale green shells. Lottie also finds a pink flowered coffee mug – new (dropped from a yacht?) – but no more mothers-of-pearl. We come, under water, suddenly upon a huge brown jelly fish. We swim backwards from it, watching it, entranced, but keeping our distance. It ha a saucer sized semi sphere of cream with brown spots. The diaphragm is brown. We watch it contract and clench to move. It tentacles are short and wispy. It is almost translucent. We watch it for ages, swimming in circles away from it, wondering if it can sense us.

We have lunch up a lane on the veranda of a house with a makeshift sign advertising fish. An olive tree drips green olives behind Lottie's head. And purple tissue paper bougainvillea streams over the steps. In front of us is the sea blocked only by pine trees, one gnarled and twisted, drooping cones over the shingle, one wreathed in fine long fishing net, one with a wicker lobster pot hanging from a broken branch stub. We eat a huge plate of chips and drink fanta and coke all for the equivalent of £3.00. The sea sparkles. The owner/waitress/cook brings us fresh water to drink – a treat on Lastavo for water is scarce: our taps run with briny desalinated liquid, disgusting to drink.

From the moment we arrive at the dive centre I know everything will be wonderful. The equipment – wetsuits, jackets, regulators - are in such good condition and are properly fitted. I am given enough weights. 'Kicks' is professional – kind, but firm and organised. We fit up our tanks ourselves under his eagle eye. There is a German woman and her daughter diving too; the girl is about three years older than Lottie. They have about the same experience as us – they did their Open Water course in Nuremberg which they said was dark and cold, so they are ecstatic about warm Croatian waters. Their motor launch is moored outside the hotel; they are here with the husband and two small brothers.

The dive boat is a rib – completely unsickmaking. We zip out to an island, a thrilling ride once 'Kicks' accelerates away from the harbour, and I flip backwards happily off the comfy rubber rim of the boat. My mask doesn't fill with water. I can see! I deflate and sink perfectly. All is perfect. For the first time I feel confident enough to look around all the time. Oh the wonder! It is like a moonscape of caves and craters, crevasses and boulders down here. An octopus oozes fat purple legs over a rock in the gloom of a cavern, silhouetted in blue light beyond. Coral is spread-eagled pinkly. Under a ledge lurks a large long vicious looking fish with glaring eyes. My swallow-tail fish dart around me. And there at my nose is a flash of fluorescent blue stripe, another pink and yellow, another with turquoise crazy-paving on his face. The colours are brilliant, shining, glossy – it's like I imagine the Caribbean to be. I have no problems with my buoyancy this time. I move dreamily just above the seabed. Sometimes ribbon strips of seaweed brush my tummy. Once or twice my fins stir lawns of brown seaweed in my wake. I can see 'Kicks' ahead – he checks us all the time – but have the time to stop and stare. I follow my favourite turquoise fish – he moves so slowly that I can – and am then distracted by yellow tiger stripes. There's a little transparent fish burrowing in seaweed and a huge flat silver fish mouths the rock. I look up: the sun shines on the surface of the sea as far up as the sky it seems. Blue shafts of light stream through the water. Lottie and I hold hands and drift.

Are we down for forty five minutes? It feels like five. 'Kicks' indicates that we should stay down at the bottom – now about 5 metres down - while he goes up to the surface to check if the boat is there (his colleague had sped off in it to pick up snorkelers from another island). I watch swallow-tail fish round my knees and don't notice him beckon us up – he comes down to get me; the first I know is him taking my hand.

"If only for that dive," I say to Lottie,"it was worth all that money and the fear."

"I liked the walls at Bol and Hvar better," she says. "My tummy hurt today. I didn't feel sick like I did at Pigeon Cave, and my ears didn't hurt, but I just felt really unwell."

"Why did your tummy hurt? Did you feel sick in the boat?"

"No, the boat was great. It was just one of those sore tummies that I get sometimes." Poor Lottie. But it goes to show – perfect dives are perfect variously and individually. I wished we could dive here again tomorrow. 'Kicks' says,

"I will be singing on the hotel terrace tonight." Do all divers sing? Or do all singers dive? But we don't go to listen to him.

The evening is beautiful and dramatic. The sun sinks orange behind the islands but the sky to the south is black and jagged with lightening. Thunder rolls in the distance. We eat utterly delicious pasta under brooding pictures of lobster in the downstairs restaurant, and go to bed early to finish reading 'Harry and the Wrinklies'.

But I don't sleep for hours – anxious maybe not to miss the alarm on my mobile for 3.45 am – the minibus leaves for Ubli at 4 am to catch the (only) catamaran to Split at 4.30 am. Lottie sleeps with her mouth open taking up three quarters of the bed. Light streaks through the louvred shutters onto the wall. I try to count fish to get to sleep – tiny brown swallow-tailed ones. I can hear singing and music from the hotel terrace – 'Kicks' I suppose.

Monday 28th August

I wake and look at my mobile to see the time. It is 2 am. It is impossible to go back to sleep – I lie waiting for the alarm. Of course, when it does go off, it wakes me. I shoot up, dress while waking Lottie and heave backpacks on. The sky is full of pinprick stars – one of the few times the night sky has been so clear this fortnight.

At the port no-one else looks as sleep-tumbled as we feel. We buy tickets and try to sleep curled up in single seats, but the tilting mechanism on Lottie's seat doesn't work and she is uncomfortable. The catamaran is full. Dawn breaks somewhere between Korchula and Hvar. It is nice to see Hvar again – familiar, known. We dock in Split at 7.30 am – Lottie feels queasy (no seasickness pills). We sit at the same café as 14 days ago and drink hot chocolate. The same waitress serves us. We leave our backpacks in a luggage office near the bus station and head into Split to explore the old town. It is a mistake – why don't we think of catching a 45 minute ferry to Supetar and back today? We don't have to be back in Split until 7 pm. We'd have done so much better to have spent the day lying on a beach and snorkelling, rather than tramping hot streets. We are too tired for a town. We find a café and have a rather repellent but nevertheless expensive melon milkshake. Perhaps we should have guessed that melon and milk wouldn't really go together. We leave to find a chemist to buy seasickness pills for the long night ferry. We trawl endless market stalls and wander the lanes of a fruit and vegetable market, buying grapes of a dubious quality that we didn't really want. The canny peasant woman slides in black grapes under the white ones that we had asked for – I suppose she wants to get rid of them; they can't be selling well. They are full of pips and bitter skinned. We wander, tired, down little alleys. Lottie finds a hungry skinny nursing cat, and seeks out her kittens – three, one an enchanting grey and white.

"Let's give her the grapes, she's hungry," Lottie suggests – but I don't think the cat wants grapes; a decent tin of 'Whiskers' more like. "I'm hungry too," Lottie says. It's only midday but feels like hours later. We find a harbour-side café with fans and umbrella shade and eat spaghetti (Lottie) and shrimp soup (me). The waiter mishears my order and brings me mushroom soup. Usually I would have been happy enough to eat that instead, but tiredness makes me less compliant, and I insist on having what I wanted and ordered. Then Lottie has a strawberry ice-cream that is an odd shade of orange.

We are running short of kuna. We find a supermarket to buy things for supper and then find a harbour-side bench to sit. It is a rather malodorous place. We are bored. We watch scanky pigeons peck at pavement cracks; people walk and talk past; ferries come or go – slowly; the traffic passes. Lottie goes off for a wander on her own – I read. She comes back quite quickly – she is hardly a chapter away. It is only 2.30 pm. We count our kuna and wonder if we have enough to pay the baggage reclaim. Suspecting that we might not, we head back to the bus station, lingering over trinkets and lavender bags on stalls. We chat to a man in a shell shop who tells us how to clean the scale and dirt off shells.

The fee for our bags is 30 kuna. We only have 17 kuna. I go to the Bureau de Change next door with my euro coins and they kindly exchange them for kuna – we even have some left over. We go to the Jadrolinja booking office and sit in their waiting room playing cards and writing diaries. The air conditioning is full on;

it is cold. By 4 pm we are hungry – or bored – or both. Lottie goes off with 10 kuna to see what she can find that we both like. She comes back and plonks a warm parcel on my lap. Pizza! Clever girl. We have half each – delicious.

"I'm so stupid," I say. "We could have stopped in Hvar today and caught a ferry here later in the day. There are quite a few ferries each day from Hvar." Lottie is kind enough not to reply.

"I need the loo. It's 3 kuna," she says.

"Try the loo in the café we were in this morning." We try and ring my mother to say happy birthday – first the network is busy, then there is no answer. We text Nicholas to find out what the situation is at airports in England now. I have heard no news of any sort for 2 weeks. I wonder if there have been any dramas? We ask him to bring jerseys to Stanstead – T-shirts and flipflops will be chilly if English weather is as normal. I try and upgrade our ferry seats for a cabin – all we are offered is ones at 700 kuna. Not worth it – well, maybe worth it, but not possible after all our diving expenditure. We are way over budget – the dives have cost us an extra £600 - but if we don't count that, our two weeks have cost us £1,200 – a bit over the £1,000 budget. That's because of parascending and renting the boat and eating in restaurants and indulging in a hotel on Lasavo (two nights there costing the same as 6 nights on Bol!).

"There's been a lot of travelling," says Lottie wearily. "To get home I mean." I wish I had been more intelligent about today. It didn't need to have felt like travelling home. It should have been a day of the holiday.

We board the ferry as soon as we are able, and make our way to the blue plush seats as before. We stretch out taking a row of three seats each. I realise why no-one else wants to come in there – it is non smoking. We are both asleep before the ferry pulls away at 9 pm.

Tuesday 29th August

Lottie wakes me up.

"We're nearly there," she says. "Come and see." I stumble up onto the deck, shivering from the cold of the air-conditioning on the ferry. It is warmer outside. The sky is grey with orangey pink edges, and we are coming into Ancona; familiar but not very pretty.

Everything is still closed. It is too early. We go to the bus stop and I work out that the buses to the airport leave every hour. We don't have to be at the airport for four hours and I don't want to make the same mistake as yesterday. These are the last moments of our last adventure, and I don't want to spend them bored, waiting for a plane, in a bleak airport departure lounge. We take a bus to the beach which is on the stretch of coastline between Ancona town and Ancona airport. The one we had seen on the way here.

There is sand. Grey sand, but sand. There is a café, just opening. We order hot chocolate. Then we paddle in the sea and look for shells. We collect hundreds,; little curved semi-circles painted with purple inside. They will be good for an art activity at school. We play cards. The sun comes weakly out. Lottie does handstands. A trinket seller appears up the beach.

"Oh cool!" says Lottie." Look! What fun!" I know that we'll never get rid of him now.

"You're not having anything," I warn Lottie.

The beach seller kneels down on the sand beside us.

"No, thank you," I say. But I am right. Lottie's enthusiasm gives him hope and he stays embarrassingly long.

It is a good way to spend the hours, but there is still something rather sad about this morning. Partly perhaps the watery sunshine. The colours are all changed. Partly too that end-of-an-era feeling. Post-joy tristesse. We are rather quiet.

The bus takes us to the airport. The plane is, of course, delayed. The waiting is, of course, boring. Moments enliven the wait: the security men laugh at the security screen pictures of our coca-cola bottles filled with sea-urchin shells; a woman disciplines her not so very rude child with exaggerated and loud, dramatic firmness – we try, and fail, not to stare; we giggle about the disgusting smell of the expensive moisturisers in the shop.

"I am really looking forward to Moreton Show on Saturday," says Lottie. "And I am so excited about school. The Upper Sixes! Big Desks! And Mr D-C will love my 'Eye Spy Diary'. Can we get the photos developed today so that I can put them in?"

England is, as ever, green from above. Home. It is not as cold as we had thought it would be. Nicholas is there to meet us – and we don't wear the jerseys he has brought. The marmite that we forgot is still in his car. We are sick of honey in a way we never got fed up of endless marmite.

Things change. Children grow up – and rightly. They have been good these years - good memories, with good photographs to jog the memories, good times. But that, as it turned out, was the end of the mother and daughter travels.

"Next year I really would like a friend to come too," says Lottie in bed that night. "Not that I haven't loved travelling with you, Mummy, but I really would like a friend to hang out with."

"I understand, but I couldn't afford it," I reply. "And actually I'm not sure that I would want to travel like that."

We don't need to say more. Lottie squeezes my hand and I kiss her goodnight.